SECRETS
IN THE DARK

OTHER BOOKS BY FREDERICK BUECHNER

The Alphabet of Grace
Beyond Words
The Book of Bebb
Brendan
The Clown in the Belfry
The Entrance to Purlock
The Eyes of the Heart
Godric
The Hungering Dark
Listening to Your Life
A Long Day's Dying
The Longing for Home
The Magnificent Defeat
Now and Then
On the Road with the Archangel
Peculiar Treasures
The Return of Angel Gibbs
A Room Called Remember
The Sacred Journey
The Season's Difference
The Son of Laughter
Speak What We Feel
The Storm
Telling Secrets
Telling the Truth
Treasure Hunt
Whistling in the Dark
Wishful Thinking
The Wizard's Tide

SECRETS
IN THE DARK

A LIFE IN SERMONS

Frederick Buechner

Foreword by Brian D. McLaren

HarperOne
An Imprint of HarperCollinsPublishers

HarperOne

All biblical quotations are taken from the Revised Standard Version unless otherwise noted.
"Air for Two Voices" was originally published in *To God Be the Glory* edited by Theodore Gill © 1973 Abingdon Press. Used by permission.
"Paul Sends His Love" was originally published in *Incarnation* edited by Alfred Corn © 1990 Viking Penguin. Used by permission.

HarperCollins books may be purchased for educational, business, or sales promotional use. For information please write: Special Markets Department, HarperCollins Publishers, 10 East 53rd Street, New York, NY 10022.

HarperCollins Web site: http://www.harpercollins.com

HarperCollins®, ■®, and HarperOne™ are trademarks of HarperCollins Publishers

FIRST HARPERCOLLINS PAPERBACK EDITION PUBLISHED IN 2007

Library of Congress Cataloging-in-Publication Data is available upon request.

ISBN: 978–0–06–114661–9

ISBN-10: 0–06–114661–7

12 RRD(H) 10 9

For my son-in-law David with love and astonishment

CONTENTS

FOREWORD

People who are afflicted with the twin passions of preaching and writing will probably agree that each benefits the other. For example, in writing, when you slowly and painstakingly fold a clever crease in syntax, when you layer and lean parallelisms one upon another just so, when you learn to signal your logical connections with sturdy connecting words like *indeed, however,* and *for example,* you practice skills that are likely to sneak out when you preach—to your surprise and your hearers' delight.

And similarly, preaching can't help but teach you something about writing. You learn to feel the rhythm of a sentence. You imagine actual readers encountering your words in real time. You learn to simplify, which is harder than it looks. You learn to write in a whisper, maybe; to romance your readers with a tiny scrap of punctuation—just as you might do with a gesture or sigh when you preach. In fact, if you practice enough writing and preaching, and if you are blessed with extraordinary natural aptitudes from the start, you have the chance of spiraling into greatness. You may even excel beyond that and become a Frederick Buechner.

I have no desire to analyze what makes Buechner's writing and preaching so extraordinary. Neither do I want to account for Bob Dylan's raspy mystique, the peculiar beauty of a rainbow trout in a riffle, or a thunderstorm's magnetic terror. I simply want to enjoy them. They all knock me out of analysis and smack me clear into pleasure and awe.

So, in Buechner's case, please spare me the burden of analysis and permit me the pleasure of observation—the kind of thing you might say to your spouse or best friend when you have a favorite CD playing on a long drive, or are on vacation when the afternoon sky grows angry dark, or are cooling your feet in a creek: *Did you catch that line in "Every Grain of Sand"? Whoa—did you see that flash of lightning? Look, there, in that still patch downstream from that boulder—see it?*

If we were sitting on a park bench together, reading these sermons of Fred Buechner, I'd keep interrupting you with similarly annoying questions. Do you see why, in "The Two Stories," for example, his narrative approach is a far cry from telling little anecdotes to illustrate points? In "The Truth of Stories," did you catch how the story is not like an orange rind, but that it is itself the point, or at least the thing that points beyond itself to something more?

Did you catch how, in the shepherd's monologue in "The Birth," Buechner does a kind of reverse on Sartre's Roquentin in *La Nausée*? Remember how Sartre's character, sitting on a park bench and staring at a root protruding beneath his feet, saw through existence into the *nihil*, the absence of essence—and the vision made him retch? See how Buechner's shepherd sees into (not through) existence and goes ecstatic by encountering glory? And when Buechner shares one of his own visions of glory—entering New York, in "The Kingdom of God," or at Sea World (of all places) watching killer whales, in "The Great Dance"—didn't you almost feel it too? And did you realize that you had in fact seen it, a thousand times, but only at that moment of reading did you realize you had seen it?

Will you ever be able to read the Noah's ark story the same way again after reading "A Sprig of Hope"? And did you notice how, against the darkness and stench of that not-really-for-children story, Buechner manages to talk sincerely about peace and love? What could be more clichéd than that? Yet he never sounds the slightest bit corny. Why is his modest little title so much bigger and robust than "The Depth of the Flood" or "Noah's Escape from Despair" would have been?

Did you notice the way Buechner guides us beyond the things fundamentalists and liberals always argue about—in "Come and See," for example, or in "The Seeing Heart"? If you're a preacher yourself, did you notice that many of the best sermons are the shortest ones, and did you feel embarrassed and stupid for being so long-winded so often, as I did? Have you ever read a better introduction to the Bible than "The Good Book as a Good Book" or a better overview of a book of the Bible than "Paul Sends His Love"?

What? You'd like me to shut up? You'd like me to stop telling you what I noticed and enjoyed in these sermons, so you can embark on your own reading—and notice things for yourself? No worries and no offense taken. I understand exactly how you feel.

A new generation of preachers is coming up, and I can't think of anyone more enjoyable and exemplary for them to read than Buechner. They need to observe his art in creating an old woman with thick glasses, eating popcorn at the movies, or a fat man in a pickup, complete with gun rack and *Jesus Loves You* sticker (in "The Church"). They need to reflect on how these characters—sketched so minimally—do something that elegant points or abstractions never could have, especially when Buechner brings them back later in the sermon, adding one devastating detail to each. The next generation of preachers will learn something precious from Buechner in this and a dozen other ways, not, we hope, so they can analyze it or talk about it, but so they can actually catch something of his art, his eye, his heart, so they unconsciously, accidentally, might trade in a few of their points and abstractions for a teenage girl with acne, smoking a cigarette, or the young bride in high heels wobbling down the aisle on her father's arm.

This new generation of preachers will have a natural affinity to Buechner because he, unlike a popular painter known as the "painter of light," never paints light without shadows. Buechner's faith carries freight because it has not come easy; it dances and sometimes street-fights with doubt. He calls himself "this skeptical old believer, this believing old skeptic." The young preachers I know are tired to death of easy answers and simple steps and cozy scenes with serene porch lights and perfect picket fences. They don't live in that world. They live in a world of thick glasses, gun racks, acne, and cancer. And so do the people they preach to.

Which is the world Buechner celebrates in his sermons. This world is the very one in which he keeps bumping into the living God, or vice versa. Which is why young preachers need to read these sermons.

In "Faith and Fiction," Buechner describes writing as whistling in the dark. And, no doubt, he'd say preaching is something like that too: maybe in part both are attempts to convince yourself "that dark is not all there is." But surely both are more: disciplines—like Godric's bath in frigid water—to remind yourself that beyond all dark is a shining river of light, and "all the death that ever was, set next to life, would scarcely fill a cup."

—BRIAN D. MCLAREN

INTRODUCTION

The earliest sermon in this collection is "The Magnificent Defeat," which I preached at Phillips Exeter Academy around 1959 or so when, fresh out of seminary, I was starting in as the new school minister. Exeter was for only boys in those days—hence the heavy use of masculine pronouns and references—and most of the ones who came to hear me did so only because it was a school requirement. Left to themselves, they would have stayed in bed. In keeping with the spirit of their time and generation, the majority of them were against almost everything—the Vietnam war, the government, anybody over thirty including their parents, the school, and especially religion because all the people they were against were always telling them it was good for them. They were there against their principles and under protest.

They dismissed all sermons as hogwash even before the preacher started preaching them, they slouched in their pews and stared up at the ceiling, yet every once in a while you could tell they were listening in spite of themselves. And that is what I can still remember their doing as I tried to describe the great scene of Jacob at the river Jabbok in Genesis. I don't think it was so much my words that held them as it was just the haunting power of the biblical narrative itself—the stranger leaping out of the darkness, the struggle by the river bank, the strangled cry for blessing—and in some deep way I was apparently haunted myself because it turned out to be the germ of a novel about Jacob, *The Son of Laughter,* which I wrote some thirty years later.

There are a number of other sermons from those early Exeter days here including three Christmas monologues entitled "The Birth." A church in

Beverly Hills, California, presented a dramatic reading of them in 1965 with Raymond Massey doing the Wise Man, Edward G. Robinson the Shepherd, and (best of all) the English actor Frederic Worlock the Innkeeper, and if ever I have occasion to read back over them, it is those three remarkable voices that I hear in my mind.

I had a strong suspicion that once they left Exeter, most of my captive listeners would never be caught dead in church again, and that gave me a strong sense of urgency about what I was doing. It might be the last time anybody would try to persuade them that religious faith was not as boring, banal, irrelevant, and outmoded as they thought it was, so if I didn't do it right, that would be the end of it. I tried every way I could think of to catch their attention and make them listen. I avoided traditional religious language and imagery as much as possible as well as the kind of fuzziness, bombast, and sentimentality that preachers are apt to resort to when all else fails. In sermons like "A Sprig of Hope," "Message in the Stars," "The Sign by the Highway," and "The Face in the Sky" I tried to be as dramatic and vivid as I could without going overboard, to tell a story or set a scene that I hoped would capture their imaginations. I tried not to let them ever see where I was going next, to keep them on their toes, to keep them wondering what on earth I was getting at until suddenly and unexpectedly, if I was lucky, we all of us got there together. I tried to be suggestive, elusive, and unpredictable rather than systematic, dogmatic, and pontifical. I never took it for granted that they believed any of even the most basic affirmations of the Christian faith concerning such matters as God and Jesus, sin and salvation, but always tried to speak to their skepticism and to honor their doubts. I made a point of never urging on them anything I did not believe myself. I was candid about what, like them, I was puzzled by and uncertain of. I tried to be myself. I tried to be honest.

All of this went on during the years, culminating in the Cuban Missile Crisis of 1962, when thermonuclear holocaust seemed such a constant and imminent possibility that people were building and stocking fallout shelters and the school designated places where students were to go in the event of an enemy attack. With all that in the air, I found myself dealing more and more with such issues as the U.S.-Soviet arms race, the folly of fighting a war that might bring about the end of civilization, and the Christian hope that not even death can separate us from the love of God. Leaning heavily on lectures I had heard given by the faith healer Agnes Sanford, I spoke about the crucial importance of prayer, and about how we must learn to ignore the voice of the skeptic in all of us and go on praying in spite of it. We should not let the fear that our prayers would be unanswered keep us from praying them. *Adeste fidelis*, I told them. If they wanted to know whether prayer has real power or not, the only way they would ever find out was to try it for themselves.

After leaving Exeter in 1967, I never had my own pulpit again, but preached pretty much wherever I was asked to in places as varied as the little Congregational church in Rupert, Vermont, which figures in "The Clown in the Belfry," the National Cathedral in Washington, where, the first time I was there, I forgot to switch on the microphone so that only the first few rows in that football field–sized nave could hear me, and Westminster Abbey, where the evening before I preached "Two Narrow Words" the Dean, Michael Mayne, who has since become a dear friend, took my wife and me on an after-dinner tour of that central shrine of the English-speaking world, which apart from the three of us was entirely empty except for the ghosts of the mighty and the soaring, vaulted darkness. All of these have been published in one of my collections or another, but there are also some that appear in print here for the first time—"The Seeing Heart," "Let Jesus Show," "Jairus's Daughter," "Waiting," "The Word of Life," and "A 250th Birthday."

It was William James who used the term "the More" to refer to the Mystery beyond space and time in which we all of us live and move and have our being whether we acknowledge its existence or not, and my purpose in these more recent sermons especially has been not to try to describe what is by definition indescribable, but to try to put into words how it seems to me we catch glimpses of it, hear whispers of it, or are sometimes moved to our depths by it as we encounter it now and then in the everydayness of what happens to us. "Listen to your life" might well serve as a distillation of all of them.

Add to that only that, as I looked out from all those different lecterns at all those different congregations, I always remembered that first congregation of some forty years ago now, who by and large thought the whole religious enterprise was for the birds, as in my darker moments I am sometimes tempted to believe may indeed be the case. It seems to me there is an Exeter student in each of us, even those of us who are churchiest and most outwardly conforming, who asks the ultimate question "Can it really be *true?*" and every time I have ever preached I have tried to speak to that question—not just to proclaim the Yes in its glory, but one way or another to acknowledge and do justice to the possibility of the No. In other words what I have been essentially doing from the pulpit all these more than fifty years is to tell the story of my life.

Just for good measure there are pieces here that are not sermons at all including the talk I was invited to give at the New York Public Library on the subject of "Faith and Fiction," in which I tried to suggest that, despite what at first glance seems a mutual contradiction between them, they have important elements in common. "The Good Book as a Good Book" is a chapter I contributed to Lee Ryken's *A Literary Guide to the Bible,* and in it I say some things about the Scriptures in general in addition to trying to state in a few words what seems to me is their basic plot. "Paul Sends His Love" is a kind of disquisition on the First Letter to the Corinthians originally published in a volume entitled *Incarnation,* in which various literary figures, including John Updike, Annie Dillard, John Hersey, and Reynolds Price, contributed essays on twenty-three books of the New Testament. "A 250th Birthday" and "The Newness of Things" were both written for academic occasions, the first for Princeton's bisesquicentennial and the second for the installation of my friend Douglas Hale as headmaster of Mercersburg Academy. And finally there is "Adolescence and the Stewardship of Pain," which I delivered at St. Paul's School before a small group of educators that included my old friend Bill Coffin, whose extraordinary career as prophet and Christian activist always makes me feel more than usually dim and irrelevant.

So here they all are, arranged more or less chronologically—a culling from *The Magnificent Defeat, The Hungering Dark, A Room Called Remember, The Clown in the Belfry,* and *The Longing for Home,* in that order, together with the most recent and hitherto unpublished ones. Not wanting my nearly eighty-year-old self to drown out my thirty-year-old self, I have let them stand more or less just as I originally wrote them. For better or worse.

Needless to say, I have changed a good deal over the years, just as my major themes have changed along with my way of saying things and seeing things and feeling about things, but by and large there is nothing in these pages that I wouldn't be willing to sign my name to still. I can only hope my readers will find it in their hearts to be accepting and merciful.

1.

The Magnificent Defeat

The same night he arose and took his two wives, his two maids, and his eleven children, and crossed the ford of the Jabbok. He took them and sent them across the stream, and likewise everything that he had. And Jacob was left alone; and a man wrestled with him until the breaking of the day. When the man saw that he did not prevail against Jacob, he touched the hollow of his thigh; and Jacob's thigh was put out of joint as he wrestled with him. Then he said, "Let me go, for the day is breaking." But Jacob said, "I will not let you go, unless you bless me." And he said to him, "What is your name?" And he said, "Jacob." Then he said, "Your name shall no more be called Jacob, but Israel, for you have striven with God and with men, and have prevailed." Then Jacob asked him, "Tell me, I pray, your name." But he said, "Why is it that you ask my name?" And there he blessed him. So Jacob called the name of the place Peniel, saying, "For I have seen God face to face, and yet my life is preserved." The sun rose upon him as he passed Penuel, limping because of his thigh.

—GENESIS 32:22–31

When a minister reads out of the Bible, I am sure that at least nine times out of ten the people who happen to be listening at all hear not what is really being read but only what they expect to hear read. And I think that what most people expect to hear read from the Bible is an edifying story, an uplifting thought, a moral lesson—something elevating, obvious, and boring. So that is exactly what very often they do hear. Only that is too bad because if you really listen—and maybe you have to forget that it is the Bible being read and a minister who is reading it—there is no telling what you might hear.

The story of Jacob at the river Jabbok, for instance. This stranger leaping out of the night to do terrible battle for God knows what reason. Jacob crying out to know his name but getting no answer. Jacob crippled, defeated, but clinging on like a drowning man and choking out the words, "I will not let you go, unless you bless me." Then the stranger trying to break away before the sun rises. A ghost? A demon? The faith of Israel goes back some five thousand years to the time of Abraham, but there are elements in this story that were already old before Abraham was born, almost as old as humankind itself. It is an ancient, jagged-edged story, dangerous and crude as a stone knife. If it means anything, what does it mean? And let us not assume that it means anything very neat or very edifying. Maybe there is more terror in it or glory in it than edification. But in any event, the place where you have to start is Jacob: Jacob the son of Isaac, the beloved of Rachel and Leah, the despair of Esau, his brother. Jacob, the father of the twelve tribes of Israel. Who and what was he?

An old man sits alone in his tent. Outside, the day is coming to a close so that the light in the tent is poor, but that is of no concern to the old man because he is virtually blind, and all he can make out is a brightness where the curtain of the tent is open to the sky. He is looking that way now, his head trembling under the weight of his great age, his eyes cobwebbed around with many wrinkles, the ancient, sightless eyes. A fly buzzes through the still air, then lands somewhere.

For the old man there is no longer much difference between life and death, but for the sake of his family and his family's destiny, there are things he has to do before the last day comes, the loose ends of a whole long life to gather together and somehow tie up. And one of these in particular will not let him sleep until he has done it: to call his elder son to him and give him his blessing, but not a blessing in our sense of the word—a pious formality, a vague expression of good will that we might use when someone is going on a journey and we say, "God bless you." For the old man, a blessing is the speaking of a word of great power; it is the conveying of something of the very energy and vitality of his soul to the one he blesses; and this final blessing of his firstborn son is to be the most powerful of all, so much so that once it is given it can never be taken back. And here even for us something of this remains true: we also know that words spoken in deep love or deep hate set things in motion within the human heart that can never be reversed.

So the old man is waiting now for his elder son, Esau, to appear, and after a while he hears someone enter and say, "My father." But in the dark one voice sounds much like another, and the old man, who lives now only in the dark, asks, "Who are you, my son?" The boy lies and says he is Esau. He says it boldly, and disguised as he is in Esau's clothes and imitating Esau's voice—the flat, blunt tones of his brother—one can imagine that he has almost convinced himself that what he says is true. But the silence that follows his words is too silent, or a shadow falls between them—something—and the old man reaches forward as if to touch the face he cannot see and asks again, "Are you really my son Esau?" The boy lies a second time, only perhaps not boldly now, perhaps in a whisper, perhaps not even bothering to disguise his voice in the half hope that his father will see through the deception. It is hard to know what the blind see and what they do not see; and maybe it was hard for the old man to distinguish clearly between what he believed and what he wanted to believe. But anyway, in the silence of his black goat-skin tent, the old man stretches out both of his arms and says, "Come near and kiss me, my son." So the boy comes near and kisses him, and the old man smells the smell of his garments and gives him the blessing, saying, "See, the smell of my son is as the smell of a field which the Lord has blessed" (Gen. 27:18–27). The boy who thus by the most calculating stealth stole the blessing was of course Jacob, whose very name in Hebrew may mean "he who supplants" or, more colloquially translated, "the go-getter."

It is not, I am afraid, a very edifying story. And if you consider the aftermath, it becomes a great deal less edifying still. What I mean is that if Jacob, as the result of duping his blind old father, had fallen on evil times, if he had been ostracized by his family and friends and sent off into the wilderness somewhere to suffer the pangs of a guilty conscience and to repent his evil ways, then of course the moralists would have a comparatively easy time of it. As a man sows, so shall he reap. Honesty is the best policy. But this is just not the way that things fell out at all.

On the contrary. Once his dishonesty is exposed and the truth emerges, there is really surprisingly little fuss. Old Isaac seemed to take the news so much in his stride that you almost wonder if perhaps in some intuitive way he knew that it had been Jacob all along and blessed him anyway, believing in his heart that he would make the worthier successor. Rebekah, the mother, had favored the younger son from the start, so of course there were no hard words from her. In fact, only Esau behaved as you might have expected. He was furious at having been cheated, and he vowed to kill Jacob the first chance he got. But for all his raging, nobody apparently felt very sorry for him because the truth of the matter is that Esau seems to have been pretty much of a fool.

One remembers the story of how, before being cheated out of the blessing, he sold his birthright for some bread and some lentil soup simply because Jacob had come to him at a time when he was ravenously hungry after a long day in the fields—his birthright looking pale and intangible beside the fragrant reality of a good meal. So, although everybody saw that Esau had been given a raw deal, there seems to have been the feeling that maybe it was no more than what he deserved, and that he probably would not have known what to do with a square deal anyway.

In other words, far from suffering for his dishonesty, Jacob clearly profited from it. Not only was the blessing his, not to mention the birthright, but nobody seems to have thought much the worse of him for it, and there are no signs in the narrative that his conscience troubled him in the least. The only price he had to pay was to go away for a while until Esau's anger cooled down; and although one can imagine that this was not easy for him, he was more than compensated for his pains by the extraordinary thing that happened to him on his way.

For anyone who is still trying to find an easy moral here, this is the place to despair: because in the very process of trying to escape the wrath of the brother he had cheated, this betrayer of his father camped for the night in the hill country to the north, lay down with a stone for his pillow, and then dreamed not the nightmare of the guilty but a dream that nearly brings tears to the eyes with its beauty. The wonderful unexpectedness of it—of life itself, of God himself. He dreamed of a great ladder set up on the earth with the top of it reaching into heaven and the angels ascending and descending upon it; and there above it in the blazing starlight stood the Lord God himself, speaking to Jacob words of great benediction and great comfort: "The land on which you lie I will give to your descendants; and your descendants will be like the dust of the earth.... Behold, I am with you and will keep you wherever you go" (Gen. 28:13–15).

Do not misunderstand me about moralists. The ecclesiastical body to which I am answerable as a minister would, I am sure, take a rather dim view of it if I were to say, "Down with moralists!" But as a matter of fact that is neither what I want to say nor what I feel. Moralists have their point, and in the long run, and very profoundly too, honesty is the best policy. But the thing to remember is that one cannot say that until one has said something else first. And that something else is that, practically speaking, dishonesty is not a bad policy either.

I do not mean extreme dishonesty—larceny, blackmail, perjury, and so on—because, practically speaking, that is a bad policy if only on the grounds that either it lands the individual in jail or keeps him so busy trying to stay out of jail that he hardly has time to enjoy his ill-gotten gains once he has gotten them. I mean Jacob's kind of dishonesty, which is also apt to be your kind and mine. This is a policy that can take a man a long way in this world, and we are fools either to forget it or to pretend that it is not so.

This is not a very noble truth about life, but I think that it is a truth nonetheless, and as such it has to be faced, just as in their relentless wisdom the recorders of this ancient cycle of stories faced it. It can be stated quite simply: the shrewd and ambitious man who is strong on guts and weak on conscience, who knows very well what he wants and directs all his energies toward getting it, the Jacobs of this world, all in all do pretty well. Again, I do not mean the criminal who is willing to break the law to get what he wants or even to take somebody's life if that becomes necessary. I mean the man who stays within the law and would never seriously consider taking other people's lives, but who from time to time might simply manipulate them a little for his own purposes or maybe just remain indifferent to them. There is no law against taking advantage of somebody else's stupidity, for instance. The world is full of Esaus, of suckers, and there is no need to worry about giving a sucker an even break because the chances are that he will never know what hit him and thus keeps on getting hit—if not by us, by somebody else. So why not by us?

And the world is full of Isaacs, of people who cannot help loving us no matter what we do and whose love we are free to use pretty much as we please, knowing perfectly well that they will go on loving us anyway—and without really hurting them either, or at least not in a way that they mind, feeling the way they do. One is not doing anything wrong by all this, not in a way the world objects to, and if he plays it with any kind of sensitivity, a man is not going to be ostracized by anybody or even much criticized. On the contrary, he can remain by and large what the world calls a "good guy," and I do not use that term altogether ironically either. I mean "gooder" than many, good enough so that God in his infinite mercy can still touch that man's heart with blessed dreams.

Only what does it all get him? I know what you expect the preacher to say: that it gets him nothing. But even preachers must be honest. I think it can get him a good deal, this policy of dishonesty where necessary. It can get him the invitation or the promotion. It can get him the job. It can get him the pat on the back and the admiring wink that mean so much. And these, in large measure, are what we mean by happiness. Do not underestimate them.

Then it comes time for Jacob to go home again. He has lived long enough in the hill country to the north, long enough to marry and to get rich. He is a successful man and, as the world goes, a happy man. Old Isaac has long since died, and there is every reason to think that Esau is willing to let bygones be bygones. Good old Esau. Jacob wants to go home again, back to the land that God promised to Abraham, to Isaac, and now to him, as a gift. A gift. God's gift. And now Jacob, who knows what he wants and what he can get and how to get it, goes back to get that gift. And I mean *get*, and you can be sure that Jacob means it too.

When he reaches the river Jabbok, which is all that stands between him and the Promised Land, he sends his family and his servants across ahead of him, but he remains behind to spend the night on the near shore alone. One wonders why. Maybe in order to savor to its fullest this moment of greatest achievement, this moment for which all his earlier moments have been preparing and from which only a river separates him now.

And then it happens. Out of the deep of the night a stranger leaps. He hurls himself at Jacob, and they fall to the ground, their bodies lashing through the darkness. It is terrible enough not to see the attacker's face, and his strength is more terrible still, the strength of more than a man. All the night through they struggle in silence until just before morning, when it looks as though a miracle might happen. Jacob is winning. The stranger cries out to be set free before the sun rises. Then, suddenly, all is reversed.

He merely touches the hollow of Jacob's thigh, and in a moment Jacob is lying there crippled and helpless. The sense we have, which Jacob must have had, that the whole battle was from the beginning fated to end this way, that the stranger had simply held back until now, letting Jacob exert all his strength and almost win so that when he was defeated, he would know that he was truly defeated; so that he would know that not all the shrewdness, will, brute force that he could muster were enough to get this. Jacob will not release his grip, only now it is a grip not of violence but of need, like the grip of a drowning man.

The darkness has faded just enough so that for the first time he can dimly see his opponent's face. And what he sees is something more terrible than the face of death—the face of love. It is vast and strong, half ruined with suffering and fierce with joy, the face a man flees down all the darkness of his days until at last he cries out, "I will not let you go, unless you bless me!" Not a blessing that he can have now by the strength of his cunning or the force of his will, but a blessing that he can have only as a gift.

Power, success, happiness, as the world knows them, are his who will fight for them hard enough; but peace, love, joy are only from God. And God is the enemy whom Jacob fought there by the river, of course, and whom in one way or another we all of us fight—God, the beloved enemy. Our enemy because, before giving us everything, he demands of us everything; before giving us life, he demands our lives—our selves, our wills, our treasure.

Will we give them, you and I? I do not know. Only remember the last glimpse we have of Jacob, limping home against the great conflagration of the dawn. Remember Jesus of Nazareth, staggering on broken feet out of the tomb toward the resurrection, bearing on his body the proud insignia of the defeat that is victory, the magnificent defeat of the human soul at the hands of God.

2.
The Birth

THE INNKEEPER

> And she gave birth to her first-born son and wrapped him in
> swaddling cloths, and laid him in a manger, because there was
> no place for them in the inn.
>
> —LUKE 2:7

"That was a long, long time ago," said the Innkeeper, "and a long, long way
away. But the memories of men are also long, and nobody has forgotten
anything about my own sad, queer part in it all unless maybe they have forgotten the truth about it. But you can never blame people for forgetting the
truth because it is, after all, such a subtle and evasive commodity. In fact,
all that distinguishes a truth from a lie may finally be no more than just the
flutter of an eyelid or the tone of a voice. If I were to say, 'I BELIEVE!' that
would be a lie, but if I were to say, 'I believe …,' that might be the truth.
So I do not blame posterity for forgetting the subtleties and making me out
to be the black villain of the piece—the heartless one who said, 'No room!
No room!' I'll even grant you that a kind of villainy may be part of the
truth. But if you want to speak the whole truth, then you will have to call
me a villain with a catch in your voice, at least a tremor, a hesitation maybe,

with even the glitter of almost a tear in your eye. Because nothing is entirely black, you know. Not even the human heart.

"I speak to you as men of the world," said the Innkeeper. "Not as idealists, but as realists. Do you know what it is like to run an inn—to run a business, a family, to run anything in this world for that matter, even your own life? It is like being lost in a forest of a million trees," said the Innkeeper, "and each tree is a thing to be done. Is there fresh linen on all the beds? Did the children put on their coats before they went out? Has the letter been written, the book read? Is there money enough left in the bank? Today we have food in our bellies and clothes on our backs, but what can we do to make sure that we will have them still tomorrow? A million trees. A million things.

"Until finally we have eyes for nothing else, and whatever we see turns into a thing. The sparrow lying in the dust at your feet—just a thing to be kicked out of the way, not the mystery of death. The calling of children outside your window—just a distraction, an irrelevance, not life, not the wildest miracle of them all. That whispering in the air that comes sudden and soft from nowhere—only the wind, the wind …

"Of course I remember very well the evening they arrived. I was working on my accounts and looked up just in time to see the woman coming through the door. She walked in that slow, heavy-footed way that women have in the last months, as though they are walking in a dream or at the bottom of the sea. Her husband stood a little behind her—a tongue-tied, helpless kind of man, I thought. I cannot remember either of them saying anything, although I suppose some words must have passed. But at least it was mostly silence. The clumsy silence of the poor. You know what I mean. It was clear enough what they wanted.

"The stars had come out. I remember the stars perfectly though I don't know why I should, sitting inside as I was. And my wife's cat jumped up onto the table where I was sitting. I had not stood up, of course. There was mainly just silence. Then it happened much in the way that you have heard. I did not lie about there being no room left—there really was none—though perhaps if there had been a room, I might have lied. As much for their sakes as for the sake of the inn. Their kind would have felt more at home in a stable, that's all, and I do not mean that unkindly either. God knows.

"Later that night, when the baby came, I was not there," the Innkeeper said. "I was lost in the forest somewhere, the unenchanted forest of a million trees. Fifteen steps to the cellar, and watch out for your head going down. Firewood to the left. If the fire goes out, the heart freezes. Only the wind, the wind. I speak to you as men of the world. So when the baby came, I was not around, and I saw none of it. As for what I heard—just at that moment itself of birth when nobody turns into somebody—I do not rightly know what I heard.

"But this I do know. My own true love. All your life long, you wait for your own true love to come—we all of us do—our destiny, our joy, our heart's desire. So how am I to say it, gentlemen? When he came, I missed him.

"Pray for me, brothers and sisters. Pray for the Innkeeper. Pray for me, and for us all, my own true love."

THE WISE MAN

Now when Jesus was born in Bethlehem of Judea in the days of Herod the king, behold, wise men from the East came to Jerusalem, saying, "Where is he who has been born king of the Jews? For we have seen his star in the East, and have come to worship him."

—MATTHEW 2:1–2

"'Beware of beautiful strangers,'" said one of the magi-astrologers, the wise men, "'and on Friday avoid travel by water. The sun is moving into the house of Venus, so affairs of the heart will prosper.' We said this to Herod, or something along those lines, and of course it meant next to nothing. To have told him anything of real value, we would have had to spend weeks of study, months, calculating the conjunction of the planets at the precise moment of his birth and at the births of his parents and their parents back to the fourth generation. But Herod knew nothing of this, and he jumped at the nonsense we threw him like a hungry dog and thanked us for it. A lost man, you see, even though he was a king. Neither really a Jew nor really a Roman, he was at home nowhere. And he believed in nothing, neither

Olympian Zeus nor the Holy One of Israel, who cannot be named. So he was ready to jump at anything, and he swallowed our little jingle whole. But it could hardly have been more obvious that jingles were the least of what he wanted from us.

"'Go and find me the child,' the king told us, and as he spoke, his fingers trembled so that the emeralds rattled together like teeth. 'Because I want to come and worship him,' he said, and when he said that, his hands were still as death. Death. I ask you, does a man need the stars to tell him that no king has ever yet bowed down to another king? He took us for children, that sly, lost old fox, and so it was like children that we answered him. 'Yes, of course,' we said, and went our way. His hands fluttered to his throat like moths.

"Why did we travel so far to be there when it happened? Why was it not enough just to know the secret without having to be there ourselves to behold it? To this, not even the stars had an answer. The stars said simply that he would be born. It was another voice altogether that said to go—a voice as deep within ourselves as the stars are deep within the sky.

"But why did we go? I could not tell you now, and I could not have told you then, not even as we were in the very process of going. Not that we had no motive, but that we had so many. Curiosity, I suppose: to be wise is to be eternally curious, and we were very wise. We wanted to see for ourselves this One before whom even the stars are said to bow down—to see perhaps if it was really true because even the wise have their doubts. And longing. Longing. Why will a man who is dying of thirst crawl miles across sands as hot as fire at simply the possibility of water? But if we longed to receive, we longed also to give. Why will a man labor and struggle all the days of his life so that in the end he has something to give the one he loves?

"So finally we got to the place where the star pointed us. It was at night. Very cold. The Innkeeper showed us the way that we did not need to be shown. A harebrained, busy man. The odor of the hay was sweet, and the cattle's breath came out in little puffs of mist. The man and the woman. Between them the king. We did not stay long. Only a few minutes as the clock goes, ten thousand, thousand years. We set our foolish gifts down on the straw and left.

"I will tell you two terrible things. What we saw on the face of the newborn child was his death. A fool could have seen it as well. It sat on his head like a crown or a bat, this death that he would die. And we saw, as sure as the earth beneath our feet, that to stay with him would be to share that death, and that is why we left—giving only our gifts, withholding the rest.

"And now, brothers, I will ask you a terrible question, and God knows I ask it also of myself. Is the truth beyond all truths, beyond the stars, just this: that to live without him is the real death, that to die with him is the only life?"

THE SHEPHERD

And in that region there were shepherds out in the field, keeping watch over their flock by night. And an angel of the Lord appeared to them, and the glory of the Lord shone around them, and they were filled with fear. And the angel said to them, "Be not afraid; for behold, I bring you good news of a great joy which will come to all the people; for to you is born this day in the city of David a Savior, who is Christ the Lord. And this will be a sign for you: you will find a babe wrapped in swaddling cloths and lying in a manger." And suddenly there was with the angel a multitude of the heavenly host praising God and saying, "Glory to God in the highest, and on earth peace among men with whom he is pleased!" When the angels went away from them into heaven, the shepherds said to one another, "Let us go over to Bethlehem and see this thing that has happened, which the Lord has made known to us." And they went with haste, and found Mary and Joseph, and the babe lying in a manger. And when they saw it they made known the saying which had been told them concerning this child; and all who heard it wondered at what the shepherds told them.

—LUKE 2:8–18

"Night was coming on, and it was cold," the shepherd said, "and I was terribly hungry. I had finished all the bread I had in my sack, and my gut still ached for more. Then I noticed my friend, a shepherd like me, about to throw away a crust he didn't want. So I said, 'Throw the crust to me, friend!' and he did throw it to me, but it landed between us in the mud where the sheep had mucked it up. But I grabbed it anyway and stuffed it, mud and all, into my mouth. And as I was eating it, I suddenly saw—myself. It was as if I was not only a man eating but a man watching the man eating. And I thought, 'This is who I am. I am a man who eats muddy bread.' And I thought, 'The bread is very good.' And I thought, 'Ah, and the mud is very good too.' So I opened my muddy man's mouth full of bread, and I yelled to my friends, 'By God, it's good, brothers!' And they thought I was a terrible fool, but they saw what I meant. We saw everything that night, everything. Everything!

"Can I make you understand, I wonder? Have you ever had this happen to you? You have been working hard all day. You're dog-tired, bone-tired. So you call it quits for a while. You slump down under a tree or against a rock or something and just sit there in a daze for half an hour or a million years, I don't know, and all this time your eyes are wide open looking straight ahead someplace, but they're so tired and glassy they don't see a thing. Nothing. You could be dead for all you notice. Then, little by little, you begin to come to, then your eyes begin to come to, and all of a sudden you find out you've been looking at something the whole time except it's only now you really see it—one of the ewe lambs maybe, with its foot caught under a rock, or the moon scorching a hole through the clouds. It was there all the time, and you were looking at it all the time, but you didn't see it till just now.

"That's how it was this night, anyway. Like finally coming to—not things coming out of nowhere that had never been there before, but things just coming into focus that had been there always. And such things! The air wasn't just emptiness anymore. It was alive. Brightness everywhere, dipping and wheeling like a flock of birds. And what you always thought was silence stopped being silent and turned into the beating of wings, thousands and thousands of them. Only not just wings, as you came to more, but voices—high, wild, like trumpets. The words I could never remember later, but something like what I'd yelled with my mouth full of bread. 'By God, it's good, brothers! The crust. The mud. Everything. Everything!'

"Oh well. If you think we were out of our minds, you are right, of course. And do you know, it was just like being out of jail. I can see us still. The squint-eyed one who always complained of sore feet. The little sawed-off one who could outswear a Roman. The young one who blushed like a girl. We all tore off across that muddy field like drunks at a fair, and drunk we were, crazy drunk, splashing through a sea of wings and moonlight and the silvery wool of the sheep. Was it night? Was it day? Did our feet touch the ground?

"'Shh, shh, you'll wake up my guests,' said the Innkeeper we met coming in the other direction with his arms full of wood. And when we got to the shed out back, one of the three foreigners who were there held a finger to his lips.

"At the eye of the storm, you know, there's no wind—nothing moves—nothing breathes—even silence keeps silent. So hush now. Hush. There he is. You see him? You see him?

"By Almighty God, brothers. Open your eyes. Listen."

3.

Message in the Stars

Not that I have already obtained this or am already perfect; but I press on to make it my own, because Christ Jesus has made me his own. Brethren, I do not consider that I have made it my own; but one thing I do, forgetting what lies behind and straining forward to what lies ahead, I press on toward the goal for the prize of the upward call of God in Christ Jesus.... Therefore, my brethren, whom I love and long for, my joy and crown, stand firm thus in the Lord, my beloved.... Rejoice in the Lord always; again I will say, Rejoice. Let all men know your forbearance. The Lord is at hand. Have no anxiety about anything, but in everything by prayer and supplication with thanksgiving let your requests be made known to God. And the peace of God, which passes all understanding, will keep your hearts and your minds in Christ Jesus.

—PHILIPPIANS 3:12–4:7

If God really exists, why in heaven's name does God not prove that he exists instead of leaving us here in our terrible uncertainty? Why does he not show his face so that at last a despairing world can have hope? At one time or another, everyone asks such a question. In some objectifiably verifiable and convincing way, we want God himself to demonstrate his own existence.

Deep in our hearts, I suspect that this is what all of us want, unbelievers no less than believers. And I have wondered sometimes what would happen if God were to do just that. What would happen if God did set about demonstrating his existence in some dramatic and irrefutable way?

Suppose, for instance, that God were to take the great, dim river of the Milky Way as we see it from down here flowing across the night sky and were to brighten it up a little and then rearrange it so that all of a sudden one night the world would step outside and look up at the heavens and see not the usual haphazard scattering of stars but, written out in letters light-years tall, the sentence I REALLY EXIST or GOD IS. If I were going to try to write a story or a play about such an event, I would start, of course, with the first night that this great theological headline appeared there in the stars, with suns and moons to dot the *i*'s and the tails of comets to cross the *t*'s. And I would try to show some of the ways I can imagine people might respond to it. I would show some of them sinking to their knees, not because they are especially religious people but just because it might seem somehow the only natural thing to do under the circumstances. They would perhaps do it without even thinking about it, just crumpling down on their knees there in the tall grass out behind the garage. Some of them I would show running back into their houses in terror—guilty ones in terror of judgment, sophisticated ones in terror at the stark and terrible simplicity of it—just GOD IS written up there in the fire of the stars—and maybe in everyone some degree of terror at just the sheer and awesome vastness of the Unknown suddenly making itself known.

There would be a good many tears of regret, I suspect—people thinking that if only they had known it before, what different lives they might have had. And in many a person the sudden, wild upsurge of hope—the sick old man lying in bed where he cannot sleep and looking up through his bedroom window. On the table his clock ticktocks his time away, but there in the sky he sees proof at last of a reality beyond time. And I would want to touch at least on the peculiar astonishment of preachers and theologians, who spend so much of their lives talking about God that, unless they are very careful, God starts to lose all reality for them and to become just a subject for metaphysical speculation. For them too there would be this great affirmation in the night, and they would discover that they had been right after all, more right than perhaps they had ever quite been able to believe, and they would marvel at the strangeness of it.

What I would be trying to suggest in my story would be that the initial impact of God's supplying the world with this kind of objective proof of his existence would be extraordinary. Churches would have to overflow into football stadiums and open fields, wars would stop, crime would stop, a kind of uncanny hush would fall over the world. But as my story ended, I am afraid that in honesty I would have to suggest something else.

Several years would go by and God's proof of himself would still be blazing away every night for all to read. In order to convince people that the message was not just some million-to-one freak of nature, I would be tempted to have God keep on rewriting it in different languages, sometimes accompanying it with bursts of pure color or with music so celestial that finally the last hardened skeptic would be convinced that God must indeed exist after all. Then the way that I would have it end might be this. I would have a child look up at the sky some night, just a plain, garden-variety child with perhaps a wad of bubble gum in his cheek. If this were to be a movie, I would have a close-up here of just the child's eyes with the stars reflected in them, and I would have him spell out the message syllable by syllable. Let us say that this night it happens to be in French—*J'existe quand-même. C'est moi, le bon Dieu.* And deep in the heavens there would be the usual strains of sublime music. And then I would have the child turn to his father, or maybe, with the crazy courage of childhood, I would have him turn to God himself, and the words that I would have him speak would be words to make the angels gasp. "So what if God exists?" he would say. "What difference does *that* make?" And in the twinkling of an eye the message would fade away for good and the celestial music would be heard no more, or maybe they would continue for centuries to come, but it would no longer make any difference.

We all want to be certain, we all want proof, but the kind of proof we tend to want—scientifically or philosophically demonstrable proof that would silence all doubts once and for all—would not in the long run, I think, answer the fearful depths of our need at all. For what we need to know, of course, is not just that God exists, not just that beyond the steely brightness of the stars there is a cosmic intelligence of some kind that keeps the whole show going, but that there is a God right here in the thick of our day-by-day lives who may not be writing messages about himself in the stars but who in one way or another is trying to get messages through our blindness as we move around down here knee-deep in the fragrant muck and misery and marvel of the world. It is not objective proof of God's existence that we want but, whether we use religious language for it or not, the experience of God's presence. That is the miracle that we are really after. And that is also, I think, the miracle that we really get.

I believe that we know much more about God than we admit that we know, than perhaps we altogether know that we know. God speaks to us, I would say, much more often than we realize or than we choose to realize. Before the sun sets every evening, he speaks to each of us in an intensely personal and unmistakable way. His message is not written out in starlight, which in the long run would make no difference; rather, it is written out for each of us in the humdrum, helter-skelter events of each day; it is a message that in the long run might just make all the difference.

Who knows what he will say to me today or to you today or into the midst of what kind of unlikely moment he will choose to say it. Not knowing is what makes today a holy mystery as every day is a holy mystery. But I believe that there are some things that by and large God is always saying to each of us. All of us, for instance, carry around inside ourselves, I believe, a certain emptiness—a sense that something is missing, a restlessness, the deep feeling that somehow all is not right inside our skin. Psychologists sometimes call it anxiety, theologians sometimes call it estrangement, but whatever you call it, I doubt that there are many who do not recognize the experience itself, especially no one of our age, which has been variously termed the age of anxiety, the lost generation, the beat generation, the lonely crowd. Part of the inner world of everyone is this sense of emptiness, unease, incompleteness, and I believe that this in itself is a word from God, that this is the sound that God's voice makes in a world that has explained him away. In such a world, I suspect that maybe God speaks to us most clearly through his silence, his absence, so that we know him best through our missing him.

But he also speaks to us about ourselves, about what he wants us to do and what he wants us to become; and this is the area where I believe we know so much more about him than we admit even to ourselves, where people hear God speak even if they do not believe in him. A face comes toward us down the street. Do we raise our eyes or do we keep them lowered, passing by in silence? Somebody says something about somebody else, and what he says happens to be not only cruel but also funny, and everybody laughs. Do we laugh too, or do we speak the truth? When a friend has hurt us, do we take pleasure in hating him, because hate has its pleasures as well as love, or do we try to build back some flimsy little bridge? Sometimes when we are alone, thoughts come swarming into our heads like bees—some of them destructive, ugly, self-defeating thoughts, some of them creative and glad. Which thoughts do we choose to think then, as much as we have the choice? Will we be brave today or a coward today? Not in some big way probably but in some little foolish way, yet brave still. Will we be honest today or a liar? Just some little pint-sized honesty, but honest still. Will we be a friend or cold as ice today?

All the absurd little meetings, decisions, inner skirmishes that go to make up our days. It all adds up to very little, and yet it all adds up to very much. Our days are full of nonsense, and yet not, because it is precisely into the nonsense of our days that God speaks to us words of great significance—not words that are written in the stars but words that are written into the raw stuff and nonsense of our days, which are not nonsense just because God speaks into the midst of them. And the words that he says, to each of us differently, are *"Be brave ... be merciful ... feed my lambs ... press on toward the goal."*

But they are not all trivia and routine and nonsense, our lives. There are the crises too, crises that shake to the foundations both the great world of the nations and the little world of the individual. And we hear God speak through the crises too, many different kinds of words but sometimes, I think, a word quite different from the others. I am thinking of the great international crises that threaten the world itself with annihilation, and in terms of the individual I am thinking of the deaths of people we love and of the failures and betrayals and of all that rises to imperil our inner peace.

In one of the last letters that St. Paul very likely ever wrote, a letter that he sent off from prison on his way to Rome and death, he has this to say at the end. "Rejoice in the Lord always; again I will say, Rejoice.... The Lord is at hand. Have no anxiety about anything, but in everything by prayer and supplication with thanksgiving let your requests be made known to God." And through the great crises of our times and through the little crises of each of our times, I believe that this is a deep part of what God says to us. Yes, take your times seriously. Yes, know that you are judged by the terrible sins of your times. Yes, you do well to faint with fear and foreboding at what is coming on the world. And yet rejoice. Rejoice. The Lord is at hand. Have no anxiety. Pray.

These words that God speaks to us in our own lives are the real miracles. They are not miracles that create faith as we might think that a message written in the stars would create faith, but they are miracles that it takes faith to see—faith in the sense of openness, faith in the sense of willingness to wait, to watch, to listen, for the incredible presence of God here in the world among us.

4.

The Face in the Sky

And in that region there were shepherds out in the field, keeping watch over their flock by night. And an angel of the Lord appeared to them, and the glory of the Lord shone around them, and they were filled with fear. And the angel said to them, "Be not afraid; for behold, I bring you good news of a great joy, which will come to all the people; for to you is born this day in the city of David a Savior, who is Christ the Lord. And this will be a sign for you: you will find a babe wrapped in swaddling clothes and lying in a manger.

—LUKE 2:8–12

As the Italian film *La Dolce Vita* opens, a helicopter is flying slowly through the sky not very high above the ground. Hanging down from the helicopter in a kind of halter is the life-size statue of a man dressed in robes with his arms outstretched so that he looks almost as if he is flying by himself, especially when every once in a while the camera cuts out the helicopter and all you can see is the statue itself with the rope around it. It flies over a field where some men are working in tractors and causes a good deal of excitement. They wave their hats and hop around and yell, and then one of them recognizes who it is a statue of and shouts in Italian, "Hey, it's Jesus!" whereupon some of them start running along under the plane, waving and calling to it. But the helicopter keeps on going, and after a while it reaches the outskirts of Rome, where it passes over a building on the roof of which there is a swimming pool surrounded by a number of girls in bikinis basking in the sun. Of course they look up too and start waving, and this time the helicopter does a double take as the young men flying it get a good look at the girls and come circling back again to hover over the pool where, above the roar of the engine, they try to get the girls' telephone numbers, explaining that they are taking the statue to the Vatican and will be only too happy to return as soon as their mission is accomplished.

During all of this the reaction of the audience in the little college town where I saw the film was of course to laugh at the incongruity of the whole thing. There was the sacred statue dangling from the sky, on the one hand, and the profane young Italians and the bosomy young bathing beauties, on the other hand—the one made of stone, so remote, so out of place there in the sky on the end of its rope; the others made of flesh, so bursting with life. Nobody in the audience was in any doubt as to which of the two came out ahead or at whose expense the laughter was. But then the helicopter continues on its way, and the great dome of St. Peter's looms up from below, and for the first time the camera starts to zoom in on the statue itself with its arms stretched out, until for a moment the screen is almost filled with just the bearded face of Christ—and at that moment there was no laughter at all in that theater full of students and their dates and paper cups full of buttery popcorn and *la dolce vita* college-style. Nobody laughed during that moment because there was something about that face, for a few seconds there on the screen, that made them be silent—the face hovering there in the sky and the outspread arms. For a moment, not very long to be sure, there was no sound, as if the face were their face somehow, their secret face that they had never seen before but that they knew belonged to them, or the face that they had never seen before but that they knew, if only for a moment, they belonged to.

I think that is much of what the Christian faith is. It is for a moment, just for a little while, seeing the face and being still, that is all. There is so much about the whole religious enterprise that seems superannuated and irrelevant and as out of place in our age as an antique statue is out of place in the sky. But just for the moment itself, say, of Christmas, there can be only silence as something comes to life, some spirit, some hope; as something is born again into the world that is so strange and new and precious that not even a cynic can laugh although he might be tempted to weep.

The face in the sky. The child born in the night among beasts. The sweet breath and steaming dung of beasts. And nothing is ever the same again.

Those who believe in God can never in a way be sure of him again. Once they have seen him in a stable, they can never be sure where he will appear or to what lengths he will go or to what ludicrous depths of self-humiliation he will descend in his wild pursuit of humankind. If holiness and the awful power and majesty of God were present in this least auspicious of all events, this birth of a peasant's child, then there is no place or time so lowly and earthbound but that holiness can be present there too. And this means that we are never safe, that there is no place where we can hide from God, no place where we are safe from his power to break in two and recreate the human heart, because it is just where he seems most helpless that he is most strong, and just where we least expect him that he comes most fully.

For those who believe in God, it means, this birth, that God himself is never safe from us, and maybe that is the dark side of Christmas, the terror of the silence. He comes in such a way that we can always turn him down, as we could crack the baby's skull like an eggshell or nail him up when he gets too big for that. God comes to us in the hungry people we do not have to feed, comes to us in the lonely people we do not have to comfort, comes to us in all the desperate human need of people everywhere that we are always free to turn our backs upon. It means that God puts himself at our mercy not only in the sense of the suffering that we can cause him by our blindness and coldness and cruelty, but the suffering that we can cause him simply by suffering ourselves. Because that is the way love works, and when someone we love suffers, we suffer with him, and we would not have it otherwise because the suffering and the love are one, just as it is with God's love for us.

The child is born in the night—the mother's exhausted flesh, the father's face clenched like a fist—and nothing is ever the same again. Nothing is ever the same again for those who believe in God, and nothing is ever the same again for those who do not believe in God either, because once the birth has happened, it is no longer just God whom they have to deny, but it is also this event that they have to deny. Those who do not believe must also fall silent in the presence of the newborn child, but their silence can have only tears at its heart because for them this can only be another child born to die as every child is born to die, and no matter how bravely and well he lives it, his life can have no meaning beyond the meaning that he gives it, and then like all life it must be like a dream once it has been dreamed. For those who do not believe, all the great poetry of the birth—the angels, the star, the three kings coming out of the night to lay their gifts in the straw—can be only like words that for all their beauty are written on the sand, not poetry that points beyond itself to the very heart of reality, which is beyond the power of time and change to touch.

But what of those who both believe and do not believe, cannot believe—which is some people all of the time and all people some of the time? The statue with its outstretched arms hovers in the sky, the still face looks down, and they recognize the face and call its name. They wave and go running a little way along the uneven ground beneath it. The night deepens and grows still, and maybe the only sound is the birth cry, the little agony of new life coming alive, or maybe there is also the sound of legions of unseen voices raised in joy.

For them too, the believing unbelievers, nothing is ever quite the same again either, because what they have seen and heard in that moment of stillness is, just possibly, possibly, the hope of the world. And what they feel in their hearts as they wave—maybe only with one hand, a little wave, not very certain, but with his name on their lips—is the stirring of new life, new courage, new gladness seeking to be born in them even as he is born, if only they too, we too, the wide world too, will stretch out our arms to those arms and raise our empty faces to that bewildering face.

Lord Jesus Christ, thou Son of the Most High, Prince of Peace, be born again into our world. Wherever there is war in this world, wherever there is pain, wherever there is loneliness, wherever there is no hope, come, thou long-expected one, with healing in thy wings.

Holy Child, whom the shepherds and the kings and the dumb beasts adored, be born again. Wherever there is boredom, wherever there is fear of failure, wherever there is temptation too strong to resist, wherever there is bitterness of heart, come, thou Blessed One, with healing in thy wings.

Savior, be born in each of us as we raise our faces to thy face, not knowing fully who we are or who thou art, knowing only that thy love is beyond our knowing and that no other has the power to make us whole. Come, Lord Jesus, to each who longs for thee even though we have forgotten thy name. Come quickly. Amen.

5.

The Sign by the Highway

Two others also, who were criminals, were led away to be put to death with him. And when they came to the place which is called The Skull, there they crucified him, and the criminals, one on the right and one on the left. And Jesus said, "Father, forgive them; for they know not what they do." And they cast lots to divide his garments. And the people stood by, watching; but the rulers scoffed at him, saying, "He saved others; let him save himself, if he is the Christ of God, his Chosen One!" The soldiers also mocked him, coming up and offering him vinegar, and saying, "If you are the King of the Jews, save yourself!" There was also an inscription over him, "This is the King of the Jews."

One of the criminals who were hanged railed at him, saying, "Are you not the Christ? Save yourself and us!" But the other rebuked him, saying, "Do you not fear God, since you are under the same sentence of condemnation? And we indeed justly; for we are receiving the due reward of our deeds; but this man has done nothing wrong." And he said, "Jesus, remember me when you come in your kingly power." And he said to him, "Truly, I say to you, today you will be with me in Paradise."

—LUKE 23:32–43

A man drives along the highway in his car or a bus, or alongside the high-way in a train, and he sees this and that: the signs and billboards—BURMA SHAVE, CHILDREN GO SLOW, PRINCE OF PIZZA. He sees the wash hanging out back, the reflection in the window of his own face whipped by the tele-phone poles that rush by or the dusty trees. And then maybe once in a while he looks up at the side of a cliff so high that he does not know how anybody ever got up there to do it, or at the concrete abutment of a bridge, and he sees written out in large, clumsy letters, usually done in white paint that has trickled down from the bottoms of the letters as though they were falling apart or melting, the message JESUS SAVES—just that, JESUS SAVES—with all the other signs going on with whatever they are saying too. And if that man is like most of the people I know, including myself much of the time and in many ways, he will wince at the message; and that is really a very strange and interesting thing, both the message and the wincing.

God only knows what kind of a person must have crawled up there with his bucket and brush to slap the words on: a man or a woman, young or old, drunk or sober, by daylight or dark. And God only knows what reason he may have had for doing it, just that way, just there. But in our strange times, among people more or less like us, the effect at least of the words is clear enough: *Jesus Saves*. The effect more or less is that we do wince. And one way or another, I believe, we wince because we are embar-rassed, and embarrassed for all kinds of reasons.

Embarrassed because the words remind us of old-time religion and the sawdust trail and pulpit-pounding, corn-belt parsons, of evangelism in the sense of emotionalism and fundamentalism. We wince because there is something in the name "Jesus" itself that embarrasses us when it stands naked and alone like that, just *Jesus* with no title to soften the blow. It seems to me that the words "Christ Saves" would not bother us half so much because they have a kind of objective, theological ring to them, whereas "Jesus Saves" seems cringingly, painfully personal—somebody named Jesus, of all names, saving somebody named whatever your name happens to be. It is something very personal written up in a place that is very public, like the names of lov-ers carved into the back of a park bench or on an outhouse wall.

Maybe *Jesus Saves* written up there on the cliff or the abutment of the bridge is embarrassing because in one way or another religion in general has become embarrassing: embarrassing to the unreligious man because, although he does not have it anymore, he has never really rooted it out of his soul either, and it still festers there as a kind of reproach; embarrassing to the religious man because, although in one form or another he still does have it, it seldom looks more threadbare or beside the point than when you set it against very much the same kind of seventy-five-mile-per-hour, neon-lit, cluttered, and clamorous world that is represented by the highway that the sign itself looks down upon there.

And maybe, at a deeper level still, *Jesus Saves* is embarrassing because if you can hear it at all through your wincing, if any part at all of what it is trying to mean gets through, what it says to everybody who passes by, and most importantly and unforgivably of all of course what it says to you, is that you need to be saved. Rich man, poor man; young man, old man; educated and uneducated; religious and unreligious—the word is in its way an offense to all of them, all of us, because what it says in effect to all of us is, "You have no peace inside your skin. You are not happy, not whole." That is an unpardonable thing to say to a man whether it is true or false, but especially if it is true, because there he is, trying so hard to be happy, all of us are, to find some kind of inner peace and all in all maybe not making too bad a job of it considering the odds, so that what could be worse psychologically, humanly, than to say to him what amounts to "You will never make it. You have not and you will not, at least not without help"?

And what could be more presumptuous, more absurd, more pathetic, than for some poor fool with a cut-rate brush and a bucket of white paint to claim that the one to give that help is Jesus? If he said God, at least that would be an idea, and if you reject it, it is only an idea that you are rejecting on some kind of intellectual grounds. But by saying "Jesus" he puts it on a level where what you accept or reject is not an idea at all but a person; where what you accept or reject, however dim and far away and disfigured by time, is still just barely recognizable as a human face. Because behind the poor fool with his bucket there always stands of course the Prince of Fools himself, blessed be he, in his own way more presumptuous, more absurd and pathetic than anyone has ever managed to be since.

Jesus Saves.... And the bad thief, the one who according to tradition was strung up on his left, managed to choke out the words that in one form or another men have been choking out ever since whenever they have found themselves crossed up by the world: "Are you the Christ? Then save yourself and us." With the accent on the "us." If you are the savior, whatever that means, then why don't you save us, whatever that involves, save us from whatever it is that crosses us all up before we're done, from the world without and the world within that crosses us all out. Save us from and for and in the midst of the seventy-five-mile-per-hour, neon-lit crisscross of roads that we all travel in this world. And then the good thief, the one on his right, rebuked the bad one for what he had said angrily, and then in effect said it again himself, only not angrily, God knows not angrily—said, "Jesus, remember me when you come in your kingly power." And finally the words of Jesus's answer, "Truly, I say to you, today you will be with me in Paradise," which are words no less crude than the ones trickling down the cliff side, in their way no less presumptuous, absurd, pathetic; words that express no theological idea as an idea, but words that it took a mouth of flesh to say and an ear of flesh to hear. I can imagine that the guards who had been posted there to see that the execution was carried out properly might themselves have felt something like embarrassment and turned away from the sheer lunacy of the scene.

Such a one as that save me? That one—the spindle-shanked crackpot who thinks he is God's son, bloodshot and drunk with his own torture, no less crossed up, crossed out than any other mother's son. Such a one as that—*Jesus,* scrawled up there on the concrete among the four-letter words and the names of lovers? Only somehow then, little by little, a deeper secret of the embarrassment begins to show through: not can such a one as that save me, but can such a one as that save me? Because I suspect that at its heart the painful wincing is directed less to the preposterousness of the claim that Jesus saves than it is directed to the preposterousness of the claim that people like ourselves are savable—not that we are such sinners that we do not deserve saving, but that we are so much ourselves, so hopelessly who we are—no better, no worse—that we wonder if it is possible for us to be saved. I suspect the reason why the name "Jesus" embarrasses us when it stands naked is that it inevitably, if only half consciously, recalls to us our own names, our own nakedness. Jesus saves ... whom? Saves Joe, saves Charlie, Ellen, saves me, saves you—just the names without any Mr.

or Mrs., without any degrees or titles or Social Security numbers; just who we are, no more, no less. I suspect that it is at our own nakedness that we finally wince.

And I suspect also that we know that in one sense anyway the words are right—right at least that, Jesus or no Jesus, something of great importance in our lives is missing, the one piece that all the other pieces have got to fit into if the entire picture of who we are is going to come together and be whole. Something whose name we do not know is missing, in the same way that sometimes in a room with friends we have the unaccountable feeling that some person is missing, someone who is supposed to be there and whom we need and want to be there, even though we cannot think who it is and know him only by his absence.

The message on the cliff side calls us by name, and it is at our own names that I believe we wince most painfully, because we know that we are less than our names: we are our names minus whatever belongs in the empty place. And the question a man is apt to ask in the darkest moments of his life is what salvation can there be, from anywhere, for the man who is less than his name.

A friend of mine had a dream that I think was a dream about this question. He dreamed he was standing in an open place out under the sky, and there was a woman also standing there dressed in some coarse material like burlap. He could not see her face distinctly, but the impression he had was that she was beautiful, and he went up to her and asked her a question. This friend of mine described himself to me once as a believing unbeliever, and the question that he asked her was the same one that Pontius Pilate asked Jesus, only he did not ask it the way you can imagine Pilate did—urbanely, with his eyes narrowed—but instead he asked it with great urgency, as if his life depended on the answer, as perhaps it did. He went up to the woman in his dream and asked, "What is the truth?" Then he reached out for her hand, and she took it. Only instead of a hand, she had the claw of a bird, and as she answered his question, she grasped his hand so tightly in that claw that the pain was almost unendurable and prevented him from hearing her answer. So again he asked her, "What is the truth?" and again she pressed his hand, and again the pain drowned out her words. And then once more, a third time, and once more the terrible pain and behind it the answer he could not hear. And the dream ended. What is the truth for the man who believes and cannot believe that there is a truth beyond all truths, to know which is to be himself made whole and true?

A child on Christmas Eve or on the day before his birthday lives for the presents that he will open the next day, and in this sense we all live like children. There are so many presents still to be opened—tomorrow, next month, next year—and in a way it is our looking forward to the presents that keeps us going. The unexpected friendship, the new job, seeing our names in the paper, falling in love, the birth of a child—all of these are presents that life gives if we want them badly enough and if we are lucky enough, and in a way every new day is a present to be opened just as today was and tomorrow will be. The old saying is that where there is life, there is hope, and I think that the hope that there is is the hope that, if not tomorrow or the next day, then some fine day, somehow, life will finally give us the present that, when we open it, will turn out to be the one we have waited for so long, the one that will fill the empty place, which is the peace that passeth all understanding, which is the truth, salvation, whatever we want to call it. But one by one, as we open the presents, no matter how rich and wondrous they are, we discover that not one of them by itself, nor even all of them taken together, is the one of our deepest desiring—that ultimately, although her face is beautiful and draws us to her, life by herself does not have that final present to give. And to know that is the pain of it as again and again we reach out our hands to life for what we need most deeply, only to have it seized in the terrible grasp. My friend in his dream asked, "What is the truth?" and it might have seemed that the answer was the pain itself; that the ultimate truth is the pain of discovering that there is no ultimate truth. Except that beyond the pain was the answer that, because of the pain, he could not hear.

What is the truth? Take my hand. The truth is not in my hand. It is not mine to give, is not life's to give. What is the truth? It is not the answer to any question that we know how to ask. Can there be a truth that saves, can there be salvation, for those who have learned of life not to believe in salvation? Only on the other side of pain, the dream said. On the other side of the pained embarrassment at the words *Jesus Saves,* which at its heart is a pained embarrassment at our own nakedness and incompleteness. On the other side of the bird-claw pain that brought tears to the eyes of the dreamer, which is the pain of hope betrayed. On the other side of the pain of the good thief, which is the pain of surrender, the pain of acknowledging finally our utter helplessness to save ourselves. In the depths of his own pain the good thief said, "Jesus, remember me when you come in your kingly power." Remember me. Remember me.

Jesus said, "I will." He said, preposterously, "Today you will be with me in Paradise." Spindle-shanked crackpot, Mary's boy, God's son, flattened out on the face of a cliff, like a spider he scrambles up past the four-letter words and the names of lovers to slap up his preposterous pitch—*Jesus Saves*—and the preposterousness, the vulgarity almost, of those words that make us wince is finally, of course, the vulgarity of God himself. The vulgarity of a God who adorns the sky at sunrise and sundown with colors no decent painter would dream of placing together on a single canvas, the vulgarity of a God who created a world full of hybrids like us—half ape, half human—and who keeps breaking back into the muck of this world. The vulgarity of a God who was born into a cave among hicks and the steaming dung of beasts only to grow up and die on a cross between crooks. The vulgarity of a God who tampers with the lives of crooks, of clowns like me to the point where we come among crooks and clowns like you with white paint and a brush of our own and nothing more profound to say, nothing more precious and crucial to say finally, than just "Yes, it is true. He does save—Jesus. He gives life, he makes whole, and if you choose to be, you will be with him in Paradise."

If it is not true, then all our religion or lack of it is only futility, busyness. If it is true, then it is we who are the crackpots, the preposterous of the earth, if we do not draw near to him who saves. How? I do not know, except that through wanting to draw near, we have already drawn nearer. Through the moments of our own lives when something of his truth, his life, breaks through as it does in the sign by the highway and our wincing at it, as it breaks through in the sight of our own lonely and searching and most unsaved faces when we see them reflected in the train window whipped by the telegraph poles, as it breaks through in the occasional dream that is a holy dream. Moments like these.

How do we draw near? Through the prayers not just that we pray in a church, God knows, but through the anytime, anywhere prayer that is

"Remember me, even though I don't remember you" that is "What is the truth?" which is also a prayer. We draw near to him by following him even on clumsy and reluctant feet and without knowing more than two cents' worth at first about what is involved in following him—into the seventy-five-mile-per-hour, neon-lit pain of our world.

And if he is the truth and the life, we will find it out soon enough for ourselves, you can be sure of that. If we want to find it out, if we are willing to draw near in whatever idiotic way we can, all our reservations and doubts notwithstanding, because little by little we find out then that to be where he is, to go where he goes, to see through eyes and work with hands like his is to feel like ourselves at last, is to become fully ourselves at last and fully each other's at last, and to become finally more even than that: to become fully his at last.

Almighty and everlasting God, only speak to us that we may hear thee. Then speak to us again and yet again so that when in our hearts we answer thee by saying No, we may at least know well to whom we say it, and what it costs us to say it, and what it costs our brothers, and what it costs thee. And when at those moments that we can never foretell we say Yes to thee, forgive our halfheartedness, accept us as we are, work thy miracle within us, and of thy grace give us strength to follow wherever love may lead.

We bless thee for him who shows us the way and is the way and who will be, we pray, at the end of all our ways. Grant that even on stumbling feet we may follow him into the terrible needs of the human heart. Remember us. Remember us. For thy mercy's sake. Amen.

6.

The Calling of Voices

In the year that King Uzziah died I saw the Lord sitting upon a throne, high and lifted up; and his train filled the temple. Above him stood the seraphim; each had six wings: with two he covered his face, and with two he covered his feet, and with two he flew. And one called to another and said: "Holy, holy, holy is the Lord of hosts; the whole earth is full of his glory." And the foundations of the thresholds shook at the voice of him who called, and the house was filled with smoke. And I said: "Woe is me! For I am lost; for I am a man of unclean lips, and I dwell in the midst of a people of unclean lips; for my eyes have seen the King, the Lord of hosts!"

Then flew one of the seraphim to me, having in his hand a burning coal which he had taken with tongs from the altar. And he touched my mouth, and said: "Behold, this has touched your lips; your guilt is taken away, and your sin forgiven." And I heard the voice of the Lord saying, "Whom shall I send, and who will go for us?" Then I said, "Here I am! Send me." And he said, "Go ..."

—ISAIAH 6:1–9

"Man shall not live by bread alone, but by every word that proceeds from the mouth of God."

—MATTHEW 4:4

The telephone rings late one night, and you jump out of your skin. You try for a while to pretend that it is not ringing, but after a while you answer it because otherwise you will never know who it is, and it might be anybody—anybody. Then a voice says, "Listen, something has happened. Something has got to be done. I know you are busy. I know you have lots on your mind. But you've got to come. For God's sake."

Or you are walking along an empty beach toward the end of the day, and there is a gray wind blowing, and a seagull with a mussel shell in its beak flaps up and up and then lets the shell drop to the rocks below, and there is something so wild and brave and beautiful about it that you have to write it into a poem or paint it into a picture or sing it into a song; or if you are no good at any of these, you have to live out at least the rest of that day in a way that is somehow true to the little scrap of wonder that you have seen.

Or I think of the school church that I served for a time where the offering each week was given to an institution for mentally handicapped children, and when the plate was passed around, some of the students, resentful of having to go to church at all, would drop in their penny or would drop in nothing at all. Then maybe someday a friend would drag one of them down to where the money went, and he would get to know one of the children a little, and when he went back another day, the child would come running up to him in a way that made him suddenly see, with a kind of panic almost, that for that child, the sight of him was Christmas morning and a rocket to the moon and the no-school whistle on a snowy morning. And then it was like the phone ringing in the night again or the seagull riding the gray wind. It was a summons that he had to answer somehow or, at considerable cost, not answer.

Or in the year that King Uzziah died, or in the year that John F. Kennedy died, or in the year that somebody you loved died, you go into the temple if that is your taste, or you hide your face in the little padded temple of your hands, and a voice says, "Whom shall I send into the pain of a world where people die?" and if you are not careful, you may find yourself answering, "Send me." You may hear the voice say, "Go." Just *go*.

Like "duty," "law," and "religion," the word "vocation" has a dull ring to it, but in terms of what it means, it is really not dull at all. *Vocare,* "to call," of

course, and our vocation is our calling. It is the work that we are called to
in this world, the thing that we are summoned to spend our lives doing.
We can speak of ourselves as choosing our vocations, but perhaps it is at
least as accurate to speak of our vocations choosing us, of a call's being
given and lives our hearing it, or not hearing it. And maybe that is the
place to start: the business of listening and hearing. Our lives are full of all
sorts of voices calling us in all sorts of directions. Some of them are voices
from inside and some of them are voices from outside. The more alive
and alert we are, the more clamorous our lives are. Which do we listen to?
What kind of voice do we listen for?

There is a sad and dangerous little game we play when we get to be a certain age. It is a form of solitaire. We get out our class yearbook, look at the pictures of the classmates we knew best, and recall the days when we first knew
them in school, all those years ago. We think about all the exciting, crazy,
wonderfully characteristic things they used to be interested in and about the
kind of dreams we had about what we were going to do when we graduated
and about the kind of dreams that maybe we had for some of them. Then
we think about what those classmates actually did with their lives, what we
are doing with them now ten or twenty years later. I make no claim that the
game is always sad or that when it seems to be sad our judgment is always
right, but once or twice when I have played it myself, sadness has been a large
part of what I have felt. Because in my class, at the school I went to, as in any
class at any school, there were students who had a real flair, a real talent, for
something. Maybe it was for writing or acting or sports. Maybe it was an interest and a joy in working with people toward some common goal, a sense of
responsibility for people who in some way had less than they had or were less.
Sometimes it was just their capacity for being so alive that made you more
alive to be with them. Yet now, a good many years later, I have the feeling that
more than just a few of them are spending their lives at work in which none
of these gifts is being used, at work they seem to be working at with neither
much pleasure nor any sense of accomplishment. This is the sadness of the
game, and the danger of it is that maybe we find that in some measure we are
among them or that we are too blind to see that we are.

When you are young, I think, your hearing is in some ways better than
it is ever going to be again. You hear better than most people the voices that

call to you out of your own life to give yourself to this work or that work. When you are young, before you accumulate responsibilities, you are freer than most people to choose among all the voices and to answer the one that speaks most powerfully to who you are and to what you really want to do with your life. But the danger is that there are so many voices and they all in their ways sound so promising. The danger is that you will not listen to the voice that speaks to you through the seagull mounting the gray wind, say, or the vision in the temple, that you do not listen to the voice inside you or to the voice that speaks from outside but specifically to you out of the specific events of your life, but that instead you listen to the great blaring, boring, banal voice of our mass culture, which threatens to deafen us all by blasting forth that the only thing that really matters about your work is how much it will get you in the way of salary and status, and that if it is gladness you are after, you can save that for weekends. In fact one of the grimmer notions that we seem to inherit from our Puritan forebears is that work is not even supposed to be glad but, rather, a kind of penance, a way of working off the guilt that you accumulate during the hours when you are not working.

The world is full of people who seem to have listened to the wrong voice and are now engaged in a life's work in which they find no pleasure or purpose and who run the risk of suddenly realizing someday that they have spent the only years that they are ever going to get in this world doing something that could not matter less to themselves or to anyone else. This does not mean, of course, people who are doing work that from the outside looks unglamorous and humdrum, because obviously such work as that may be a crucial form of service and deeply creative. But it means people who are doing work that seems simply irrelevant not only to the great human needs and issues of our time but also to their own need to grow and develop as humans.

In John Marquand's novel *Point of No Return,* for instance, after years of apple-polishing and bucking for promotion and dedicating all his energies to a single goal, Charlie Gray finally gets to be vice president of the fancy little New York bank where he works; and then the terrible moment comes when he realizes that it is really not what he wanted after all, when the prize that he has spent his life trying to win suddenly turns to ashes in his hands. His promotion assures him and his family of all the security and standing that he has always sought, but Marquand leaves you with the feeling that maybe the best way Charlie Gray could have supported his family would have been by giving his life to the kind of work where he could have expressed himself and fulfilled himself in such a way as to become in himself, as a person, the kind of support they really needed.

There is also the moment in the Gospels where Jesus is portrayed as going into the wilderness for forty days and nights and being tempted there by the devil. And one of the ways that the devil tempts him is to wait until Jesus is very hungry from fasting and then to suggest that he simply turn the stones into bread and eat. Jesus answers, "Man shall not live by bread alone," and this just happens to be, among other things, true, and very close to the same truth that Charlie Gray comes to when he realizes too late that he was not made to live on status and salary alone, but that something crucially important was missing from his life even though he was not sure what it was any more than, perhaps, Marquand himself was sure what it was.

There is nothing moralistic or sentimental about this truth. It means for us simply that we must be careful with our lives, for Christ's sake, because it would seem that they are the only lives we are going to have in this puzzling and perilous world, and so they are very precious and what we do with them matters enormously. Everybody knows that. We need no one to tell it to us. Yet in another way perhaps we do always need to be told, because there is always the temptation to believe that we have all the time in the world, whereas the truth of it is that we do not. We have only one life, and the choice of how we are going to live it must be our own choice, not one that we let the world make for us. Because surely Marquand was right that for each of us there comes a point of no return, a point beyond which we no longer have life enough left to go back and start all over again.

To Isaiah, the voice said, "Go," and for each of us there are many voices that say it, but the question is which one will we obey with our lives, which of the voices that call is to be the one we answer. No one can say, of course, except each for himself, but I believe that it is possible to say at least this in general to all of us: we should go with our lives where we most need to go and where we are most needed.

Where we most need to go. Maybe that means that the voice we should listen to most as we choose a vocation is the voice that we might think we should listen to least, and that is the voice of our own gladness. What can we do that makes us gladdest, what can we do that leaves us with the strongest sense of sailing true north and of peace, which is much of what gladness is? Is it making things with our hands out of wood or stone or paint on canvas? Or is it making something we hope like truth out of words? Or is it making people laugh or weep in a way that cleanses their spirit? I believe that if it is a thing that makes us truly glad, then it is a good thing and it is our thing and it is the calling voice that we were made to answer with our lives.

And also, where we are most needed. In a world where there is so much drudgery, so much grief, so much emptiness and fear and pain, our gladness in our work is as much needed as we ourselves need to be glad. If we keep our eyes and ears open, our hearts open, we will find the place surely. The phone will ring and we will jump not so much out of our skin as into our skin. If we keep our lives open, the right place will find us.

Jesus said, "Man shall not live by bread alone, but by every word that proceeds from the mouth of God," and in the end every word that proceeds from the mouth of God is the same word, and the word is Christ himself. And in the end that is the vocation, the calling of all of us, the calling to be Christs. To be Christs in whatever way we are able to be. To be Christs with whatever gladness we have and in whatever place, among whatever brothers we are called to. That is the vocation, the destiny to which we were all of us called even before the foundations of the world.

O thou, who art the God no less of those who know thee not than of those who love thee well, be present with us at the times of choosing when time stands still and all that lies behind and all that lies ahead are caught up in the mystery of a moment. Be present especially with the young who must choose between many voices. Help them to know how much an old world needs their youth and gladness. Help them to know that there are words of truth and healing that will never be spoken unless they speak them, and deeds of compassion and cour-age that will never be done unless they do them. Help them never to mistake success for victory or failure for defeat. Grant that they may never be entirely content with whatever bounty the world may

bestow upon them, but that they may know at last that they were
created not for happiness but for joy, and that joy is to them alone
who, sometimes with tears in their eyes, commit themselves in love
to thee and to others. Lead them and all the world ever deeper into
the knowledge that finally all people are one and that there can never
really be joy for any until there is joy for all. In Christ's name we ask
it and for his sake. Amen.

7.

A Sprig of Hope

Now the earth was corrupt in God's sight, and the earth was filled with violence. And God saw the earth, and behold, it was corrupt; for all flesh had corrupted their way upon the earth. And God said to Noah, "I have determined to make an end of all flesh; for the earth is filled with violence through them.... For behold, I will bring a flood of waters upon the earth, to destroy all flesh in which is the breath of life.... Make yourself an ark of gopher wood; make rooms in the ark, and cover it inside and out with pitch.... And of every living thing of all flesh, you shall bring two of every sort into the ark, to keep them alive with you; they shall be male and female.... For in seven days I will send rain upon the earth forty days and forty nights; and every living thing that I have made I will blot out from the face of the ground." And Noah did all that the Lord had commanded him....

In the sixth hundredth year of Noah's life, in the second month, on the seventeenth day of the month, on that day all the fountains of the great deep burst forth, and the windows of the heavens were opened.... The flood continued forty days upon the earth; and the waters increased, and bore up the ark, and it rose high above the earth. The waters prevailed and increased greatly upon the earth; and the ark floated on the face of the waters. And the waters prevailed so mightily upon the earth that all the high mountains under the whole heaven were covered ... fifteen cubits deep.... Only Noah was left, and those that were with him in the ark....

At the end of forty days Noah opened the window of the ark which he had made.... Then he sent forth a dove from him, to see if the waters had subsided from the face of the ground; but the dove found no place to set her foot, and she returned to him to the ark, for the waters were still on the face of the whole earth. So he put forth his hand ... and brought her into the ark with him. He waited another seven days, and again he sent forth the dove out of the ark; and the dove came back to him in the evening, and lo, in her mouth a freshly plucked olive leaf.

—GENESIS 6:11–8:11, PASSIM

It is an ironic fact that this ancient legend about Noah survives in our age mainly as a children's story. When I was a child, I had a Noah's ark made of wood with a roof that came off so you could take the animals out and put them in again, and my children have one too. Yet if you stop to look at it at all, this is really as dark a tale as there is in the Bible, which is full of dark tales. It is a tale of God's terrible despair over the human race and his decision to visit them with a great flood that would destroy them all except for this one old man, Noah, and his family. Only now we give it to children to read. One wonders why.

Not, I suspect, because children particularly want to read it, but more because their elders particularly do not want to read it, or at least do not want to read it for what it actually says and so make it instead into a fairy tale, which no one has to take seriously—just the way we make black jokes about disease and death so that we can laugh instead of weep at them; just the way we translate murder and lust into sixth-rate television melodramas, which is to reduce them to a size that anybody can cope with; just the way we take the nightmares of our age, the sinister, brutal forces that dwell in the human heart threatening always to overwhelm us and present them as the Addams family or monster dolls, which we give, again, to children. *Gulliver's Travels* is too bitter about humankind, so we make it into an animated cartoon; *Moby Dick* is too bitter about God, so we make it into an adventure story for boys; Noah's ark is too something-or-other else, so it becomes a toy with a roof that comes off so you can take the little animals out. This is one way of dealing with the harsher realities of our existence, and since the alternative is, by facing them head on, to risk adding more to our burden of anxiety than we are able to bear, it may not be such a bad way at that. But for all our stratagems, the legends, the myths persist among us, and even in the guise of fairy tales for the young they continue to embody truths or intuitions that in the long run it is perhaps more dangerous to evade than to confront.

So what, then, are the truths embodied in this tale of Noah and his ark? Let us start with the story itself, more particularly let us start with the moment when God first spoke to Noah, more particularly let us start with Noah's face at that moment when God first spoke to him.

When somebody speaks to you, you turn your face to look in the direction the voice comes from; but if the voice comes from no direction at all, if the voice comes from within and comes wordlessly, and more powerfully for being wordless, then in a sense you stop looking at anything at all. Your eyes become unseeing, and if someone were to pass a hand in front of them, you would hardly notice the hand. If you can be said to be looking at anything then, you are probably looking at, without really seeing, something of no importance whatever, like the branch of a tree stirring in the wind or the frayed cuff of your shirt where your arm rests on the windowsill. Your face goes vacant because for the moment you have vacated it and are living somewhere beneath your face, wherever it is that the voice comes from. So it was maybe with Noah's face when he heard the words that he heard, or when he heard what he heard translated clumsily into words: that the earth was corrupt in God's sight, filled with violence and pain and unlove—that the earth was doomed.

It was presumably nothing that Noah had not known already, nothing that any of us who have ever lived on this earth with our eyes open have not known. But because it came upon him sudden and strong, he had to face it more squarely than people usually do, and it rose up in him like a pain in his own belly. And then maybe, like Kierkegaard's Abraham, Noah asked whether it was God who was speaking or only the pain in his belly; whether it was a vision of the glory of the world as it first emerged from the hand of the Creator that led him to the knowledge of how far the world had fallen, or whether it was just his pathetic human longing for a glory that had never been and would never be. If that was his question, perhaps a flicker of bewilderment passed across his vacant face—the lines between his eyes deepening, his mouth going loose, a little stupid. A penny for your thoughts, old Noah.

But then came the crux of the thing because the voice that was either God's voice or an undigested matzoh ball shifted from the indicative of doom to the imperative of command and it told him that, although the world was doomed, he, Noah, had a commission to perform that would have much to do with the saving of the world. "Make yourself an ark of gopher wood," the voice said, "and, behold, I will bring a flood of waters upon the earth to destroy all flesh in which is the breath of life." So Noah had to decide, and the decision was not just a theological one—yes, it is God; no, it is not; and you live your life the same way in either case—because if the voice proceeded not from the mystery of the human belly but from the mystery and depth of life itself, then Noah had to obey, and Noah knew it. And out of common humanity this is the point to shift our gaze from his face, because things are happening there that no stranger should be allowed to see, and to look instead at his feet, because when we have to decide which way we are going to bet our entire lives, it is very often our feet that finally tell the tale.

There are Noah's feet—dusty, a little slew-footed, Chaplinesque, stock still. You watch them. Even the birds in the trees watch. Which direction will the feet move, or will they move at all? It comes down to that with all of us finally. And finally they do move. Maybe with no spring in the step, maybe dragging a little, but they move nevertheless. And they move in the direction of . . . the lumber yard . . . as he bets his life on his voice.

There are so many things to say about Noah, whoever he was, if ever he was, the old landlubber with the watery, watery eyes; but the one thing that is certain is that he must have looked like an awful fool for a while, for all those days it took him to knock together the great and ponderous craft. Three hundred cubits long and fifty cubits wide and thirty cubits high, all three decks of it covered inside and out with pitch, and he had nothing more plausible in the way of an explanation than that he was building it—and building it many a mile from the nearest port—because a voice had told him to, which was maybe God's voice or maybe hardening of the arteries. Only a fool would heed such a voice at all when every other voice for miles around could tell him, and probably did, that our proper business is to keep busy: to work, to play, to make love, to watch out for our own interests as everybody else does, and to leave the whole shadowy business of God to those who have a taste for shadows. So Noah building his ark becomes the bearded joke draped in a sheet who walks down Broadway with his sandwich-board inscribed REPENT; and Noah's face becomes the great white moon face of the clown looking up with anguish at the ones who act out their dance of death on the high wire. A penny for your thoughts, old Noah, as you pound together your zany craft while the world goes about its business as usual and there is not a cloud in the sky.

His thoughts, one imagines, were of water, and as the windows of heaven were opened and all the fountains of the great deep burst forth so that the sea crept in over the earth, and where there had been dry land and order all was disorder and violence, perhaps Noah knew that it had always been so. Perhaps Noah knew that all the order and busyness of people had been at best an illusion and that, left to themselves, they had always been doomed. The waters came scudding in over forest and field, sliding in across kitchen floors and down cellar stairs, rising high above television aerials and the steeples of churches, and death was everywhere as death is always everywhere, people trapped alone as they are always trapped, always alone, in office or locker room, bedroom or bar, people grasping out for something solid and sure to keep themselves from drowning, everybody fighting for the few remaining pieces of dry ground. Maybe the chaos was no greater than it has ever been. Only wetter.

The ark rose free from its moorings, cumbersome old tub creaking and pitching in the wilderness of waves with the two of everything down below and a clown for a captain who did not know his port from his starboard. But it stayed afloat, by God, this Toonerville trolley of vessels, clouted from side to side by the waves and staggering like a drunk. It was not much, God knows, but it was enough, and it stayed afloat, and granted that it was noisy as hell and stank to heaven, creatures took comfort from each other's creatureliness, and the wolf lay down with the lamb, and the lion ate straw like the ox, and life lived on in the ark while all around there was only chaos and death.

Then finally, after many days, Noah sent forth a dove from the ark to see if the waters had subsided from the earth, and that evening she returned, and lo, in her mouth a freshly plucked olive leaf. Once again, for the last time, the place to look, I think, is Noah's face. The dove stands there with her delicate, scarlet feet on the calluses of his upturned palm. His cheek just touches her breast so that he can feel the tiny panic of her heart. His eyes are closed, the lashes watery wet. Only what he weeps with now, the old clown, is no longer anguish, but wild and irrepressible hope. That is not the end of the story in Genesis, but maybe that is the end of it for most of us—just a little sprig of hope held up against the end of the world.

All these old tales are about us, of course, and I suppose that is why we can never altogether forget them; that is why, even if we do not read them anymore ourselves, we give them to children to read so that they will never be entirely lost, because if they were, part of the truth about us would be lost too. The truth, for instance, that, left to ourselves, as a race we *are* doomed—what else can we conclude?—doomed if only by our own insatiable lust for doom. Despair and destruction and death are the ancient enemies, and yet we are always so helplessly drawn to them that it is as if we are more than half in love with our enemies. Even our noblest impulses and purest dreams get all tangled up with them just as in Vietnam, in the name of human dignity and freedom, the bombs are falling on both the just and the unjust and we recoil at the horror of little children with their faces burned off, except that somehow that is the way the world has always been and is, with nightmare and noble dream all tangled up together. That is the way we are doomed—doomed to be what we are, doomed to seek our own doom. And the turbulent waters of chaos and nightmare are always threatening to burst forth and flood the earth. We hardly need the tale of Noah to tell us that. The *New York Times* tells us just as well, and our own hearts tell us well too, because chaos and nightmare have their little days there also. But the tale of Noah tells other truths as well.

It tells about the ark, for one, which somehow managed to ride out the storm. God knows the ark is not much—if anybody knows it is not much, God knows—and the old joke seems true that if it were not for the storm without, you could never stand the stench within. But the ark was enough, is enough. Because the ark is wherever human beings come together as human beings in such a way that the differences between them stop being barriers—the way if people meet at the wedding, say, of someone they both love, all the differences of age between them, all the real and imagined differences of color, of wealth, of education, no longer divide them but become for each a source of strength and delight, and although they may go right on looking at each other as very odd fish indeed, it becomes an oddness to gladden the heart, and there is no shyness anymore, no awkwardness or fear of each other. Sometimes even in a church we can look into each other's faces and see that, beneath the differences, we are all of us outward bound on a voyage for parts unknown.

The ark is wherever people come together because this is a stormy world where nothing stays put for long among the crazy waves and where at the end of every voyage there is a burial at sea. The ark is where, just because it is such a world, we really need each other and know very well that we do. The ark is wherever human beings come together because in their heart of hearts all of them—white and black, believer and unbeliever, hippie and square—dream the same dream, which is a dream of peace—peace between the nations, between the races, between the brothers—and thus ultimately a dream of love. Love not as an excuse for the mushy and innocuous, but love as a summons to battle against all that is unlovely and unloving in the world. The ark, in other words, is where we have each other and where we have hope.

Noah looked like a fool in his faith, but he saved the world from drowning, and we must not forget the one whom Noah foreshadows and who also looked like a fool spread-eagled up there, cross-eyed with pain, but who also saved the world from drowning. We must not forget him because he saves the world still, and wherever the ark is, wherever we meet and touch in something like love, it is because he also is there, brother and father of us all. So into his gracious and puzzling hands we must commend ourselves through all the days of our voyaging, wherever it takes us, and at the end of all our voyages. We must build our arks with love and ride out the storm with courage and know that the little sprig of green in the dove's mouth betokens a reality beyond the storm more precious than the likes of us can imagine.

*How can we pray to thee, thou holy and hidden God, whose ways
are not our ways, who reignest in awful mystery beyond the realm of
space and time? Yet how can we not pray to thee, Heavenly Father,
who knowest what it is to be a man because thou hast walked among
us as a man, breaking with us the bread of our affliction and drinking deep of the cup of our despair? How can we not pray to thee when
it is thy very Spirit alive within us that moves our lips in prayer?*

*Hear, O God, the prayers of all thy children everywhere: for
forgiveness and healing, for courage, for faith; prayers for the needs
of others; prayers for peace among the desperate nations. Whether
thou givest or withholdest what we ask, whether thou answerest us in
words that burn like fire or in silence that burns like fire, increase in
us the knowledge that thou art always more near to us than breathing, that thy will for us is love.*

*And deep beneath all our asking, so deep beneath that we are all
but deaf to it ourselves, hear, O God, the secret song of every human
heart praising thee for being what thou art, rejoicing with the morning stars that thou art our God and we thy children. Make strong
and wild this secret song within until it bursts forth at last to thy
glory and our saving. Through Jesus Christ our Lord. Amen.*

8.
Come and See

The people who walked in darkness have seen a great light; those who dwelt in a land of deep darkness, on them has light shined. Thou hast multiplied the nation, thou hast increased its joy; they rejoice before thee as with joy at the harvest, as men rejoice when they divide the spoil. For the yoke of his burden, and the staff for his shoulder, the rod of his oppressor, thou hast broken as on the day of Midian. For every boot of the tramping warrior in battle tumult and every garment rolled in blood will be burned as fuel for the fire. For to us a child is born, to us a son is given; and the government will be upon his shoulder, and his name will be called "Wonderful Counselor, Mighty God, Everlasting Father, Prince of Peace."

—ISAIAH 9:2–6

In one respect if in no other this metaphor of Isaiah's is a very relevant one for us and our age because we are also, God knows, a people who walk in darkness. There seems little need to explain. If darkness is meant to suggest a world where nobody can see very well—either themselves, or each other, or where they are heading, or even where they are standing at the moment; if darkness is meant to convey a sense of uncertainty, of being lost, of being afraid; if darkness suggests conflict, conflict between races, between nations, between individuals all pretty much out for themselves when you come right down to it; then we live in a world that knows much about darkness. Darkness is what our newspapers are about. Darkness is what most of our best contemporary literature is about. Darkness fills the skies over our own cities no less than over the cities of our enemies. And in our single lives, we know much about darkness too. If we are people who pray, darkness is apt to be a lot of what our prayers are about. If we are people who do not pray, it is apt to be darkness in one form or another that has stopped our mouths.

But the prophecy of Isaiah is that into this darkness a great light will shine, and of course the proclamation of the gospel, especially the wild and joy-drunk proclamation of Christmas, is that into this darkness there has already shone a light to dazzle the world with its glory and its terror, for if there is a terror about darkness because we cannot see, there is also a terror about light because we *can* see. There is a terror about light because much of what we see in the light about ourselves and our world we would rather not see, would rather not have be seen. The first thing that the angel said to the shepherds was, "Be not afraid," and he said it with the glory of the Lord shining round about them there in the fields, because there was terror as well as splendor in the light of the glory of the Lord.

In the darkness of a church, the candles burn. They hold the darkness back, just barely hold it back. In the darkness of that Judean night, in the midst of nowhere, to parents who were nobody, the child was born, and whoever it was that delivered him slapped his bare backside to start the breath going, and he cried out, as each one of us cried out, at the shock and strangeness of being born into the darkness of the world. Then, as the Gospels picture it, all heaven broke loose.

The darkness was shattered like glass, and the glory flooded through with the light of a thousand suns. A new star blazed forth where there had never been a star before, and the air was filled with the bright wings of angels, the night sky came alive with the glittering armies of God, and a great hymn of victory rose up from them—"Glory to God in the highest"—and strange kings arrived out of the East to lay kingly gifts at the feet of this even stranger and more kingly child. This is how, after all the weary centuries of waiting, the light is said finally to have come into the world, as Luke proclaims it and Matthew, and they proclaim it of course in the language of faith and from the standpoint of faith.

But there is also the standpoint of history and the blunt language of fact. We live in a skeptical age where the assumption that most of us go by, consciously or otherwise, is that nothing is entirely real that cannot somehow be verified by science. It seems to me at best a dubious assumption, but it is part of the air we breathe, so let us be as skeptical as our age about this story of Christmas. Let us assume that if we had been there that night when he was born, we would have seen nothing untoward at all. Let us assume that the darkness would have looked very much like any darkness. Maybe there were a few stars, the same old stars, or the moon. For a long time the only sound perhaps was the rough, rapid breathing of the woman in labor. If the tradition of the manger is accurate, there was the smell of hay, the great moist eyes of the cattle. The father was there, possibly a shepherd or two attracted by the light, if there was any light. There was a last cry of pain from the mother as the child was born, and then the cry of the child. In the distance maybe the lonely barking of a dog. The mother stares up at the rafters from where she is lying, too exhausted even to think of the child. Someone has taken him from her to wrap him up against the cold and darkness of the world. Maybe a mouse burrows deeper into the straw.

Maybe that is all we would have seen if we had been there because maybe that or something like that was all that really happened. In the Letters of St. Paul, which are the earliest New Testament writings, there is no suggestion that the birth of Jesus was accompanied by any miracle, and in the Gospel of Mark, which is probably the earliest of the four, the birth plays no part. So a great many biblical scholars would agree with the skeptics that the great nativity stories of Luke and Matthew are simply the legendary accretions, the poetry, of a later generation, and that were we to have been present, we would have seen a birth no more or less marvelous than any other birth.

But if that is the case, what do we do with the legends of the wise men and the star, the shepherds and the angels and the great hymn of joy that the angels sang? Do we dismiss them as fairy tales, the subject for pageants to sentimentalize over once a year come Christmas, the lovely dream that never came true? Only if we are fools do we do that, although there are many in our age who have done it and there are moments of darkness when each one of us is tempted to do it. A lovely dream. That is all.

Who knows what the facts of Jesus's birth actually were? As for myself, the longer I live, the more inclined I am to believe in miracle, the more I suspect that if we had been there at the birth, we might well have seen and heard things that would be hard to reconcile with modern science. But of course that is not the point, because the Gospel writers are not really interested primarily in the facts of the birth but in the significance, the meaning for them of that birth, just as the people who love us are not really interested primarily in the facts of our births but in what it meant to them when we were born and how for them the world was never the same again, how their whole lives were charged with new significance. Whether there were ten million angels there or just the woman herself and her husband when that child was born, the whole course of history was changed. That is a fact as hard and blunt as any fact. Art, music, literature, our culture itself, our political institutions, our whole understanding of ourselves and our world—it is impossible to conceive of how differently world history would have developed if that child had not been born. And in terms of faith, much more must be said because for faith the birth of the child into the darkness of the world made possible not just a new way of understanding life but a new way of living life.

Ever since the child was born, there have been people who have gotten drunk on him no less than they can get drunk on hard liquor. Or if that metaphor seems crude, all the way down the centuries since that child was born, there have been countless different kinds of people who in count-less different kinds of ways have been filled with his spirit, who have been grasped by him, caught up into his life, who have found themselves in deep and private ways healed and transformed by their relationships with him, so much so that they simply have no choice but to go on proclaiming what the writers of the Gospels first proclaimed: that he was indeed the long expected one, the Christ, Wonderful Counselor, Mighty God, Everlasting Father, Prince of Peace—all these curious and forbidding terms that Christians keep on using in their attempt to express in language one thing and one thing only. That in this child, in the man he grew up to be, there is the power of God to bring light into our darkness, to make us whole, to give a new kind of life to anybody who turns toward him in faith, even to such as you and me.

This is what Matthew and Luke are trying to say in their stories about how he was born, and this is the truth that no language seemed too miraculous to them to convey. This is the only truth that matters, and the wise men, the shepherds, the star are important only as ways of pointing to this truth. So what is left to us then is the greatest question of them all. How do we know whether or not this truth is true? How do we find out for ourselves whether in this child born so long ago there really is the power to give us a new kind of life in which both suffering and joy are immeasurably deepened, a new kind of life in which little by little we begin to be able to love even our friends, at moments maybe even our enemies, maybe at last even ourselves, even God?

Adeste fidelis. That is the only answer I know for people who want to find out whether or not this is true. Come all ye faithful, and all ye who would like to be faithful if only you could, all ye who walk in darkness and hunger for light. Have faith enough, hope enough, despair enough, foolishness enough at least to draw near to see for yourselves.

He says to ask and it will be given you, to seek and you will find. In other words, he says that if you pray for him, he will come to you, and as far as I know, there is only one way to find out whether that is true, and that is to try it. Pray for him and see if he comes, in ways that only you will recognize. He says to follow him, to walk as he did into the world's darkness, to throw yourself away as he threw himself away for love of the dark world. And he says that if you follow him, you will end up on some kind of cross, but that beyond your cross and even on your cross you will also find your heart's desire, the peace that passes all understanding. And again, as far as I know there is only one way to find out whether that is true, and that is to try it. Follow him and see. And if the going gets too tough, you can always back out. Maybe you can always back out.

Adeste fidelis. Come and behold him, born the king of angels. Speak to him or be silent before him. In whatever way seems right to you and at whatever time, come to him with your empty hands. The great promise is that to come to him who was born at Bethlehem is to find coming to birth within ourselves something stronger and braver, gladder and kinder and holier, than ever we knew before or than ever we could have known without him.

Dear God, in the darkness of the virgin's womb the holy child grows. In the darkness of the world's pain, the blessed light begins to kindle. In the darkness of our own doubting of thee and of ourselves, the great hope begins to rise again like a lump in the throat: the hope that thou wilt come to us truly, that the child will be born again in our midst, the Prince of Peace in a world at war, the hope that thou wilt ransom us and our world from the darkness that seeks to destroy us.

O Lord, the gift of new life, new light, can be a gift truly only if we open ourselves to receive it. So this is our prayer, Lord: that thou wilt open our eyes to see thy glory in the coming again of light each day, open our ears to hear the angels' hymn in the stirring within us of joy at the coming of the child, open our hearts to the transforming power of thy love as it comes to us through the love of all those who hold us most dear and have sacrificed most for us.

Be born among us that we may ourselves be born. Be born within us that by words and deeds of love we may bear the tidings of thy birth to a world that dies for lack of love. We ask it in the child's name. Amen.

9.

A Room Called Remember

And they brought in the ark of God, and set it inside the tent which David had pitched for it; and they offered burnt offerings and peace offerings before God. . . . Then on that day David first appointed that thanksgiving be sung to the Lord by Asaph and his brethren: "O give thanks to the Lord, call on his name, make known his deeds among the peoples! . . . Glory in his holy name; let the hearts of those who seek the Lord rejoice! Seek the Lord and his strength, seek his presence continually! Remember the wonderful works that he has done, the wonders he wrought, the judgments he uttered."

—1 CHRONICLES 16:1, 7–12

And he said, "Jesus, remember me when you come in your kingly power." And he said to him, "Truly, I say to you, today you will be with me in Paradise."

—LUKE 23:42–43

Every once in a while, if you're like me, you have a dream that wakes you up. Sometimes it's a bad dream—a dream in which the shadows become so menacing that your heart skips a beat and you come awake to the knowledge that not even the actual darkness of night is as fearsome as the dreamed darkness, not even the shadows without as formidable as the shadows within. Sometimes it's a sad dream—a dream sad enough to bring real tears to your sleeping eyes so that it's your tears that you wake up by, wake up to. Or again, if you're like me, there are dreams that take a turn so absurd that you wake laughing—as if you need to be awake to savor the full richness of the comedy. Rarest of all is the dream that wakes you with what I can only call its truth.

The path of your dream winds now this way, now that—one scene fades into another, people come and go the way they do in dreams—and then suddenly, deep out of wherever it is that dreams come from, something rises up that shakes you to your foundations. The mystery of the dream suddenly lifts like fog, and for an instant it is as if you glimpse a truth truer than any you knew that you knew, if only a truth about yourself. It is too much truth for the dream to hold anyway, and the dream breaks.

Several years ago I had such a dream, and it is still extraordinarily fresh in my mind. I dreamt that I was staying in a hotel somewhere and that the room I was given was a room that I loved. I no longer have any clear picture of what the room looked like, and even in the dream itself I think it wasn't so much the way the room looked that pleased me as it was the way it made me feel. It was a room where I felt happy and at peace, where everything seemed the way it should be and everything about myself seemed the way it should be too. Then, as the dream went on, I wandered off to other places and did other things and finally, after many adventures, ended back at the same hotel again. Only this time I was given a different room, which I didn't feel comfortable in at all. It seemed dark and cramped, and I felt dark and cramped in it. So I made my way down to the man at the desk and told him my problem. On my earlier visit, I said, I'd had this marvelous room that was just right for me in every way and that I'd very much like if possible to have again. The trouble, I explained, was that I hadn't kept track of where the room was and didn't know how to find it or how to ask for it. The clerk was very understanding. He said that he knew exactly the room I meant and that I could have it again anytime I wanted it. All I had to do, he said, was ask for it by its name. So then, of course, I asked him what the name of the room was. He would be happy to tell me, he said, and then he told me. The name of the room, he said, was Remember.

Remember, he said. The name of the room I wanted was Remember. That was what woke me. It shocked me awake, and the shock of it, the dazzling unexpectedness of it, is vivid to me still. I knew it was a good dream, and I felt that in some unfathomable way it was also a true dream. The fact that I did not understand its truth did not keep it from being in some sense also a blessed dream, a healing dream, because you do not need to understand healing to be healed or know anything about blessing to be blessed. The sense of peace that filled me in that room, the knowledge that I could return to it whenever I wanted to or needed to—that was where the healing and blessing came from. And the name of the room—that was where the mystery came from; that was at the heart of the healing though I did not fully understand why. The name of the room was Remember. *Why* Remember? What was there about remembering that brought a peace so deep, a sense of well-being so complete and intense that it jolted me awake in my bed? It was a dream that seemed true not only for me but true for everybody. What are we to remember—all of us? To what end and purpose are we to remember?

One way or another, we are always remembering, of course. There is no escaping it even if we want to, or at least no escaping it for long, though God knows there are times when we try to, don't want to remember. In one sense the past is dead and gone, never to be repeated, over and done with, but in another sense, it is of course not done with at all or at least not done with us. Every person we have ever known, every place we have ever seen, everything that has ever happened to us—it all lives and breathes deep in us somewhere whether we like it or not, and sometimes it doesn't take much to bring it back to the surface in bits and pieces. A scrap of some song that was popular years ago. A book we read as a child. A stretch of road we used to travel. An old photograph, an old letter. There is no telling what trivial thing may do it, and then suddenly there it all is—something that happened to us once—and it is there not just as a picture on the wall to stand back from and gaze at, but as a reality we are so much a part of still and that is still so much a part of us that we feel with something close to its original intensity and freshness what it felt like, say, to fall in love at the age of sixteen, or to smell the smells and hear the sounds of a house that has long since disappeared, or to laugh till the tears ran down our cheeks with somebody who died more years ago than we can easily count or for whom, in every way that matters, we might as well have died years ago ourselves. Old failures, old hurts. Times too beautiful to tell or too terrible. Memories come at us helter-skelter and unbidden, sometimes so thick and fast that they are more than we can handle in their poignance, sometimes so sparsely that we all but cry out to remember more.

But the dream seems to say more than that, to speak of a different kind of memory and to speak of remembering in a different kind of way. The kind of memories I have been naming are memories that come and go more or less on their own and apart from any choice of ours. Things remind us, and the power is the things', not ours. The room called Remember, on the other hand, is a room we can enter whenever we like so that the power of remembering becomes our own power. Also, the kind of memories we normally have are memories that stir emotions in us that are as varied as the memories that stir them. The room called Remember, on the other hand, is a room where all emotions are caught up in and transcended by an extraordinary sense of well-being. It is the room of all rooms where we feel at home and at peace. So what do these differences point to, is the ques-tion—the difference between the haphazard memories that each day brings to us willy-nilly and the memories represented by the room in the dream?

First of all, I think, they point to remembering as much more of a conscious act of the will than it normally is for us. We are all such escape artists, you and I. We don't like to get too serious about things, especially about ourselves. When we are with other people, we are apt to talk about almost anything under the sun except for what really matters to us, except for our own lives, except for what is going on inside our own skins. We pass the time of day. We chatter. We hold each other at bay, keep our distance from each other even when God knows it is precisely each other that we desperately need.

And it is the same thing when we are alone. Let's say it is late evening and everybody else has gone away or gone to bed. The time is ripe for look-ing back over the day, the week, the year, and trying to figure out where we have come from and where we are going to, for sifting through the things we have done and the things we have left undone for a clue to who we are and who, for better or worse, we are becoming. But again and again we avoid the long thoughts. We turn on the television maybe. We pick up a newspaper or a book. We find some chore to do that could easily wait for the next day. We cling to the present out of wariness of the past. We cling to the surface out of fear of what lies beneath the surface. And why not, after all? We get tired. We get confused. We need such escape as we can find. But there is a deeper need yet, I think, and that is the need—not all the time, surely, but from time to time—to enter that still room within us all where the past lives on as part of the present, where the dead are alive again, where we are most alive ourselves to the long journeys of our lives with all their twistings and turnings and to where our journeys have brought us. The name of the room is Remember—the room where with patience, with charity, with quietness of heart, we remember consciously to remember the lives we have lived.

So much has happened to us all over the years. So much has happened within us and through us. We are to take time to remember what we can about it and what we dare. That's what entering the room means, I think. It means taking time to remember on purpose. It means not picking up a book for once or turning on the radio, but letting the mind journey gravely, deliberately, back through the years that have gone by but are not gone. It means a deeper, slower kind of remembering; it means remembering as a searching and finding. The room is there for all of us to enter if we choose to, and the process of entering it is not unlike the process of praying, because praying too is a slow, grave journey—a search to find the truth of our own lives at their deepest and dearest, a search to understand, to hear and be heard.

"Nobody knows the trouble I've seen" goes the old spiritual, and of course nobody knows the trouble we have any of us seen—the hurt, the sadness, the bad mistakes, the crippling losses—but we know it. We are to remember it. And the happiness we have seen too—the precious times, the precious people, the moments in our lives when we were better than we know how to be. Nobody knows that either, but we know it. We are to remember it. And then, if my dream was really a true dream, we will find, beyond any feelings of joy or regret that one by one the memories give rise to, a profound and undergirding peace, a sense that in some unfathomable way all is well.

We have survived, you and I. Maybe that is at the heart of our remembering. After twenty years, forty years, sixty years or eighty, we have made it to this year, this day. We needn't have made it. There were times we never thought we would and nearly didn't. There were times we almost hoped we wouldn't, were ready to give the whole thing up. Each must speak for himself, for herself, but I can say for myself that I have seen sorrow and pain enough to turn the heart to stone. Who hasn't? Many times I have chosen the wrong road, or the right road for the wrong reason. Many times I have loved the people I love too much for either their good or mine, and others I might have loved I have missed loving and lost. I have followed too much the devices and desires of my own heart, as the old prayer goes, yet often when my heart called out to me to be brave, to be kind, to be honest, I have not followed at all.

To remember my life is to remember countless times when I might have given up, gone under, when humanly speaking I might have gotten lost beyond the power of any to find me. But I didn't. I have not given up. And each of you, with all the memories you have and the tales you could tell, you also have not given up. You also are survivors and are here. And what does that tell us, our surviving? It tells us that weak as we are, a strength beyond our strength has pulled us through at least this far, at least to this day. Foolish as we are, a wisdom beyond our wisdom has flickered up just often enough to light us if not to the right path through the forest, at least to a path that leads forward, that is bearable. Faint of heart as we are, a love beyond our power to love has kept our hearts alive.

So in the room called Remember it is possible to find peace—the peace that comes from looking back and remembering to remember that though most of the time we failed to see it, we were never really alone. We could never have made it this far if we had had only each other to depend on, because nobody knows better than we do ourselves the undependability and frailty of even the strongest of us. Who or what was with us all those years? Who or what do we have to thank for our survival? Our lucky stars? Maybe just that. Maybe we have nothing more to thank than that. Our lucky stars.

But David the king had more than that or thought he did. "O give thanks to the Lord," he cried out, "make known his deeds among the peoples!" He had brought the ark of the covenant into Jerusalem and placed it in a room, a tent, and to the sound of harp, lyre, cymbals, and trumpet he sang his wild and exultant song. "Remember the wonderful works that he has done," he sang, "the wonders he wrought, the judgments he uttered." *Remember* was the song David sang, and what memories he had or was to have, what a life to remember! His failure as a husband and a father, his lust for Bathsheba and the murder of her husband, his crime against Naboth and the terrible denunciation of the prophet Nathan, his failures, his betrayals, his hypocrisy. But "Tell of his salvation from day to day" (1 Chron. 16:23), his song continues nonetheless and continued all his life, and I take him to mean not just that the telling was to take place from day to day, but that salvation itself takes place from day to day. Every day, as David remembered, he had been somehow saved—saved enough to survive his own darkness and lostness and folly, saved enough to go on through thick and thin to the next day and the next day's saving and the next. "Remember the wonders he wrought, the judgments he uttered," David cries out in his song, and the place where he remembers these wonders and judgments is his own past in all its brokenness and the past of his people before him, of Abraham, Isaac, and Jacob, the Exodus, the entrance into the Promised Land, which are all part of our past too as Christ also is part of our past, that Exodus, that Promised Land, and all those mightier wonders yet. That's what he remembers and sings out for us all to remember.

"Seek the Lord and his strength, seek his presence continually" goes the song—seek him in the room in the tent where the holy ark is, seek him in the room in the dream. It is the Lord, it is God, who has been with us through all our days and years whether we knew it or not, he sings—with us in our best moments and in our worst moments, to heal us with his wonders, to wound us healingly with his judgments, to bless us in hidden ways though more often than not we had forgotten his name. It is God that David thanks and not his lucky stars. "O give thanks to the Lord ... make known his deeds among the peoples," he sings; remember and make known the deeds that he wrought among the years of your own lives. Is he right? Was it God? Is it God we have to thank, you and I, for having made it somehow to this day?

Again each of us must speak for himself, for herself. We must, each one of us, remember our own lives. Someone died whom we loved and needed, and from somewhere something came to fill our emptiness and mend us where we were broken. Was it only time that mended, only the resurging busyness of life that filled our emptiness? In anger we said something once that we could have bitten our tongues out for afterwards, or in anger somebody said something to us. But out of somewhere forgiveness came, a bridge was rebuilt; or maybe forgiveness never came, and to this day we have found no bridge back. Is the human heart the only source of its own healing? Is it the human conscience only that whispers to us that in bitterness and estrangement is death? We listen to the evening news with its usual recital of shabbiness and horror, and God, if we believe in him at all, seems remote and powerless, a child's dream. But there are other times—often the most unexpected, unlikely times—when strong as life itself comes the sense that there is a holiness deeper than shabbiness and horror and at the very heart of darkness a light unutterable. Is it only the unpredictable fluctuations of the human spirit that we have to thank? We must each of us answer for ourselves, remember for ourselves, preach to ourselves our own sermons. But "Remember the wonderful works," sings King David, because if we remember deeply and truly, he says, we will know whom to thank, and in that room of thanksgiving and remembering there is peace.

Then hope. Then at last we see what hope is and where it comes from, hope as the driving power and outermost edge of faith. Hope stands up to its knees in the past and keeps its eyes on the future. There has never been a time past when God wasn't with us as the strength beyond our strength, the wisdom beyond our wisdom, as whatever it is in our hearts—whether we believe in God or not—that keeps us human enough at least to get by despite everything in our lives that tends to wither the heart and make us less than human. To remember the past is to see that we are here today by grace, that we have survived as a gift.

And what does that mean about the future? What do we have to hope for, you and I? Humanly speaking, we have only the human best to hope for: that we will live out our days in something like peace and the ones we love with us; that if our best dreams are never to come true, neither at least will our worst fears; that something we find to do with our lives will make some little difference for good somewhere; and that when our lives end we will be remembered a little while for the little good we did. That is our human hope. But in the room called Remember we find something beyond it.

"Remember the wonderful works that he has done," goes David's song—remember what he has done in the lives of each of us; and beyond that remember what he has done in the life of the world; remember above all what he has done in Christ—remember those moments in our own lives when with only the dullest understanding but with the sharpest longing we have glimpsed that Christ's kind of life is the only life that matters and that all other kinds of life are riddled with death; remember those moments in our lives when Christ came to us in countless disguises through people who one way or another strengthened us, comforted us, healed us, judged us, by the power of Christ alive within them. All that is the past. All that is what there is to remember. And *because* that is the past, *because* we remember, we have this high and holy hope: that what he has done, he will continue to do, that what he has begun in us and our world, he will in unimaginable ways bring to fullness and fruition.

"Let the sea roar, and all that fills it, let the field exult, and everything in it! Then shall the trees of the wood sing for joy," says David (1 Chron. 16:32–33). And *shall* is the verb of hope. Then death shall be no more, neither shall there be mourning or crying. Then shall my eyes behold him and not as a stranger. Then his Kingdom shall come at last and his will shall be done in us and through us and for us. Then the trees of the wood shall sing for joy as already they sing a little even now sometimes when the wind is in them and as underneath their singing our own hearts too already sing a little sometimes at this holy hope we have.

The past and the future. Memory and expectation. Remember and hope. Remember and wait. Wait for him whose face we all of us know because somewhere in the past we have faintly seen it, whose life we all of us thirst for because somewhere in the past we have seen it lived, have maybe even had moments of living it ourselves. Remember him who himself remembers us as he promised to remember the thief who died beside him. To have faith is to remember and wait, and to wait in hope is to have what we hope for already begin to come true in us through our hoping. Praise him.

10.
Faith

By faith we understand that the world was created by the word of God, so that what is seen was made out of things which do not appear.... By faith Noah, being warned by God concerning events as yet unseen, took heed and constructed an ark for the saving of his household.... By faith Abraham ... went out, not knowing where he would go.... By faith Sarah herself received power to conceive even when she was past the age.... These all died in faith, not having received what was promised, but having seen it and greeted it from afar, and having acknowledged that they were strangers and exiles on the earth. For people who speak thus make it clear that they are seeking a homeland.

—HEBREWS 11:3, 7–14

Every once in a while, life can be very eloquent. You go along from day to day not noticing very much, not seeing or hearing very much, and then all of a sudden, when you least expect it, very often something speaks to you with such power that it catches you off guard, makes you listen whether you want to or not. Something speaks to you out of your own life with such directness that it is as if it calls you by name and forces you to look where you have not had the heart to look before, to hear something that maybe for years you have not had the wit or the courage to hear. I was on my way home from a short trip I took not long ago when such a thing happened to me—three such things actually, three images out of my journey, that haunt me still with what seems a truth that it is important to tell.

The first thing was this. I was on a train somewhere along that grim stretch of track between New Brunswick, New Jersey, and New York City. It was a gray fall day with low clouds in the sky and a scattering of rain in the air, a day as bleak and insistent as a headache. The train windows were coated with dust, but there wasn't all that much to see through them anyway except for the industrial wilderness that spread out in all directions and looked more barren and more abandoned as we approached Newark—the flat, ravaged earth, the rubble, the endless factories black as soot against the sky with their tall chimneys that every now and then are capped with flame, a landscape out of Dante. I was too tired from where I'd been to feel much like reading and still too caught up in what I'd be doing to be able to doze very satisfactorily, so after gazing more or less blindly out of the dirty window for a while, I let my eyes come to rest on the nearest bright thing there was to look at, which was a large color photograph framed on the wall up at the front end of the coach.

It was a cigarette ad, and I forget what it was in it exactly, but there was a pretty girl in it and a good-looking boy, and they were sitting together somewhere—by a mountain stream, maybe, or a lake, with a blue sky overhead, green trees. It was a crisp, sunlit scene full of beauty, of youth, full of *life* more than anything else, and thus as different as it could have been from the drabness I'd been looking at through the window until I felt just about equally drab inside myself. And then down in the lower left-hand corner of the picture, in letters large enough to read from where I was sitting, was the Surgeon General's familiar warning about how cigarette smoking can be hazardous to your health, or whatever the words are that they use for saying that cigarette smoking can cause lung cancer and kill you dead as a doornail.

It wasn't that I hadn't seen such ads thousands of times before and boggled at the macabre irony of them—those pretty pictures, that fatal message—but for some reason having to do with being tired, I suppose, and having nothing else much to look at or think about, I was so stunned by this one that I haven't forgotten it yet. "Buy this; it will kill you," the ad said. "Choose out of all that is loveliest and greenest and most innocent in the world that which can make you sick before your time and bring your world to an end. Live so you will die."

I'm not interested here in scoring a point against the advertising business or the tobacco industry, and the dangers of cigarette smoking are not what I want to talk about; what I want to talk about is something a great deal more dangerous still, which the ad seemed to be proclaiming with terrible vividness and power. We are our own worst enemies, the ad said. That's what I want to talk about. I had heard it countless times before as all of us have, but this time the ad hit me over the head with it—that old truism that is always true, spell it out and apply it however you like. As nations we stockpile new weapons and old hostilities that may well end up by destroying us all; and as individuals we do much the same. As individuals we stockpile weapons for defending ourselves against not just the things and people that threaten us but against the very things and people that seek to touch our hearts with healing and make us better and more human than we are. We stockpile weapons for holding each other at arm's length, for wounding sometimes even the ones who are closest to us. And as for hostilities—toward other people, toward ourselves, toward God if we happen to believe in God—we can all name them silently and privately for ourselves.

The world is its own worst enemy, the ad said. The world, in fact, is its *only* enemy. No sane person can deny it, I think, as suddenly the picture on the wall of the train jolted me into being sane and being unable to deny it myself. The pretty girl and the good-looking boy. The lake and trees in all their beauty. The blue sky in all its innocence and mystery. And, tucked in among it all, this small, grim warning that we will end by destroying ourselves if we're not lucky. We need no urging to choose what it is that will destroy us because again and again we choose it without urging. If we don't choose to smoke cigarettes ourselves, we choose at least to let such ads stand without batting an eye. "Buy this; it can kill you," the pretty picture said, and nobody on the train, least of all myself, stood up and said, "Look, this is madness!" Because we are more than half in love with our own destruction. All of us are. That is what the ad said. I suppose I had always known it, but for a moment—rattling along through the Jersey flats with the gray rain at the window and not enough energy to pretend otherwise for once—I more than knew it. I choked on it.

The second thing was not unlike the first in a way, as if, in order to put the point across, life had to hit me over the head with it twice. I haven't led an especially sheltered life as lives go. I've knocked around more or less like everybody else and have seen my share of the seamy side of things. I was born in New York City and lived there off and on for years. I've walked along West Forty-Second Street plenty of times and seen what there is to see there though I've tried not to see it—wanted to see it and tried not to see it at the same time. I've seen the adult bookstores and sex shops with people hanging around the doors to con you into entering. I've seen the not all that pretty girls and less than good-looking boys—many of them hardly more than children, runaways—trying to keep alive by clumsily, shiftily selling themselves for lack of anything else to sell; and staggering around in the midst of it all, or slumped like garbage against the fronts of buildings, the Forty-Second Street drunks—not amiable, comic drunks you can kid yourself into passing with a smile, but angry, bloodshot, crazy drunks, many of them members of minority groups because minorities in New York City have more to be angry and crazy about than the rest of us.

I'd seen it all before and will doubtless see it all again, but walking from my train to the Port Authority bus terminal—and with that ad, I suppose, still on my mind—I saw it almost as if for the first time. And, as before, I'm not so much interested in scoring a point against the sex industry, or against the indifference or helplessness or ineptitude of city governments, or against the plague of alcoholism; because instead, again, it was the very sight I saw that scored a point against me, against our world. I found myself suddenly so scared stiff by what I saw that if I'd known a place to hide, I would have gone and hidden there. And what scared me most was not just the brutality and ugliness of it all but how vulnerable I was to the brutality and ugliness, how vulnerable to it we all of us are and how much it is a part of us.

What scared the daylights out of me was to see suddenly how drawn we all are, I think, to the very things that appall us—to see how beneath our civilizedness, our religiousness, our humanness, there is that in all of us which remains uncivilized, religionless, subhuman and which hungers for precisely what Forty-Second Street offers, which is basically the license to be subhuman not just sexually but any other way that appeals to us—the license to use and exploit and devour each other like savages, to devour and destroy our own sweet selves. And if you and I are tempted to think we don't hunger for such things, we have only to remember some of the dreams we dream and some of the secrets we keep and the battle against darkness we all of us fight. I was scared stiff that I would somehow get lost in that awful place and never find my way out. I was scared that everybody I saw coming toward me down the crowded sidewalk—old and young, well dressed and ragged, innocent and corrupt—was in danger of getting lost. I was scared that the world itself was as lost as it was mad. And of course in a thousand ways it is.

The third thing was finally getting home. It was late and dark when I got there after a long bus ride, but there were lights on in the house. My wife and daughter were there. They had waited supper for me. There was a fire in the woodstove, and the cat was asleep on his back in front of it, one paw in the air. There are problems at home for all of us—problems as dark in their way as the dark streets of any city—but they were nowhere to be seen just then. There was nothing there just then except stillness, light, peace, and the love that had brought me back again and that I found waiting for me when I got there. Forty-Second Street was only a couple of hundred miles from my door, but in another sense it was light-years away.

Part of what I felt, being home, was guilt, because feeling guilty is one of the things we are all so good at. I felt guilty about having, at home, the kind of peace the victims and victimizers of Forty-Second Street not only don't have but don't even know exists, because that is part of the price you pay for being born into the world poor, unloved, without hope. "I was hungry and you gave me food," Christ said. "I was a stranger and you welcomed me.... I was sick and you visited me," Christ said (Matt. 25:35–36), and by coming home I was turning my back not just on Christ, but on all the sick, the hungry, the strangers in whom Christ is present and from whom I'd fled like a bat out of hell—just that, because hell was exactly where I'd been. But I wouldn't let myself feel guilty long; I fought against feeling guilty, because as I sat there in that warm, light house, safe for the moment from the darkness of night and from all darkness, I felt something else so much more powerful and real.

Warmth. Light. Peace. Stillness. Love. That was what I felt. And as I entered that room where they were present, it seemed to me that wherever these things are found in the world, they should not be a cause for guilt but treasured, nurtured, sheltered from the darkness that threatens them. I thought of all such rooms everywhere—both rooms inside houses and rooms inside people—and how in a way they are like oases in the desert where green things can grow and there is refreshment and rest surrounded by the sandy waste; how in a way they are like the monasteries of the Dark Ages, where truth, wisdom, charity were kept alive surrounded by barbarity and misrule.

The world and all of us in it are half in love with our own destruction and thus mad. The world and all of us in it are hungry to devour each other and ourselves and thus lost. That is not just a preacher's truth, a rhetorical truth, a Sunday school truth. Listen to the evening news. Watch television. Read the novels and histories and plays of our time. Read part of what there is to be read in every human face including my face and your faces. But every once in a while in the world, and every once in a while in ourselves, there is something else to read—there are places and times, inner ones and outer ones, where something like peace happens, love happens, light happens, as it happened for me that night I got home. And when they happen, we should hold on to them for dear life, because of course they are dear life. They are glimpses and whispers from afar: that peace, light, love are where life ultimately comes from, that deeper down than madness and lostness they are what at its heart life is. By faith we know this, and I think only by faith, because there is no other way to know it.

"By faith we understand that the world was created by the word of God, so that what is seen was made out of things which do not appear," says the author of Hebrews. Faith is a way of looking at what is seen and understanding it in a new sense. Faith is a way of looking at what there is to be seen in the world and in ourselves and hoping, trusting, believing against all evidence to the contrary that beneath the surface we see there is vastly more that we cannot see.

What is it "that is seen," as Hebrews puts it? What is seen is the ruined landscape I saw through the train window, the earth so ravaged you can't believe any green thing will ever grow there again. What is seen is all the streets in the world like Forty-Second Street—the crazy drunks, the child whores, the stink of loneliness, emptiness, cruelty, despair. Maybe most of all what is seen, if we're honest, is that there is in all of us what is both sickened and fascinated by such things, attracted and repelled. What is seen is a world that tries to sell us what kills us like the cigarette ad and never even gives it a second thought, as you and I rarely give it a second thought either but rush to buy what the world sells, and in our own way sell it ourselves.

Who or what created such a world? On the face of it, there seems to be only one answer to that question. We ourselves created it—that is the answer—and it is hard to see on the face of it—hard to *see*—that what created us can have been anything more than some great cosmic upheaval, some slow, blind process as empty of meaning or purpose as a glacier. But "by faith," says Hebrews, we see exactly the same world and yet reach exactly the opposite answer, which is faith's answer. "By faith we understand that the world was created by the word of God," it says, "so that what is seen was made out of things which do not appear."

By faith we understand, if we are to understand it at all, that the madness and lostness we see all around us and within us are not the last truth about the world but only the next to the last truth. Madness and lostness are the results of terrible blindness and tragic willfulness, which whole nations are involved in no less than you and I are involved in them. Faith is the eye of the heart, and by faith we see deep down beneath the face of things—by faith we struggle against all odds to be able to see—that the world is God's creation even so. It is he who made us and not we ourselves, made us out of his peace to live in peace, out of his light to dwell in light, out of his love to be above all things loved and loving. That is the last truth about the world.

Can it be true? No, of course it cannot. On the face of it, if you take the face seriously and face up to it, how can it possibly be true? Yet how can it not be true when our own hearts bear such powerful witness to it, when blessed moments out of our own lives speak of it so eloquently? And that no-man's-land between the Yes and the No, that everyman's land, is where faith stands and has always stood. Seeing but not seeing, understanding but not understanding, we all stand somewhere between the Yes and the No the way old Noah stood there before us, and Abraham, and Sarah his wife, all of them. The truth of God as the last and deepest truth—they none of them saw it in its fullness any more than we have, but they spent their lives homesick for it—seeking it like a homeland, like home, and their story is our story because we too have seen from afar what peace is, light is, love is, and we have seen it in something like that room that love brought me back to that rainy day on the train and the bus, and where I found supper waiting, found love waiting, love enough to see me through the night.

That still, light room in that house—and whatever that room represents of stillness and light and the possibility of faith, of Yes, in your own lives—is a room to find healing and hope in, but it is also a room with a view. It is a room that looks out, like the window of the train, on a landscape full of desolation—that looks out on Forty-Second Street with its crowds of hungry ones, lonely ones, sick ones, all the strangers who turn out not to be strangers after all because we are all of us seeking the same homeland together whether we know it or not, even the mad ones and lost ones who scare us half to death because in so many ways they are so much like ourselves.

Maybe in time we will even be able to love them a little—to feed them when they are hungry and maybe no farther away than our own street; to visit them when they are sick and lonely; maybe hardest of all, to let them come serve us when the hunger and sickness and loneliness are not theirs but ours. "Your faith has made you whole," Jesus said to the woman who touched the hem of his garment (Mark 5:34, KJV), and maybe by grace, by luck, by holding fast to whatever of him we can touch, such faith as we have will make us whole enough to become something like human at last—to see something of the power and the glory and the holiness beneath the world's lost face. That is the direction that home is in anyway—the homeland we have seen from afar in our dearest rooms and truest dreams, the homeland we have seen in the face of him who is himself our final home and haven, our kingdom and king.

11.

Hope

Now Moses was keeping the flock of his father-in-law, Jethro, the priest of Midian; and he led his flock to the west side of the wilderness, and came to Horeb, the mountain of God. And the angel of the Lord appeared to him in a flame of fire out of the midst of a bush; and he looked, and lo, the bush was burning, yet it was not consumed. And Moses said, "I will turn aside and see this great sight, why the bush is not burnt." When the Lord saw that he turned aside to see, God called to him out of the bush. "Moses, Moses!" And he said, "Here am I." Then he said, "Do not come near; put off your shoes from your feet, for the place on which you are standing is holy ground." And he said, "I am the God of your father, the God of Abraham, the God of Isaac, and the God of Jacob." And Moses hid his face, for he was afraid to look at God.

—Exodus 3:1–6

As he was now drawing near, at the descent of the Mount of Olives, the whole multitude of the disciples began to rejoice and praise God with a loud voice for all the mighty works that they had seen, saying, "Blessed is the King who comes in the name of the Lord! Peace in heaven and glory in the highest!" And some of the Pharisees in the

multitude said to him, "Teacher, rebuke your disciples." He answered,
"I tell you, if these were silent, the very stones would cry out."

—LUKE 19:37–40

It is one of the great moments in Old Testament history. Perhaps it is the key
moment. Moses was a stranger and exile in a strange land—in Midian, on
the east bank of the Gulf of Aqabah—the land he fled to from Egypt, where
he had murdered an Egyptian for beating a Hebrew slave. With death on
his conscience, he had fled for his life, left everything behind. He married a
Midianite woman, settled down, and was tending his father-in-law's sheep
on the slopes of Mt. Horeb in the wilderness when suddenly the moment
happened. A bush burst into flame. It blazed up, the heat of it rippling
the air around it. Leaf and stem, it became all fire, crackling, leaping, as if
the air itself was on fire. But though the bush burned, it did not burn up
because it was a miraculous fire, which is to say a fire that Moses could not
explain any more than we can explain it except by explaining it away as no
real fire at all but only a figment of Moses's fiery imagination or the pious
invention of a later time.

Then out of the flaming moment, a voice also flamed up, and of all the
conceivable things it might have said, what it said was the name of Moses
himself. "Moses," it said, "Moses," twice, and at the sound of his own name
he was caught, as we also would have been caught, because we so much *are*
our own names that at the sound of them we cannot help listening whether
we want to or not because the voice that calls us by name is a voice that
knows us by name, knows us, and has something to say to us, and for all we
know everything may depend on our listening and answering. So Moses,
the stranger and exile, stood there with the muck of the sheep on his shoes,
guilty as hell of a man's murder and listened and answered.

"Here am I," he said, waiting for God only knows what will happen
next, what lightning bolt to strike him on fire himself like the bush. Only
what happened next instead was that when the voice out of the fire spoke
again, what it said was, "Put off your shoes from your feet, for the place
on which you are standing is holy ground." That scrubby patch of upland
wilderness that the sheep had mucked up, that patch of no-man's-land that

Moses had fled to for no motive holier than to save his own skin, was holy, the voice said, because it was as aflame with God as the bush was aflame with fire. Then the voice identified itself. It was God's voice, the God of Abraham, Isaac, and Jacob, the voice said. And then Moses hid his face, the book of Exodus says, "for he was afraid to look at God," and well he might have been afraid if he had any inkling of what God was going to say next, because what God said next was as holy and fiery a word as there is in the Old Testament or anywhere else. That word was Go.

For those of us who are in the habit of putting on our best clothes and going to church from time to time, maybe it is a good idea to consider what a church is, of all things. What are all these churches we keep coming to, year in and year out? A church in the sense of a building is walls and a roof erected on the proposition that this ancient story of Moses and his burning bush is somehow true—that however you choose to explain that story, you cannot all that easily explain it away. Something extraordinary took place a long time ago on the eastern shore of the Gulf of Aqabah, and our presence in churches, and the presence of millions like us, is evidence that the reverberations of that event are felt to this day. It is the reason why churches exist. It is the reason why we go to them, though we often forget it and go for shabbier reasons. The old church walls, the old church roofs were put up in the faith that if God is present anywhere in the world, he is present everywhere, and that if the ground that Moses stood on was holy, then the little patches of ground where churches stand are holy too. The whole earth is holy because God makes himself known on it, which means that in that sense a church is no holier than any other place. God is not more in a church than he is anywhere else. But what makes a church holy in a special way is that we ourselves are more present in it.

What I mean is that if we come to a church right, we come to it more fully and nakedly ourselves, come with more of our humanness showing, than we are apt to come to most places. We come like Moses with muck on our shoes—footsore and travel-stained with the dust of our lives upon us, our failures, our deceits, our hypocrisies, because if, unlike Moses, we have never taken anybody's life, we have again and again withheld from other people, including often even those who are nearest to us, the love that might have made their lives worth living, not to mention our own.

Like Moses we come here as we are, and like him we come as strangers and exiles in our way, because wherever it is that we truly belong, whatever it is that is truly home for us, we know in our hearts that we have somehow lost it and gotten lost. Something is missing from our lives that we cannot even name—something we know best from the empty place inside us all where it belongs. We come here to find what we have lost. We come here to acknowledge that in terms of the best we could be we are lost and that we are helpless to save ourselves. We come here to confess our sins.

That is the sadness and searching of what church is, of what we are in a church—and then suddenly FIRE! The bush bursts into flame. And the voice speaks our names, whatever they are—Peter, John, Ann, Mary. The heart skips a beat. "YOU! YOU!" the voice says. Does it? Does any voice other than a human voice speak in this place? Does any flame other than a candle flame on Christmas Eve ever leap here? I think so. I think if you have your ears open, if you have your eyes open, every once in a while some word in even the most unpromising sermon will flame out, some scrap of prayer or anthem, some moment of silence even, the sudden glimpse of somebody you love sitting there near you, or of some stranger whose face without warning touches your heart, will flame out—and these are the moments that speak our names in a way we cannot help hearing. These are the moments that, in the depths of whatever our dimness and sadness and lostness are, give us an echo of a wild and bidding voice that calls us from deeper still. It is the same voice that Moses heard and that one way or another says. "GO! BE! LIVE! LOVE!" sending us off on an extraordinary and fateful journey for which there are no sure maps and whose end we will never fully know until we get there. And for as long as the moment lasts, we suspect that maybe it is true—maybe the ground on which we stand really is holy ground because we heard that voice here. It called us by name.

Is it madness to believe such a thing? That is a serious question. Is it madness to believe in God at all, let alone in a God who speaks to us through such obscure and fleeting moments as these and then asks us to believe that these moments are windows into the truest meaning and mystery of the cosmos itself? It is a kind of madness indeed. A famous scientist recently gave a definitive answer as to what the cosmos is. "The cosmos," he said, "is all there is or ever was or ever will be." Which means that if you want to understand the cosmos, there is nothing other than the cosmos itself that you can look to for your answer.

Where did the world come from and where is it going? Ask the geologists and cosmologists, such a man would say. Ask the astrophysicists, the philosophers even. They may not have all the answers today, but as government puts more money into research and as technology becomes more sophisticated, they will have them tomorrow. What is the human being? The advances in biology, biochemistry, genetics over the last few years have been extraordinary, and such problems as the structure of the brain, the nature of disease, the chemical origins and makeup of life itself come closer to a solution every day. Or maybe your questions are more practical than theoretical. How do we get on in this world with the bodies and brains that we have? How do we stay healthy, cure cancer? How do we cope with the psychological tensions of modern living? How do we keep our heads above water economically, environmentally? What about the arms race, the tens of thousands dying of starvation in Africa? What about the failed marriage? The suicidal eighteen-year-old?

There are times for all of us when life seems without purpose or meaning, when we wake to a sense of chaos like a great cat with its paws on our chests sucking our breath. What can we do? Where can we turn? Well, you can thank your lucky stars, say many among us, that the world is full of specialists who are working on all these problems; and you can turn to them, men and women who have put behind them all the ancient myths and dreams and superstitions and have dedicated themselves to finding solutions to these problems in the only place where solutions or anything else can be found—which is here in the midst of the vast complexities of the cosmos itself, which is all there is or ever was or ever will be.

The existence of the church bears witness to the belief that there is only one thing you can say to such a view and that is that it is wrong. There is only one answer you can give to this terrible sanity, and that is that it is ultimately insane. The ancient myths and dreams of a power beyond power and a love beyond love that hold the cosmos itself, hold all things, in existence reflect a reality that we can deny only to our great impoverishment; and the dream of a holiness and mystery at the heart of things that humankind with all its ingenuity and wisdom can neither explain away nor live fully without goes on being dreamed. Moments continue to go up in flames like the bush in Midian to illumine, if only for a moment, a path that stretches before us like no other path. And such moments call out in a voice that, if we only had courage and heart enough, we would follow to the end of time.

For a human being to say that the cosmos is all there is strikes me as like a worm in an apple saying that the apple is all there is. Even if we could solve all the problems of the cosmos and stood here healthy, solvent, adjusted, and proud in our knowledge at last, we would still stand here like Moses with the muck of our less-than-humanness on our shoes and the feeling in the pits of our stomachs that the cosmos can never entirely be home because we know as surely as we know anything that, though we have never seen it except in dreams, our true home lies somewhere else. Those dreams are the ultimate madness the church is built upon or, because those who call them madness are themselves madder still, the ultimate sanity.

But enough of all that. We have come to this church, and for centuries others like us have come church too, so it is to them we should turn our attention, the people who came here over the years and why they came and what they found when they got here or failed to find. People came to this church for the same reasons they came to any church anywhere, and my guess is that many of their reasons were just about as inconsequential as many of ours. They came because there wasn't all that much else to do on Sundays and there was no nine-thousand-page *New York Times* to drowse over. They came to see their friends and be seen by them. They came out of habit because they had always come, and out of tradition because their ancestors had come before them. They came to be entertained, maybe even to be edified. They came, even the ones who in their secret hearts believed very little, with the idea that just maybe there is a God who keeps track of who comes and who doesn't and it is just as well to stay on his good side. Sometimes they enjoyed themselves here, and sometimes they were bored stiff. Sometimes they were set to thinking long thoughts about themselves and their lives, but as often as not their minds probably wandered off into the same anxieties, fantasies, daydreams that they would have lost themselves in if they had been riding the bus or waiting their turn at the dentist. And in all this, their ministers were probably not all that different. Sometimes their hearts were in it, and sometimes it was just a job to get done, a sermon to be preached, a collection to take.

Ministers and congregation both, they came to church year after year, and who is to say how if at all their lives were changed as the result? If you'd stopped and asked them on any given Sunday, I suspect they would have said they weren't changed much. Yet they kept on coming anyway; and beneath all the lesser reasons they had for doing so, so far beneath that they themselves were only half aware of it, I think there was a deep reason, and if I could give only one word to characterize that reason, the word I would give is *hope*.

They came here, the awkward boys and shy girls, to get married and stood here with their hearts in their mouths and their knees knocking to mumble their wild and improbable vows in these very shadows. They came to christen their babies here—carried them in their long white dresses hoping they wouldn't scream bloody murder when the minister took them in his arms and signed their foreheads with a watery cross. They came here to bury their dead and brought in, along with the still, finished bodies, all the most un-still, unfinished love, guilt, sadness, relief that are part of what death always is for the living. In other words what they were doing essentially beneath this roof was offering up the most precious moments of their lives in the hope that there was a God to hallow them—a God to hear and seal their vows, to receive their children into his unimaginable kingdom, to raise up and cherish their dead. I see them sitting here, generations of them, a little uncomfortable in their Sunday best with their old faces closed like doors and their young faces blank as clapboard; but deep within those faces—farther down than their daydreams and boredom and way beyond any horizon of their wandering minds that they could describe—there was the hope that somewhere out of all the words and music and silences of this place, and out of a mystery even greater than the mystery of the cosmos itself, a voice that they would know from all other voices would speak their names and bless them.

I think also of a school church where I served once as chaplain. People didn't get married and christened there very much and death rarely entered because that wasn't the kind of church it was. The people in the pews weren't townspeople—the rich men, poor men, beggar men, thieves of the town—but teenage boys, hundreds of them, all shapes and sizes, from all over the map and from every sort of religious background or no religious background at all. They came because they knew they would catch bloody hell from the dean's office if they didn't. So come they did, pulling up their ties and choking down their breakfasts as they raced through drifts of autumn leaves or snow to get in before the last stroke of the last bell sounded. And what many of them brought with them was their hostility to religion in general and church in particular, their skepticism about the whole business of God, their determination, many of them, not to look interested even if they were, all of which means that in many ways they weren't as different from you and me as at first glance it might appear, because there is something in all of us that is full of doubts about religion and church and God himself, full of skepticism and hostility.

And what did they find when they got there? They didn't find ministers who had known them and their families for years but a succession of visiting preachers, many of them the great ones of their time, who preached the gospel with all the wit and eloquence they could muster in the name not only of Almighty God but of the school itself in the person of the Principal, who sat up there on the platform with them like a lion under the throne. And for nine years they also found me there—the new school minister, young and green in his job, having never ministered to anybody before, let alone to such a three-ring circus as that. So I did what I could, and what I could was to try like the others to set forth such faith as I had with all the power I could muster.

I had the feeling that for many of the boys who went there, this was the last time they would be so much as caught dead in a church ever again, which meant that this was just possibly the last chance anybody might ever have to speak to them seriously about Christ and about what life with Christ involves and what life without Christ involves too. So for nine years I ran scared and never climbed into that pulpit without my mouth going dry and my stomach in a turmoil at the sense I had of the terrible urgency of what I was about. There they would be, Sunday after Sunday, sitting in their seats much as you are sitting in yours and not wanting, most of them, to be there at all, and showing it. But as I looked out at their faces the way I look out now at yours, I had again and again the uncanny sense that from time to time, in spite of themselves, they were truly listening.

Different as that school church was from churches in general, and different as those boys were from you and me, I think that what lay at the heart of their listening was the same thing that lies no less at your heart and mine and at the hearts of all the generations who worshiped here before us. I think it is hope that lies at our hearts and hope that finally brings us all here. Hope that in spite of all the devastating evidence to the contrary, the ground we stand on is holy ground because Christ walked here and walks here still. Hope that we are known, each one of us, by name, and that out of the burning moments of our lives he will call us by our names to the lives he would have us live and the selves he would have us become. Hope that into the secret grief and pain and bewilderment of each of us and of our world he will come at last to heal and to save.

When Jesus of Nazareth rode into Jerusalem on Palm Sunday and his followers cried out, "Blessed is the King who comes in the name of the Lord," the Pharisees went to Jesus and told him to put an end to their blasphemies, and Jesus said to them, "I tell you, if these were silent, the very stones would cry out."

This church. The church on the other side of town, the other side of the world. All churches everywhere. The day will come when they will lie in ruins, every last one of them. The day will come when all the voices that were ever raised in them, including our own, will be permanently stilled. But when that day comes, I believe the tumbled stones will cry aloud of the great, deep hope that down through the centuries has been the one reason for having churches at all and is the one reason we have for coming to this one now, the hope that into the world the King does come. And in the name of the Lord. And is always coming, blessed be he. And will come afire with glory, at the end of time.

In the meantime, King Jesus, we offer all churches to you as you offer them to us. Make thyself known in them. Make thy will done in them. Make our stone hearts cry out thy kingship. Make us holy and human at last that we may do the work of thy love.

12.
The Two Stories

But thanks be to God, who in Christ always leads us in triumph, and
through us spreads the fragrance of the knowledge of him everywhere.
For we are the aroma of Christ to God among those who are being
saved and among those who are perishing, to one a fragrance from
death to death, to the other a fragrance from life to life. Who is suf-
ficient for these things? For we are not, like so many, peddlers of God's
word; but as men of sincerity, as commissioned by God, in the sight
of God we speak in Christ.

—2 Corinthians 2:14–17

A few months ago I received a letter inviting me to speak to a group of ministers on the subject of storytelling. It was a good letter and posed a number
of thoughtful questions such as: How do you use stories effectively in sermons? How do you use a story to put a point across? To what degree do you
make the point of your story clear to your listeners instead of leaving them
to work it out for themselves? And so on. They were all perfectly reasonable questions to which I think useful answers can be given, but the more I
thought about them, the more I found that something about them gave me
pause. The trouble was that they were all questions that had to do with *how*
to tell a story instead of *what* stories to tell and *to what end;* and the kind of

stories they rightly or wrongly suggested to me were stories as anecdotes, as attention-getters, as illustrations, stories to hang on sermons like lights on a Christmas tree. Maybe I did the letter writer an injustice, and that isn't what he had in mind at all, but if so, all I can say is that that's the kind of stories I have often heard in church myself. And why not? They have their place. They can help make the medicine go down. But the more I thought about it, the more I realized that even if I believed I could give some helpful literary advice along those lines, that was not what basically interested me.

And yet what the letter reminded me of is that yes, storytelling is itself immensely interesting and immensely important. Not just for preachers and preachers-to-be, but for Christians in general. Storytelling matters enormously because it is a story, of course, that stands at the heart of our faith and that more perhaps than any other form of discourse speaks to our hearts and illumines our own stories. It is related to what Paul is writing about, I think, in this passage from Corinthians. "We are not, like so many, peddlers of God's word," he says, and the image is a rich and painfully telling one.

Peddlers are people with packs on their backs full of things they want to sell, and the things they try to sell hardest are the things they think will sell best. Peddlers are less concerned with what the world needs than with what the world wants or can be made to settle for. Peddlers are salespeople who are interested less in the quality of what they're selling than in the success of their sale. So if the peddlers of God's word happen to be preachers, it's preaching as an end in itself that they're apt to concentrate on. They do their best to be effective, eloquent, original. They choose the stories that will go over best and be remembered to their credit longest. Or if we happen not to be preachers, then when it comes to just speaking of, and out of, our faith in a general way we, like them, tend to stick to the salesmanship of it and to speak of it whatever is easiest to speak and whatever we think will go down most easily.

We speak of books we've read and ideas we've had. We speak of great questions like abortion and conservation and the dangers of nuclear power, and of what we take to be the Christian answers to such questions. If we get more personal about it, we speak of problems we've had—problems with children and old age, problems with sex and marriage, ethical problems— and of Christian solutions to those problems or at least of Christian ways of viewing them. And if, in the process, we decide to tell stories, then, like the preacher as peddler, we may tell stories about ourselves as well as about other people, but not, for the most part, our real stories, not stories about what lies beneath all our other problems, which is the problem of being human, the problem of trying to hold fast somehow to Christ when much of the time, both in ourselves and in our world, it is as if Christ had never existed. Because all peddlers of God's word have that in common, I think: they tell what costs them least to tell and what will gain them most; and to tell the story of who we really are and of the battle between light and dark, between belief and unbelief, between sin and grace that is waged within us all costs plenty and may not gain us anything, we're afraid, but an uneasy silence and a fishy stare.

So one way or another we are all of us peddlers of God's word, and those of us in the ministry are more apt to be peddlers than most because as professionals we're continually being sought out to display our wares. We're invited to give commencement addresses and to speak about storytelling to people who travel miles to learn the trick. And so it's to all of us that Paul speaks. "We are not," he says (meaning we should not be, must not be, had bloody well better not be), "we are not, like so many, peddlers of God's word; but as men of sincerity, as commissioned by God, in the sight of God we speak in Christ." That's the whole point of it, he says: *to speak in Christ,* which means among other things, I assume, to speak *of* Christ. And when it comes to storytelling, that is of course the crux of it. If we are to speak, as he says, with sincerity—speak as we have been commissioned by God to speak, and with our hearts as well as our lips—then this is the one story above all others that we have in us to tell, you and I. It is his story.

The story of Christ is where we all started from, though we've come so far since then that there are times when you'd hardly know it to listen to us and when we hardly know it ourselves. The story of Christ is what once, somehow and somewhere, we came to Christ through. Maybe it happened little by little—a face coming slowly into focus that we'd been looking at for a long time without really seeing it, a voice gradually making itself heard among many other voices and in such a way that we couldn't help listening after a while, couldn't help trying somehow, in some unsatisfactory way, to answer. Or maybe there was more drama to it than that—a sudden catch of the breath at the sound of his name on somebody's lips at a moment we weren't expecting it, a sudden welling up of tears out of a place where we didn't think any tears were. Each of us has a tale to tell if we would only tell it. But however it happened, it comes to seem a long time ago and a long way away, and so many things have happened since—so many books read, so many sermons heard or preached, so much life lived—that to be reminded at this stage of the game of the story of Christ, where we all started, is like being suddenly called by your childhood name when you have all but forgotten your childhood name and maybe your childhood too.

The Jehovah's Witness appears on the doorstep, or somebody who's gotten religious corners you at a party, and embarrassing questions are asked in an embarrassing language. Have you been born again? Have you accepted Jesus Christ as your personal Lord and Savior? And yes, yes, you want to say—half humiliated, half appalled and irritated, torn in a dozen directions at once by the directness and corn of it, tongue-tied. You wouldn't be caught dead maybe using such language yourself, but oh Jesus, yes, in some sense your answer is and has to be yes, though to be asked it out of the blue that way, by a stranger you'd never have opened the door to if you'd known what he was after, makes the blood run cold. To be reminded that way or any way of the story of Jesus, where you came from, is like having somebody suddenly produce a picture of home in all its homeliness—the barn that needs cleaning, the sagging porch steps, the face in the dusty window—when you've traveled a thousand miles and a thousand years from home and are involved in a thousand new and different things. But the story of Jesus is home nonetheless—the barn, the steps, the face. You belong to it. It belongs to you. It is where you came from. God grant it is also where you are heading for. So that is the story to remember. That is the story beyond all stories to tell.

The story of Jesus is full of darkness as well as of light. It is a story that hides more than it reveals. It is the story of a mystery we must never assume we understand and that comes to us breathless and broken with unspeakable beauty at the heart of it, yet is by no means a pretty story, though that is the way we're apt to peddle it much of the time. We sand down the rough edges. We play down the obscurities and contradictions. What we can't explain, we explain away. We set Jesus forth as clear-eyed and noble-browed, whereas the chances are he can't have been anything but old before his time once the world started working him over, and once the world was through, his clear eyes were swollen shut and his noble brow as much of a shambles as the rest of him. We're apt to tell his story when we tell it at all, to sell his story, for the poetry and panacea of it. "But we are the aroma of Christ," Paul says, and the story we are given to tell is a story that smells of his life in all its aliveness, and our commission is to tell it in a way that makes it come alive as a story in all its aliveness and to make those who hear it come alive and God knows to make ourselves come alive too.

He was born, the story begins—the barn that needs cleaning, the sagging steps, the dusty face—and there are times when we have to forget all about the angels and shepherds and star of it, I think, and just let the birth as a birth be wonder enough, which heaven help us it is, this wonder of all wonders. Into a world that has never been famous for taking special care of the naked and helpless, he was born in the same old way to the same old end and in all likelihood howled bloody murder with the rest of us when they got the breath going in him and he sensed more or less what he was in for. An old man in the Temple predicted great things for him but terrible things for the mother who loved him in what seem to have been all the wrong ways. He got lost in the city and worried his parents sick. John baptized him in the river and wondered afterwards if he'd chosen the right man. It wasn't just Satan who tempted him then because for the rest of his life just about everybody tempted him—his best friend, his disciples, his mother and brothers, his enemies. They all of them tempted him one way or another not to go off the deep end but to stay on the bearable surface of things—to work miracles you could see with your eyes, to feed hungers you could feel in your belly, to heal the sickness of the flesh you could touch, to be a power among powers and to avoid the powerless, the sinful, the deadbeats like the plague in favor of the outwardly righteous, the publicly pious.

But "like a root out of dry ground," he came, Isaiah says (53:2), and it was down at the roots of things that he moved all his life like a mole—down at the undetected sickness fiercer than flesh, the buried sin, the hidden holiness. "Cleave the wood, I am there," he says in the apocryphal *Gospel of Thomas*. "Lift the stone, and you will find me there" (77), and it is always far beneath that he is to be found and deep within that his most shattering miracles happen. He made precious few friends and a mob of enemies. He taught in a way that almost nobody either understood or wanted to risk understanding, least of all the ones who were closest to him. And in the end they got him. And forget all the grim paraphernalia of his death, because the obscenity and horror have long since been ritualized out of it. They got him, that's all. He wasn't spared a damned thing. It was awful beyond telling, god-awful. And then it happened.

However we try to explain it, however we try at all costs to avoid having to explain it because it was so long ago and seems so wild and crazy and because so many other more plausible, manageable things have happened since; whatever words we can find for telling the story or for watering it down—what happened was that he wasn't dead anymore. He wasn't dead. Anymore. He was not a ghost. By comparison, it's we who are the ghosts. The worst we know of darkness, any of us, was split in two like an atom. The explosion shook history to its roots, shook even us once to our roots, though it's sometimes hard to remember. The fallout continues to this day—falls imperceptibly, without a sound, like snow or ash, like light. Only it is not death-dealing. It is life-dealing. You and I are here in this place now because of what little life it dealt us. Because of this story of Jesus, each of our own stories is in countless ways different from what it would have been otherwise, and that is why in speaking about him we must speak also about ourselves and about ourselves with him and without him too because that, of course, is the other story we have in us to remember and tell. Our own story.

We are men and women of sincerity, Paul says, and God help us if we're not because that's what we're cracked up to be, and sincerity you'd like to think would be the least of it. We are commissioned by God to speak in Christ, and to speak in Christ is to speak truth, and there is no story whose truth we are closer to than our own, than the story of what it's like to live inside ourselves. The trouble is that, like Christ's story, this too is apt to be the last we tell, partly because we are uncomfortable with it and afraid of sincerity and partly because we have half forgotten it. But tell it we must and, before we tell it to anybody else, tell it first of all to ourselves and keep on telling it, because unless we do, unless we live with, and out of, the story of who we are inside ourselves, we lose track of who we are. We live so much on the outer surface and seeming of our lives and our faith that we lose touch with the deep places that they both come from.

We have the story of our own baptism, for one—if not by water, in a river, then by fire God knows where, because there isn't one of us whose life hasn't flamed up into moments when a door opened somewhere that let the future in, moments when we moved through that door as Jesus moved out of Jordan, not perfectly cleansed but cleansed enough, with the past behind us, we hoped, and a new sense of what at its most outlandish and holiest the future might become. And God knows we have all had our wilderness and our temptations too—not the temptation to work evil probably, because by grace or luck we don't have what it takes for more than momentary longings in that direction, but the temptation to settle for the lesser good, which is evil enough and maybe a worse one—to settle for niceness and usefulness and busyness instead of for holiness; to settle for plausibility and eloquence instead of for truth. And miracles too are part of our story as well as of his, blind though we are to them most of the time and leery as we are of acknowledging them, because to acknowledge a miracle is to have to act on it somehow—to become some kind of miracles ourselves—and that's why they scare us to death. The miracle of our own births when the odds were millions to one against them. The miracle of every right turn we ever took and every healing word we ever spoke. The miracle of loving sometimes even the unlovely, and out of our own unloveliness. And the half-forgotten miracles by which we've turned up here now, such as we are, who might never have made it here at all when you consider all the hazards along the way.

And crucifixion is part of our stories too, because we too are men and women of sorrow and acquainted with grief. Maybe our crucifixion is in knowing that for all we'd like to believe to the contrary, we don't have the stomach for even such few, half-baked chances to give up something precious for him as come our way, let alone for giving up, in any sense that really matters, our selves for him. Yet we're raised up nonetheless. We're raised up, and we have that to tell of too, that part of our story. In spite of every reason to give the whole show up, we're here still just able to hope; in spite of all the griefs and failures we've known, we're here still just able to rejoice; in spite of the darkness we all of us flirt with, we are here still just a little, at least, in love with light. By miracle we survive even our own shabbiness, and for the time being maybe that is resurrection enough.

Two stories then—our own story and Jesus's story, and in the end, perhaps, they are the same story. "Cleave the wood, I am there. Life up the stone, and you will find me there." To cleave the truth of our own lives, to live and look beneath our own stories, is to see glimmers at least of his life, of his life struggling to come alive in our lives, his story whispering like a song through the babble and drone of ours. Where he is strong, we are weak, God knows. Where he is faithful, we are what we are. Where he opens himself to the worst the world can do for the sake of the best the world can be, we arm ourselves against the world with the world's hard armor for our own sweet sakes. Our stories are at best a parody of his story, and if, as Paul says, we are the fragrance of Christ, then it is like the fragrance of the sea from ten miles inland when the wind is in the right direction, like the fragrance of a rose from the other side of the street with all the world between.

Yet they meet as well as diverge, our stories and his, and even when they diverge, it is *his* they diverge from, so that by his absence as well as by his presence in our lives we know who he is and who we are and who we are not.

We have it in us to be Christs to each other and maybe in some unimaginable way to God too—that's what we have to tell finally. We have it in us to work miracles of love and healing as well as to have them worked upon us. We have it in us to bless with him and forgive with him and heal with him and once in a while maybe even to grieve with some measure of his grief at another's pain and to rejoice with some measure of his rejoicing at another's joy almost as if it were our own. And who knows but that in the end, by God's mercy, the two stories will converge for good and all, and though we would never have had the courage or the faith or the wit to die for him any more than we have ever managed to live for him very well either, his story will come true in us at last. And in the meantime, this side of Paradise, it is our business (not, like so many, peddlers of God's word, but as men and women of sincerity) to speak with our hearts (which is what sincerity means) and to bear witness to, and live out of, and live toward, and live by the true word of his holy story as it seeks to stammer itself forth through the holy stories of us all.

13.

Emmanuel

"Behold, a virgin shall conceive and bear a son, and his name shall be called Emmanuel" (which means, God with us).

—MATTHEW 1:23

"We preach Christ crucified," the apostle Paul wrote to the church at Corinth, "a stumbling block to Jews and folly to Gentiles" (1 Cor. 1:23). He could as well have written, "We preach Christ born" or "We preach Christmas," because the birth presents no fewer problems than the death does both to religious people—"the Jews"—and to everybody else—"the Gentiles." Christmas is not just Mr. Pickwick dancing a reel with the old lady at Dingley Dell or Scrooge waking up the next morning a changed man. It is not just the spirit of giving abroad in the land with a white beard and reindeer. It is not just the most famous birthday of them all and not just the annual reaffirmation of "Peace on Earth" that it is often reduced to so that people of many faiths or no faith can exchange Christmas cards without a qualm. On the contrary, if you do not hear in the message of Christmas something that must strike some as blasphemy and others as sheer fantasy, the chances are you have not heard the message for what it is. *Emmanuel* is the message in a nutshell, which is Hebrew for "God with us." Who is this God? How is he with us? That's where the problem lies.

God is "the high and lofty One who inhabits eternity," says the prophet Isaiah (57:15), and by and large, though they would use different language and symbols to express it, all the major faiths of the world would tend to agree. Judaism calls him Yahweh. Islam calls him Allah. Buddhism and Hinduism use terms like Brahman-Atman or the Void or the One. But whatever they call him, all of them point to the ultimate spiritual Ground of existence as transcendent and totally other. The reality of God is so radically different from anything we know as real that in the last analysis we can say nothing about him except what he is not. *Neti neti* is the Upanishad's famous definition: "He is not this, he is not that." "The Tao that can be expressed is not the eternal Tao," says the *Tao Te Ching* of Taoism. The Old Testament says it in characteristically concrete form as a narrative. When Moses asks to see God, God answers by saying, "You cannot see my face; for man shall not see me and live" (Exod. 33:20). As a mark of special favor, he hides Moses in the cleft of a rock and only after he has passed by in his glory takes his hand away so that Moses can see his back. According to the Protestant theologian Paul Tillich, you cannot even say that God exists in the same sense that you say a person exists, or a mountain or an idea. God is not a thing among other things. He does not take his place in a prior reality. He is that out of which reality itself arises, and to say that "he is" as we say that "we are" is to use language that is at best crudely metaphoric.

If all this sounds hopelessly abstruse, it nonetheless reflects the common experience of human beings as they contemplate the mystery that surrounds them. When a person looks up at the stars and ponders that which either goes on forever or ends at some unthinkably remote point beyond which there is Nothing; when we pray out of our deepest need to a God whom we can know only through faith; when we confront the enigma of our own life and the inevitability of our own death, all we can do is hold our tongues or say with Job, "Behold, I am of small account. I lay my hand on my mouth.... I have uttered what I did not understand, things too wonderful for me, which I did not know" (40:4; 42:3).

That is not the end of it, of course. Transcendent as God is—of another quality entirely from the world that he transcends—he nonetheless makes himself known to the world. Many would say that he is known to it because he made it, and from their earliest beginnings people have looked at the world of nature and claimed to see in it the marks of his handicraft. Where nature is beautiful and beneficent, they have seen the love of God, and where it is harsh and terrifying, his wrath. In the orderliness of nature they have seen God as lawgiver, and where this order is interrupted by the unforeseen and beneficent they have seen miracle. And the same holds true for the world of history. The prosperity of nations or individuals suggests God's favor, and disaster suggests either condemnation or warning. Even the religions of India, which see the world less as the creation of the Ultimate than as a kind of illusory reverberation of it, speak of the law of karma, which as inexorably as the law of gravity rewards the good and punishes the evil. Furthermore, though they do not see the world as a book where humankind can read of the nature and will of God, but rather as an endless cycle of death and rebirth where our only hope is to escape altogether into the ineffable bliss of nirvana, the very fact that such escape is available suggests the presence of something not entirely unlike divine intervention. Indeed, great teaching Buddhas and infinitely compassionate Bodhisattvas keep reappearing throughout the ages to show the way to nirvana, just as in the biblically based religions of Judaism, Islam, and Christianity, God keeps sending forth prophets, saints, and angels.

And in all these traditions, needless to say, God also makes himself known through the mystics. However religions differ in other ways, all of them produce men and women who, by turning their attention inward, encounter him at first hand. As different from one another as Teresa of Avila, Ramakrishna, and Thomas Merton and using language that varies from the *Bhagavad Gita* to the journals of the Quaker George Fox, they all clearly seem to be trying to express the same ecstatic and inexpressible experience that might best be summarized as, at one and the same time, the total loss and total realization of self in merging with the ultimately Real.

Back then to the essential message of Christmas, which is Emmanuel, God with us, and to the questions it raises: Who is this God and how is he with us? "The high and lofty One who inhabits eternity" is the answer to the first. The One who is with us is the One whom none can look upon because the space-and-time human mind can no more comprehend fully the spaceless, timeless Reality of the One than the eyes of the blind can comprehend light. The One who is with us is the One who has made himself known at most only partially and dimly through the pantomime of nature and history and the eloquent but always abstruse utterance of prophets, saints, and mystics.

It is the answer to the second question that seems "folly to the Gentiles" and "a stumbling block to the Jews," because the claim that Christianity makes for Christmas is that at a particular time and place God came to be with us himself. When Quirinius was governor of Syria, in a town called Bethlehem, a child was born who, beyond the power of anyone to account for, was the high and lofty One made low and helpless. The One who inhabits eternity comes to dwell in time. The One whom none can look upon and live is delivered in a stable under the soft, indifferent gaze of cattle. The Father of all mercies puts himself at our mercy.

For those who believe in the transcendence and total otherness of God, it radically diminishes him. For those who do not believe in God, it is the ultimate absurdity. For those who stand somewhere between belief and unbelief, it challenges credulity in a new way. It is not a theory that can be tested rationally because it is beyond reason and because it is not a theory, not something that theologians have thought their way to. The claim is, instead, that it is something that has happened, and reason itself is somehow tested by it, humankind's whole view of what is possible and real. Year after year the ancient tale of what happened is told—raw, preposterous, holy—and year after year the world in some measure stops to listen.

In the winter of 1947 a great snow fell on New York City. It began slowly, undramatically, like any other snow. The flakes were fine and steady and fell straight, with no wind. Little by little the sidewalks started to whiten. Shopkeepers and doormen were out with their shovels clearing paths to the street. After a while the streets began to fill and the roofs of parked cars were covered. You could no longer tell where the curb was, and even the hydrants disappeared, the melted discs over manhole covers. The plows could not keep up with it, and traffic moved more and more slowly as the drifts piled up. Businesses closed early, and people walked home from work. All evening it continued falling and much of the night. There were skiers on Park Avenue, children up way past their bedtime. By the next morning it was a different city. More striking than anything else about it was the silence. All traffic had stopped. Abandoned cars were buried. Nothing on wheels moved. The only sounds to be heard were church bells and voices. You listened because you could not help yourself.

"Ice splits starwise," Sir Thomas Browne wrote. A tap of the pick at the right point, and fissures shoot out in all directions, and the solid block falls in two at the star. The child is born, and history itself falls in two at the star. Whether you believe or do not believe, you date your letters and checks and income tax forms with a number representing how many years have gone by since what happened happened. The world of A.D. is one world, and the world of B.C. is another. Whatever the mystery was that widened the gaze of Tutankhamen's golden head, it was not this mystery. Whatever secret triggered the archaic smiles of Argive marbles or made the Bodhisattvas sit bolt upright at Angkor Wat, it was not our secret. The very voices and bells of our world ring out on a different air, and if most of the time we do not listen, at Christmas it is hard not to.

Business goes on as usual, only more so. Canned carols blast out over shopping-center blacktops before the Thanksgiving turkey is cold on the plate. Salvation Army tambourines rattle, and street-corner Santas stamp their feet against the cold. But if you have an ear for it at all, at the heart of all the hullabaloo you hear a silence, and at the heart of the silence you hear—whatever you hear.

"The Word became flesh and dwelt among us, full of grace and truth," the prologue to the Gospel of John says (1:14). A dream as old as time of the God descending hesitates on the threshold of coming true in a way to make all other truths seem dreamlike. If it is true, it is the chief of all truths. If it is not true, it is of all truths the one perhaps that people would most have be true if they could make it so. Maybe it is that longing to have it be true that is at the bottom even of the whole vast Christmas industry—the tons of cards and presents and fancy food, the plastic figures kneeling on the floodlit lawns of poorly attended churches. The world speaks of holy things in the only language it knows, which is a worldly language.

Emmanuel. We all must decide for ourselves whether it is true. Certainly the grounds on which to dismiss it are not hard to find. Christmas is commercialism. It is a pain in the neck. It is sentimentality. It is wishful thinking. With its account of the shepherds, the star, the three wise men, it smacks of a make-believe pathetically out of place in a world of energy crisis and space exploration and economic *malaise*. Yet it is never as easy to get rid of as all this makes it sound, because whereas to dismiss belief in God is to dismiss only an idea, a hypothesis, for which there are many alternatives (such as belief in no god at all or in any of the lesser gods we are always creating for ourselves like science or morality or the inevitability of human progress), to dismiss Christmas is for most of us to dismiss part of ourselves.

For one thing it is to dismiss one of the most fragile yet enduring visions of our own childhood and of the child who continues to exist in all of us. The sense of mystery and wonderment. The sense that on this one day each year two plus two adds up not to four but to a million. The leap of the heart at waking up into a winter morning that for a while at least is as different from all other mornings as the city where the great snow fell was a different city. "Let all mortal flesh keep silence," the old hymn goes, and there was a time for most of us when it did.

And it is to dismiss a face. Who knows what we would have seen if we had been present there in Quirinius's time. Whether it happened the way Luke says it did, with the angels and the star, is almost beside the point because the one thing that believer and unbeliever alike can be equally sure happened is an event that changed the course of human history. And it was a profoundly human event—the birth of a human being by whose humanness we measure our own, of a human being with a face that, though none of us has ever seen it, we would all likely recognize because for twenty centuries it has been of all faces the one that our world has been most haunted by.

More than anything else perhaps, to dismiss this particular birth as no different in kind from the birth of Socrates, say, or Moses or Gautama Buddha would be to dismiss the quality of life that it has given birth to in an astonishing variety of people over an astonishing period of time. There have been wise ones and simple ones, sophisticated ones and crude ones, respectable ones and disreputable ones. There have been medieval peasants and eighteenth-century aristocrats, nineteenth-century spinsters and twentieth-century dropouts. They need not be mystics or saints or even unusually religious in any formal, institutional sense, and there may never have been any one dramatic moment of conversion in the past that they would point to. But somewhere along the line something deep in them split starwise and they became not simply followers of Christ but bearers of his life. A birth of grace and truth took place within them scarcely less miraculous in its way than the one the Magi traveled all those miles to kneel before.

To look at the last great self-portraits of Rembrandt or to read Pascal or hear Bach's B-minor Mass is to know beyond the need for further evidence that if God is anywhere, he is with them, as he is also with the man behind the meat counter, the woman who scrubs floors at Roosevelt Memorial, the high-school math teacher who explains fractions to the bewildered child. And the step from "God with them" to Emmanuel, "God with us," may not be as great as it seems. What keeps the wild hope of Christmas alive year after year in a world notorious for dashing all hopes is the haunting dream that the child who was born that day may yet be born again even in us and our own snowbound, snowblind longing for him.

14.
Love

Hear, O Israel: The Lord our God is one Lord; and you shall love the Lord your God with all your heart, and with all your soul, and with all your might. And these words which I command you this day shall be upon your heart; and you shall teach them diligently to your children, and shall talk of them when you sit in your house, and when you walk by the way, and when you lie down, and when you rise.

—DEUTERONOMY 6:4–7

Now from the sixth hour there was darkness over all the land until the ninth hour. And about the ninth hour Jesus cried with a loud voice, "Eli, Eli, lama sabachthani?" that is "My God, my God, why hast thou forsaken me?"

—MATTHEW 27:45–46

"*Hear, O Israel!*" says the great text in Deuteronomy where Moses calls out to his people in the wilderness. Hear, O Israel! *Hear!* Listen! And not just O Israel, hear, but O World, O Everybody, O Thou, O every last man and woman of us, because we are all of us called to become Israel by hearing lest instead we become Israel by not hearing and thus like her in her apostasy instead of in her faith. Nor is it just the text in Deuteronomy that is calling out to us to hear but the entire text of the Bible as a whole. We are to hear. All of us are. That is what the whole Bible is calling out. *"Hear, O Israel!"*

But hear what? Hear what? The Bible is hundreds upon hundreds of voices all calling at once out of the past and clamoring for our attention like barkers at a fair, like air-raid sirens, like a whole barnyard of cock crows as the first long shafts of dawn fan out across the sky. Some of the voices are shouting, like Moses's voice, so all Israel, all the world, can hear, and some are so soft and halting that you can hardly hear them at all, like Job with ashes on his head and his heart broken, like old Simeon whispering, "Lord, now lettest thou thy servant depart in peace" (Luke 2:29). The prophets shrill out in their frustration, their rage, their holy hope and madness; and the priests drone on and on about the dimensions and furniture of the Temple; and the lawgivers spell out what to eat and what not to eat; and the historians list the kings, the battles, the tragic lessons of Israel's history. And somewhere in the midst of them all one particular voice speaks out that is unlike any other voice because it speaks so directly to the deepest privacy and longing and weariness of each of us that there are times when the centuries are blown away like mist and it is as if we stand with no shelter of time at all between ourselves and the one who speaks our secret name. *Come,* the voice says. *Unto me. All ye.* Every last one.

Hear! the Bible says. Hear, O Israel! And what there is to hear is so vast and varied that it can be like sitting in the thick of a crowd so huge and clamorous that you literally don't know what all the shouting is about. You have to go stand across the street somewhere under the stars. You have to elbow your way out of the great crowd. And maybe then—off by yourself with some distance to catch your breath in and to soften the sound—maybe then you hear, in a sudden burst of cheering or windy gasp of astonishment as it rises up out of the huge arena, the inner truth of what all the shouting is about.

And that, I believe, is what this text from Deuteronomy does. It gives us distance and perspective. It sounds the one crucial and definitive note that points to the heart of the great crowd's thundering. "You shall love the Lord your God with all your heart, and with all your soul, and with all your might." That is what you are to hear. That is the heart of it, Deuteronomy says. And then, century upon century later, the Pharisees come and ask, "Teacher, which is the great commandment?" and the words that Jesus answers them with are the same words. "You shall love the Lord your God with all your heart, and with all your soul, and with all your mind. This is the great and first commandment" (Matt. 22:36–38).

Love God. We have heard the words so often that we no longer hear them. They are too loud to hear, too big to take in. We know the words so much *by* heart that we scarcely know them any longer as words spoken *to* the heart out of a mystery beyond all knowing. We take the words so much for granted that we hardly stop to wonder where they are seeking to take us. Above all else, the words say, *you shall love*—not first your neighbor as yourself, because that is second and comes later. On the contrary, it is God you shall love first before you love anything else, and you shall love him with all that you are and all that you have it in you to become—whatever that means, whatever that involves. The words don't explain. They just proclaim and command.

Loving our neighbors, loving each other, is easier to talk about, easier even to do. God knows we are none of us much good at it much of the time, but at least we can see each other with our eyes. We can see each other's faces especially, and every once in a while, if we have our eyes open, we can see something of what is within those faces. Even with strangers sometimes, people we pass on the street or find sitting across from us in a bus or a waiting room; even sometimes with people we know very well but seldom take the trouble really to look at—we see something that stops us in our tracks. We catch a glimpse of some unexpected beauty or pain or need in another's face, or maybe we just notice the tilt of an old man's Agway cap, or the way a young woman rests her cheek on the palm of her hand, or the way a child looks out the window at the rain; and for a moment, then, our heart goes out to them in ways too deep for words. We would love them right if we only could. We would love them truly and forever if we only knew how. And even as things are, we love them maybe as much as we are capable of loving anybody.

But so much of our loving them has to do with seeing them—these strangers who are sometimes so precious, these precious ones who are sometimes such strangers—whereas the God we are commanded to love with all our hearts, souls, minds is the one we cannot see at all. Not even Moses could see him when he asked to, because humans shall not see him and live, God said. "I will put you in a cleft of the rock," God said, "and I will cover you with my hand until I have passed by ... and you shall see my back; but my face shall not be seen" (Exod. 33:22–23).

We also have seen God's back, or pray at least that that is what we have seen. We have seen traces of him in each other's faces and in the mystery and splendor of the creation maybe, have seen as much of him as human eyes can see in the dream each of us has of Christ's face. But him in himself, God in his full glory and power, we have not seen and cannot see, and yet it is he whom we are commanded to love above all others. *Hear, O Israel!* You shall love him.

Can we? Do we even know what loving God looks like and feels like— not just taking comfort in him as an idea, not just believing in him as a possibility, not just worshiping him (because there was never a man or woman yet who didn't have to worship something, so why not God?), but actually loving him: wanting at least to be near him, wanting at least to do things for him, because that is the least of what love seems to mean?

If we have never seen God, maybe we can say at least that we have heard him. Maybe "hearing" is a better metaphor than "seeing" and certainly a more biblical one because hearing takes place in time: we listen to one word following another in time, and it is in time, in the day-by-day events of our own times and of historic time, that God makes himself known to us if he makes himself known to us at all. And in this sense of "hearing," we can sometimes believe that we have heard him for ourselves. We have heard him in Scripture—in the passion of Jeremiah, the crying out of Job, the love of Christ. We have heard him in history. We have heard him in our own inner histories—our own passion, our own crying out, our own love.

And yet, to be honest, we must say also that there are times when we have not heard him any more than we have seen him. There are times when we have heard the Bible, the Gospels themselves, ring like a cracked bell. When we have heard truth itself go sour, banal, ambiguous, have listened to our own lives and heard mostly confusion and emptiness. Instead of hearing God, there have been times when we have heard only a Godforsaken silence. And for many of us these are the times that we know best.

Hear, O Israel! Only more often than not we hear nothing because we live in a wilderness where more often than not there is nothing of God to hear. And of course it was in just such a wilderness that the great words of Moses were trumpeted forth in the first place, and the people who first heard them were in the wilderness with him, as wandering and lost as we are, with nothing to keep them going but the hope of a Promised Land, which much of the time seemed a promise so remote and improbable that even the bondage they had left behind them in Egypt looked hopeful by comparison. To be commanded to love God at all, let alone in the wilderness, is like being commanded to be well when we are sick, to sing for joy when we are dying of thirst, to run when our legs are broken. But this is the great and first commandment nonetheless. Even in the wilderness—especially in the wilderness—you shall love him.

We know that wilderness well, you and I—all of us do—because there isn't one of us who hasn't wandered there, lost, and who will not wander there again before our time is done. Let me speak for a moment of once when I wandered there myself. The wilderness was a strange city three thousand miles from home. In a hospital in that city there was somebody I loved as much as I have ever loved anybody, and she was in danger of dying. Apparently not even death itself was as terrifying to her as life was, and for that reason she was fighting against her own healing. With part of herself she didn't want to be well. She had lost track of what being well meant, and day after day my wife and I drove to the hospital to see her, parked the car in the parking lot, went up in the elevator. We played games with her. We rubbed her back. We read aloud. She weighed less as a young woman than she had as a child. We had known her since the day she was born, but if we had passed her in the corridor, we wouldn't have been able to recognize her.

When the worst finally happens, or almost happens, a kind of peace comes. I had passed beyond grief, beyond terror, all but beyond hope, and it was there, in that wilderness, that for the first time in my life I caught sight of something of what it must be like to love God truly. It was only a glimpse, but it was like stumbling on fresh water in the desert, like remembering something so huge and extraordinary that my memory had been unable to contain it. Though God was nowhere to be clearly seen, nowhere to be clearly heard, I had to be near him—even in the elevator riding up to her floor, even walking down the corridor to the one door among all those doors that had her name taped on it. I loved him because there was nothing else left. I loved him because he seemed to have made himself as helpless in his might as I was in my helplessness. I loved him not so much in spite of there being nothing in it for me, but almost because there was nothing in it for me. For the first time in my life, there in that wilderness, I caught a glimpse of what it must be like to love God truly, for his own sake, to love him no matter what. If I loved him with less than all my heart, soul, mind, I loved him with at least as much of them as I had left for loving anything.

And in that wilderness several small things happened that were not of that wilderness because they were of a far country. Two total strangers found their way to me, both of them ministers, offering more than just help, because what they offered was themselves in a way that made me understand for the first time what the word *Christendom* means—Christ's domain or dominion, the King's kingdom. And one night I heard compline sung in a great, bare church—sat in the coolness and dimness of it with nothing I had to say or be or do except just to let the chanting voices—grave, dispassionate, unearthly—wash over me like air from a far country. And quite by accident—if there are such things as accidents at times like these—I opened the Bible one evening to Psalm 131, which, if I'd ever read it before, I had read only as words, but which became now—of all words—the ones I most needed to hear: "O Lord, my heart is not lifted up, my eyes are not raised too high; I do not occupy myself with things too great and too marvelous for me. But I have calmed and quieted my soul, like a child quieted at its mother's breast; like a child that is quieted is my soul. O Israel, hope in the Lord from this time forth and for evermore."

I did not love God, God knows, because I was some sort of saint or hero. I did not love him because I suddenly saw the light (there was almost no light at all) or because I hoped by loving him to persuade him to heal the young woman I loved. I loved him because I couldn't help myself. I loved him because the one who commands us to love is the one who also empowers us to love, as there in the wilderness of that dark and terrible time I was, through no doing of my own, empowered to love him at least a little, at least enough to survive. And in the midst of it, these small things happened that were as big as heaven and earth because through them a hope beyond hopelessness happened. "O Israel, hope in the Lord from this time forth and for evermore."

O Israel, hope. Have faith. Above all, love. You shall love the Lord your God. That is the first and greatest. And I suppose the truth of it is something like this: that as the farthest reach of our love for each other is loving our enemies, and as the farthest reach of God's love for us is loving us at our most unlovable and unlovely, so the farthest reach of our love for God is loving him when in almost every way that matters we can neither see him nor hear him, and when he himself might as well be our enemy for all he comes to us in the ways we want him to come, and when the worst of the wilderness for us is the fear that he has forsaken us if indeed he exists at all.

"My God, my God, why hast thou forsaken me?" As Christ speaks those words, he too is in the wilderness. He speaks them when all is lost. He speaks them when there is nothing even he can hear except for the croak of his own voice and when as far as even he can see there is no God to hear him. And in a way his words are a love song, the greatest love song of them all. In a way his words are the words we all of us must speak before we know what it means to love God as we are commanded to love him.

"*My* God, *my* God." Though God is not there for him to see or hear, he calls on him still because he can do no other. Not even the cross, not even death, not even life can destroy his love for God. Not even God can destroy his love for God because the love he loves God with is God's love empowering him to love in return with all his heart even when his heart is all but broken.

That is the love that you and I are called to move toward both through the wilderness times, on broken legs, and through times when we catch glimpses and hear whispers from beyond the wilderness. Nobody ever claimed the journey was going to be an easy one. It is not easy to love God with all your heart and soul and mind when much of the time you have all but forgotten his name. But to love God is not a goal we have to struggle toward on our own, because what at its heart the gospel is all about is that God himself moves us toward it even when we believe he has forsaken us.

The final secret, I think, is this: that the words "You shall love the Lord your God" become in the end less a command than a promise. And the promise is that, yes, on the weary feet of faith and the fragile wings of hope, we will come to love him at last as from the first he has loved us—loved us even in the wilderness, especially in the wilderness, because he has been in the wilderness with us. He has been in the wilderness for us. He has been acquainted with our grief. And, loving him, we will come at last to love each other too so that, in the end, the name taped on every door will be the name of the one we love.

"And these words which I command you this day shall be upon your heart; and you shall teach them diligently to your children, and you shall talk of them when you sit in your house, and when you walk by the way, and when you lie down, and when you rise."

And rise we shall, out of the wilderness, every last one of us, even as out of the wilderness Christ rose before us. That is the promise, and the greatest of all promises.

15.

Delay

The people who walked in darkness have seen a great light; those who dwelt in a land of deep darkness, on them has light shined. Thou hast multiplied the nation, thou hast increased its joy.... For every boot of the tramping warrior in battle tumult and every garment rolled in blood will be burned as fuel for the fire. For to us a child is born, to us a son is given; and the government will be upon his shoulder, and his name will be called "Wonderful Counselor, Mighty God, Everlasting Father, Prince of Peace." Of the increase of his government and of peace there shall be no end, upon the throne of David, and over his kingdom, to establish it and to uphold it with justice and with righteousness, from this time forth and for evermore. The zeal of the Lord of hosts will do this.

—ISAIAH 9:2–7

Philip found Nathanael, and said to him, "We have found him of whom Moses in the law and also the prophets wrote, Jesus of Nazareth, the son of Joseph." Nathanael said to him, "Can anything good come out of Nazareth?" Philip said to him, "Come and see." Jesus saw Nathanael coming to him, and said of him, "Behold, an Israelite indeed, in whom is no guile!" Nathanael said to him, "How do you know me?" Jesus answered him, "Before Philip called you, when you were under the fig tree, I saw you." Nathanael answered him, "Rabbi, you are the Son of God! You are the King of Israel!" Jesus answered him, "Because I said to you, I saw you under the fig tree, do you believe? You shall see greater things than these." And he said to him, "Truly, truly, I say to you, you will see heaven opened, and the angels of God ascending and descending upon the Son of man."

—JOHN 1:45–51

Delay

You have to take a long drive somewhere, say, and set out well before dawn to make a good start. It is winter, and the snow is coming down heavily. The headlights catch the tumbling flakes a little way ahead of you, but otherwise, all around you, there is nothing you can see. The darkness is so complete that it seems less an absence of light than itself a presence, a darkness so dense and impenetrable, like the snow itself, that what little light you have on your own can barely survive in it. It is hard to believe that it will ever be day again. There is no sky for the sun to rise in, and except for the short stretch of road that your car lights up, there is no earth; there is nothing to get your bearings by, nobody anywhere to point you on your way or reassure you by the sound of a human voice. As you travel slowly into the night, it's as if night travels slowly into you until the darkness without starts to become indistinguishable from the darkness within, darkness piling up in you like snow. It's as if it's not just someplace far away out there that you're moving toward but someplace even farther away in here, in you. Daybreak is what in every sense you're hoping toward, the coming of light into every kind of darkness. Light to see by—to see the road and whatever awaits at the road's end, to see another human being, to see yourself as human. It is winter. It is deep night. The snow muffles all sound except the faint hum of the engine, the ticking of the dashboard clock. Like an ancient pagan at the winter solstice, you feel there is maybe nothing too precious to sacrifice, nothing you would not be willing to give or do or be, if you only knew what, to make day come.

Or say instead that on just such another winter night it is not you who are journeying out, but somebody who is journeying home to you. The roads are icy, and the radio has been full of accident reports. You've been waiting a long time. There comes a point where you can't bear just to sit there any longer; you go stand at the window to watch for the lights of cars. Every once in a while one appears out of the dark, and with your eyes, more than your eyes, you follow it up the long hill and around the bend, waiting to hear it slow down as it nears your house, waiting to see the little directional signal flicker a turn into your drive. But one after another, the cars all pass by and continue up the hill out of sight with stretches of silence in between them so long and empty that it's hard to believe in even the possibility of another car ever breaking that silence again—a silence too deep for any sound ever to well up out of it, a dark too thick for any light to pierce.

An hour late becomes an hour and a half, two hours late. You try to find something to take your mind off it—a book to read, the dishwasher to empty, a prayer to pray—but there's too much more of you involved by now than just your mind, and you can feel your face grow gray with waiting. Will the telephone ring like a fire alarm? Or will there be only more darkness, more silence? Or will your prayer finally be answered? So deep is your hoping that at moments hope itself drives back the night a little; and in your mind, if nowhere else, in the darkness of your waiting, what you hope to happen all but does happen. You all but see a light move slowly up the hill. You all but hear a car slow down as if to turn. Can it conceivably be? Silence fills your ears, darkness fills your eyes and more than your eyes. Is it only inside yourself that somewhere you hear a door opening? The sound of footsteps in the hall? From some distant part of the house, some deep and distant part of who you are, the one voice out of all the voices in the world you wait for calls out your name. Does it? Will it? Will the one you hope for ever come out of the hopelessness of such a night?

Or say, finally, that it is night, and you are home, and no one you love is in danger. You alone are in danger. The hospital has taken certain tests, say, and how they will turn out only time will tell. Your life may just depend on how they turn out. So you lie there in the dark straining to hear time's tale ahead of time, because waiting time is always time strained, time searched and listened to, till past time, present time, future time all start to whisper at once—the past in all its preciousness and never more precious than now; the present in all its dark impenetrability; the future in whatever form it is to come. Morning will come at last, and with it the word you wait for will be spoken at last, the word that you hope for, long for, until you can all but hear it already, which is the word, of course, that gives you back your life again.

For light to come. For the one you love to come. For the word of life to be spoken. Faith is a way of waiting—never quite knowing, never quite hearing or seeing, because in the darkness we are all but a little lost. There is doubt hard on the heels of every belief, fear hard on the heels of every hope, and many holy things lie in ruins because the world has ruined them and we have ruined them. But faith waits even so, delivered at least from that final despair which gives up waiting altogether because it sees nothing left worth waiting for. Faith waits—for the opening of a door, the sound of footsteps in the hall, that beloved voice delayed, delayed so long that there are times when you all but give up hope of ever hearing it. And when at moments you think you do hear it (if only faintly, from far away) the question is: Can it possibly be, impossibly be, that one voice of all voices?

"Come and see," Philip says, says it to Nathanael, to all of us. "We have found him," Philip says. Found whom? Found what? "The one of whom Moses in the law and also the prophets wrote," Philip says. He means holiness itself, of course, giver of light and life, the beloved one whom all the world has been awaiting and will always await whether it knows it does or not. There are times when you can sense even the trees waiting, the stones, the dumb beasts. It's as if not just Nathanael, whoever he was, but all of us, whoever we are, hold our breath—history itself holds its breath—to hear who it is that Philip has found. Then Philip tells. "Jesus," he says, a name like any other name. "From Nazareth," he says, a place like any other place. Joseph's child.

The longing is so rich. Philip's words are so meager. "Jesus of Nazareth," he says. It seems hardly more than the brushing of snow against the windshield, the creak of the old house as you watch at the window, the beat of your own heart as you lie in bed waiting for morning. Do you laugh? Do you cry? Nathanael in a way does both with his half bitter, half sad little shrug of a joke. "Can anything good come out of Nazareth?" he asks. Can anything that matters so much come out of anywhere that seems to matter so little, let alone can something that matters more than anything else in the world because that is what Jesus is, Philip says. That is how Jesus matters. For thousands of years, since Moses's time, he is the one we've been waiting for, Philip says. The light that the darkness has been waiting for. Joseph's child. Out of no place, nowhere.

Nathanael's shrug is the shrug of us all if we're honest, I think. Can any one life shed light on the mystery of life itself? In some new and shattering way, can any one life make us come alive ourselves, because that is of course what we wait for, what religion is about—what churches are about, what our hymns and preaching and prayers are all about, though there are times you would hardly know it. *Life:* that's what we all hunger for, wait for always, whether we keep coming back to places like church to find it or whether we avoid places like church like the plague as the last places on earth to find it: both delivered in part and derelict in part, immigrants and mongrels all of us. It's life as we've never really known it but only dreamed it that we wait for. Life with each other. Life for each other. Life with the darkness gone. And they have found it, Philip says. They have found him. Can it be true?

The danger is that we'll say yes too easily, that we'll say it because all these centuries the church has been saying it and because for years we have been saying it ourselves. To say yes too easily, too much out of old habit, is to say it as if we really know who Jesus is, as if he is somehow *our* Jesus. He is not ours. If anything, we are his. He is Joseph's child. He is also Mystery's child. Who he is for our world, for us, we can know only from him. "Come and see," Philip says, and there is no other way for any of us. There was just a little way for Nathanael to travel—just around the bend in the road and across a patch of field—but in a sense Nathanael had been traveling there his whole life long as in a sense you and I have too: to see at last and to be seen, to know and to be known, to find and to be found.

There is a game we play sometimes. If we could somehow meet one of the great ones of history, which one would we choose? Would it be Shakespeare, maybe, because nobody knew better than he the Hamlet of us and the Ophelia of us, nobody knew better than he this midsummer night's dream of a darkly enchanted world. Or maybe it would be Abraham Lincoln, with feet no less of clay than our own feet, but whose face, in those last great photographs, seems somehow to have not only all of human suffering in it but traces of goodness and compassion that seem more than human. Or maybe it would be St. Joan, the Maid of Orleans, whose very weakness was her strength, her innocence her armor, lighting up the dark skies of the fifteenth century like a star. But the great ones of the world, if you and I were to meet them, would have nothing to give us but their greatness, nothing to ask of us but our admiration; and we would go to such a meeting full of awe to be sure, but knowing more or less what to expect. In the saints and heroes of the past we would find someone greater than we are, more human, more complete, but cut from the same cloth as we are after all, someone who was as often lost, as full of doubt, as full of hope, waiting no less than you and I wait for we're not sure what to deliver us at last.

But if Philip is right, it is not just somebody greater than we whom we go to meet, and it is not just out of the past that he comes to meet us, and it is not just his greatness that he has to give us. It is himself that he has to give us. It is ourselves that he has to give us. That is our faith. And it is not just our admiration that he asks. Who of us knows fully what he has to ask any more than we know fully what he has to give? And it is our not knowing that makes our meeting with him more momentous than any other we can imagine. It is the one whom Moses and the prophets foretold, Philip says. It is the Word made flesh. It is the word of all words that speaks out of deepest mystery to the flesh and blood of all of us.

Around the bend in the road and across the patch of field. Driving through the snowy night. Standing at the dark window. Lying in bed waiting for dawn to bring whatever word dawn brings. The one we await is the one whom for all these years we have prayed to, prayed through. We are Nathanael. Come and see, Philip tells us.

So we come as Nathanael came, to see for ourselves if it is true what Philip says and what for all our lives we sometimes believed and sometimes failed to believe. We are men and women of the world, all of us are. We don't believe in fairy tales, at least not many of them, not often. Many of our best dreams have turned out to be only dreams. Many of our dearest hopes for ourselves and for the people we love have died stillborn, and the world has long since taught us to be prepared always for the worst. But we come nevertheless—come in faith. We make our way to where he stands beyond a little grove of trees, whoever we are—a retired schoolteacher half sick with boredom and loneliness, a young dancer at the peak of her career, an out-of-work black woman facing a mastectomy, a middle-aged couple trying to hold their marriage together, a boy and girl in love. And you and I come with them—like them, the bearers of secrets we have never told, the guardians of memories more precious than gold and sadder than an empty house. As we make our way through the trees, a figure comes into view. It is dusk, and he stands dark against the gray sky. At the sound of our footsteps, he glances our way. We stand for a moment with our eyes lowered, not daring to look up and see his face, for fear both of what it may be and of what it may fail to be. We have waited so long. We have traveled so far.

What Nathanael saw when he raised his eyes at last and looked up into that face we do not know, and we do not know either what you and I will see if such a moment should come also for us when we too shall stand before his justice and his love at last with all our secrets laid bare. But I believe that for us, as for Nathanael, it will be a face we recognize because at some level of our being it is a face that we have always known the way the birds of the air know from a distance of a thousand miles their place of nesting, the way the trees of the forest, even in winter, are rooted deep in the promise of spring. We will know him when we see him, and, more crucial still, he will know us.

"Behold, an Israelite indeed, in whom is no guile," Jesus says to Nathanael before Nathanael has found a tongue to say anything to him; and we picture this Nathanael standing there in all his guilenesses with mud on his shoes and his jaw hanging loose before he says finally, whispers it, I suspect, "Rabbi, you are the Son of God! You are the King of Israel!" And I picture you and me standing there too, not guileless by a long shot if you're anything like me, but full of all that the world has filled us with—and that we have filled the world with—in the way of disillusion and doubt and self-seeking and love and fear and deceit and hope and everything else that makes us, each in our own unrepeatable way, human.

Behold us for what we truly and helplessly are. Behold us each for what we have it in us to become and at our best moments pray to become and again and again choose not to become, can find no way of becoming. Behold every man and woman of us, everywhere, who spend most of our lives believing that we wait only for morning to break, for the beloved to return, for some word of comfort to be spoken. Behold all of us who, half blinded by all that blinds us, find it hard to believe that we ourselves have been awaited ever since the creation of the world.

"The people who walked in darkness have seen a great light; those who dwelt in a land of deep darkness, on them has the light shined." Deep is the darkness of our time—of our land and of all lands and of all of us. And most of what light comes our way is as random and elusive as the lights of cars winding up the long hill at night. It is not a great light we have seen but only a small light. But we have come here anyway because somewhere, sometime, once, for all of us, an exodus happened, a grim sea parted, and we were delivered enough from bondage to ourselves to see at least where true deliverance lies. We have come here because, although there is always much in the world and much in ourselves that drives us toward despair, and although we ourselves are often among those who lay waste the Temple in its holiness, we have never been abandoned in our dereliction by the one whom no Temple can ever contain. And the great light that our small light foretells is that the one who from the beginning has led us out, led us forth, and who has been with us through the perpetual ruins we have wandered in ever since and, through the long delay, is the one whom we wait for in great hope and who in great hope waits also for us. Listen to your lives for the sound of him. Search even in the dark for the light and the love and the life because they are there also, and we are known each one by name.

And the name of the one who waits for us? It is Wonderful Counselor, Mighty God. It is Everlasting Father, Mother, Princess and Prince of Peace. "And you shall see greater things than this" are the words that come to us as they came to Nathanael before us. Much that we hold fast to we will have to let loose, and much that we have lost we will have to find again; and for those as long accustomed to the dark as we, the great light will doubtless bring great tribulation as well as great benediction before we rise up in the splendor of it whole and new at last. But greater things than this we shall see is the promise, and, by God's grace, greater things than this we shall become.

"Truly, truly, I say to you, you will see heaven opened, and the angels of God ascending and descending upon the Son of man" and upon us all. May we never deceive ourselves that we know what those words mean. If we think they are no more than the florid poetry of another age we only reveal how captive we are to the narrow presuppositions of our own. If we think they are to be taken as literally as a child would take them, I suspect we are more nearly right, but only clumsily, partially, in the manner of children. Who can know fully what Christ means when he says that we will see him in his glory? But because we have already seen him in the glory of our long delayed but dearest hope, I believe that the faith is by no means blind that sees his word as not just a poem, and only a poem, but as high and unimaginable truth. Amen. Come, Lord Jesus.

16.

Air for Two Voices

In the beginning was the Word, and the Word was with God, and the Word was God. He was in the beginning with God; all things were made through him, and without him was not anything made that was made. In him was life, and the life was the light of men. The light shines in the darkness, and the darkness has not overcome it.

There was a man sent from God, whose name was John. He came for testimony, to bear witness to the light, that all might believe through him. He was not the light, but came to bear witness to the light.

The true light that enlightens every man was coming into the world. He was in the world, and the world was made through him, and yet the world knew him not. He came to his own home, and his own people received him not. But to all who received him, who believed in his name, he gave power to become children of God; who were born, not of blood nor of the will of the flesh nor of the will of man, but of God.

And the Word became flesh and dwelt among us, full of grace and truth; we have beheld his glory, glory as of the only Son from the Father. (John bore witness to him, and cried, "This was he of whom I said, 'He who comes after me ranks before me, for he was before me.'") And from his fullness have we all received, grace upon grace.

—JOHN 1:1–16

There are two voices in this extraordinary text from John. The first of them is a voice chanting, a cantor's voice, a muezzin's voice, a poet's voice, a choirboy's voice before it has changed—ghostly, virginal, remote, and cool as stone. "In the beginning was the Word, and the Word was with God, and the Word was God. He was in the beginning with God." It is sung, not said, a hymn, not a homily. It is a hymn to perform surgery with, a heart-transplanting voice.

The second voice is insistent and overearnest, a little nasal. It is a voice that wants to make sure, a voice that's trying hard to get everything straight. It is above all a down-to-earth voice. It keeps interrupting. This troublesome confusion about just who the Messiah was, the second voice says: not John the Baptist certainly, whatever may have been rumored in certain circles. It is a point that cannot be made too clearly or too emphatically. It was not the Baptist. It was Jesus. Right from the beginning Jesus was without any question who it was.

"In him was life, and the life was the light of men. The light shines in darkness, and the darkness has not overcome it," the first voice sings far above all sublunary distinctions, the great Logos hymn.

And then the second voice again. Yes, it says. Only to come back to the Baptist for a moment. He came for testimony, to bear witness to the light. He was not the light, but came to bear *witness* to the light, the perspiration beading out on the upper lip, the knuckles whitening.

"And the Word became flesh and dwelt among us," the cry soars up to the great rose window, toward the Pleiades, the battlements of jasper and topaz and amethyst: "*In principio erat verbum* and dwelt among us, full of grace and truth."

And that is true, says the second voice. The Baptist made it absolutely clear when he said—I remember the very words he used—"He who comes after me ranks before me, for he was before me." The Baptist said so himself.

It is good to have both the voices. The sound the second voice makes is a very human sound, and you need a very human sound to get your bearings by in the midst of the first voice's unearthly music. It is also good to have the interruptions. There should be interruptions in sermons too: the sound of a baby crying, a toilet being flushed—something to remind us of just what this flesh is that the Word became, the Word that was with God, that was God. What it smells and sounds and tastes like, this flesh the Word buckled on like battle dress. When the host is being raised before the altar to the tinkling of bells, it is very meet and right if not his bounden duty for the sexton to walk through with the vacuum cleaner. The New Testament itself is written that way: the risen Christ coming back at dawn to the Sea of Tiberias, Jesus with the mystery of life and death upon him, standing there on the beach saying, "Have you any fish?" (John 21:5).

Have you any *fish*, for Christ's sweet sake! Precisely that. The Christ and the chowder. The Messiah and the mackerel. The Word and the flesh. The first voice and the second voice. It is what the great text is all about, of course, this mystery, this tension and scandal; and the text itself, with this antiphony of voices, is its own illustration.

Somebody has to do the vacuuming. Somebody has to keep the accounts and put out the cat. And we are grateful for these things to the second voice, which is also of course our own voice, puny and inexhaustible as Faulkner said. It is a human voice. It is the only voice the universe has for speaking of itself and to itself. It is a voice with its own message, its own mystery, and it is important to be told that it was not the Baptist, it was Jesus—not that one standing over there bony and strident in the Jordan, but this one with the queer north-country accent, full of grace and truth. Behold, the Baptist said, that is the lamb of God. Not this one, but *that* one. We need to know.

But it is the first voice that prevails here, and the first voice that haunts and humbles us—muezzin, cantor, Christ Church chorister—and it is a voice that haunts us at first less with what it means than with how it sounds, with the music before the message, whatever the message is; with the cadences and chords, the silences. "*Im Anfang war das Wort, und das Wort war bei Gott, und Gott war das Wort,*" the first voice incants, "*et omnia per ipsum facta sunt, et sine ipso factum est nihil quod factum est.*" It hardly matters what it means at first. "*Et la Parole a été faite chair, et elle a habité parmi nous, pleine de grâce et de vérité.*" It hardly matters what it means any more than it matters what the sound of the surf means, the organ notes winging like trapped birds toward some break in the gothic dusk. "And from this fullness have we all received, grace upon grace, *Gnade um Gnade, gratiam pro gratia.* He was in the world," the voice sings, "yet the world knew him not," and *"Siehe, das ist Gottes Lamm,"* John says, *"qui ôte le péché du monde. Ecce Agnus Dei qui tollit peccatum mundi.* Behold, the Lamb of God, who takes away the sin of the world" (1:29).

Shout "Fire!" Cry "Havoc!" Cry "Help" or "Hallelujah, Hosanna!" A siren in the night. A trumpet at sunup. A woman singing in the rain, or a man singing, or weeping, or yelling bloody murder. When you hear it, what happens is that the pulse quickens. It is simply the sound that stirs the heart, literally as well as figuratively stirs it. The sound of the word sung or shouted, its music, literally as well as figuratively, stirs it. The sound of the word sung or shout ed, its music literally makes the heart beat faster, makes the blood run quicker and hotter, which is to say the word stirs life. Whatever it is at the level of meaning, at the level of sound, rhythm, breath, the word has the power to stir life. And again this is both what John is saying here and what with his own words he is illustrating: that the Word stirs life even as his own words stir life, stir something. It is hard to hear this prologue read in any tongue without something inside quickening.

The Word becomes flesh. As the word of terror in the night makes the flesh crawl, as the word of desire makes the flesh burn, as other words make the scalp run cold and set the feet running, in maybe some such way this Logos Word of God becomes flesh, becomes Jesus. Jesus so responds to this Word, which is God's, that he himself becomes the Word, as simple and as complicated as that.

Things get into the air, we say—violence gets into the air, or hate, or panic, or joy—and we catch these things from the air or get caught up in them to the point where the violence or the joy becomes ours or we theirs. The Word becoming flesh means something like that maybe. God was in the air, and Jesus got so caught up, let this Word of God that was in the air get so under his skin, so in his hair, took it so to heart what there was of God in the air that what was in the air became who he was. He opened his mouth to answer the Word, and like air it filled his mouth.

Or God is poet, say, searching for the right word. Tries Noah, but Noah is a drinking man, and tries Abraham, but Abraham is a little too Mesopotamian with all those wives and whiskers. Tries Moses, but Moses himself is trying too hard; and David, too handsome for his own good; Elisha, who sicks the bears on the children. Tries John the Baptist with his locusts and honey, who might almost have worked except for something small but crucial like a sense of the ridiculous or a balanced diet.

Word after word God tries and then finally tries once more to say it right, to get it all into one final Word what he is and what human is and why the suffering of love is precious and how the peace of God is a tiger in the blood. And the Word that God finds—who could have guessed it?—is this one, Jesus of Nazareth, all of it coming alive at last in this life, Jesus this implausible Jew, the Word made finally flesh in Jesus's flesh. Jesus as the *mot juste* of God.

The poetry of the first voice fleshed out in the prose of the second. The Word becoming flesh and dwelling among us full of grace and truth, and that is not all that being flesh involves being full of, so full of that too, like the rest of us, and full of beans too, full of baloney—the scandal of the incarnation, the unimaginable *kenosis* and humbling of God. John means certainly no less than this and almost certainly more.

"In the beginning," he says, "was the Word," and although it is a poem he is writing, we assume that he is being more than just poetic. "*In principio,*" he says, and we assume he means no less than what Genesis means with *bereshith,* which is to say "in the beginning" quite literally: before anything yet had been made that was to be made, before whatever it was that happened to make it possible for Being to happen. You can't speak literally about such things, of course, but we assume that he is speaking as seriously as physicists also speak seriously about the possibility at least of a time beyond time before creation happened. At that point where everything was nothing or nothing everything, before the Big Bang banged or the Steady State was stated, when there was no up and no down, no life and no death, no here and no there, at the very beginning, John says, there was this Word, which was God and through which all things were made.

The Bible is usually very universal and makes you want to *see* something—some image to imagine it by. "The light shines in the darkness," John says, and maybe you see an agonizing burst of light with the darkness folding back like petals, like hands. But the imagery of John is based rather on sound than on sight. It is a Word you hear breaking through the unimaginable silence—a creating word, a word that calls forth, a word that stirs life and is life because it is God's word, John says, and has God in it as your words have you in them, have in them your breath and spirit and tell of who you are. Light and dark, the visual, occur in space, but sound, this Word spoken, occurs in time and starts time going. "Let there *be*," the Word comes, and then there is, creation is. Something is where before there was nothing, and the morning stars sing together and all the Sons of God shout for joy because sequence has begun, time has begun, a story has begun.

All of which is to say that John will stop at nothing and here at the start of his Gospel asks us to believe no less than everything. He asks us to believe that the Word that became flesh, that became flesh like our flesh, that stood there in the moonshine asking "Have you any fish?" was not a last-minute word and not just one word among many words, but was The Word, the primal, cosmic Word in which was life and light. All that God had from the beginning meant was here in this flesh. The secret of life and death was here.

Behold, the Lamb of God who takes away the sin of the world. The Lamb of God approaches slowly along the river bank. The Baptist sees him coming, and here the second voice interrupts again. Forget all this about the primal, cosmic Word, the second voice says, and about how it was in the beginning. Just watch the one who is approaching—not the Baptist there in the water, but the one who is walking toward the Baptist along the edge of the water. *Siehe, das ist Gottes Lamm.* Nothing matters except him. See how the air stirs, bending the rushes in front of him. Watch his face as he picks his way along—nobody else's face. His. Everything that matters is in his face. Everything that matters is in his hands.

In his hands is the meaning and purpose of creation, the first voice says. In his hands is your life, the second voice says. Behold, he takes away the sins of the world. *Das ist Gottes Lamm.* His foot slips in the mud. The Baptist waits in the water up to his waist. He cannot see yet whether the one who is coming is the One he has been expecting or not. There is mud on the man's hands now where he grabbed out to keep himself from falling. Perhaps the Baptist is afraid—either afraid that the one who is coming won't be the One or afraid that he will be the One.

Mary, the mother, was also afraid—a little afraid when the angel first came with his announcement, but that was the least of it. He had come so quietly, with an Easter lily in his hand. She had been wearing blue Florentine velvet at the time with her hair hanging down her back like a girl's. Sunlight lay on the tiles like a carpet. The angel stood so still that he could have been one of the columns in the loggia where they met. She had trouble hearing what he said and afterwards thought it might have been a dream. It was not until much later that the real terror came. The real terror came when what the angel had told her would happen happened but in a way she could never have dreamed: squatting there in the straw with her thighs wrenched apart and out of her pain dropping into the howling world something that looked like nothing so much as raw beefsteak: which was the one the angel said was to be called Holy, the Son of the Most High: which was the Word fleshed in, of all flesh, hers.

We have reason, all of us, to be among other things afraid. Like the Baptist waiting there in the river, afraid that the one who is coming along the slippery bank is after all not the One who has been awaited for so long; afraid that the one who is coming and who by now has slipped several times more and has gotten mud all over everything—either he is out of his head or just isn't looking where he's going—afraid that he is simply not the One at all. Afraid that he is not the Word made flesh because there was no Word in the first place and there was no first place either. In the beginning there was nothing much of anything and still isn't if you add up all there is and place it next to all there is not. Afraid that Jesus and the Baptist meet there in the river like Laurel and Hardy, and as the water rises, their derby hats go floating off toward the Dead Sea.

Or, like the Baptist, afraid that the one who is coming is the One. Behold the Lamb of God who takes away … all that is going to have to be taken away. The Lamb of God who gives …, God help us, "the power to become children of God," John says. Just suppose for the sake of an admittedly fantastic argument that he is the One who is to come, full of grace and truth and all that. Have you ever considered, have I whose trade it is to consider it, ever really considered seriously just what it is that the Lamb of God is going to have to take away?

I mean if I have any inclination at all, or you, to start being whatever in God's name it means to be "a child of God"—and let's say there is no argument for having such an inclination, but let's just suppose that at certain unguarded moments we have it, this inclination to *start* being children of God—have we any idea at all what by the grace of God we are in all likelihood going to have to stop being, stop doing, stop having, stop pretending, stop smacking our lips over, stop hating, stop being scared of, stop chasing after till we're blue in the face and sick at the stomach? O God, deliver us from the Lamb of God who takes away the sin of the world, because the sin of the world is our heart's desire, our uniform, our derby hat. O Lamb of God, have mercy upon us. Christ have mercy upon us.

We have reason, all of us, to be afraid as Mary was afraid, squatting in the straw. She was afraid, I suppose, of giving birth, and why shouldn't she have been? It is by all accounts a painful, bloody process at best. We all have reason to be among other things afraid of giving birth: the wrenching and tearing of it; the risk that we will die in giving birth; more than the risk, the certainty, that if there is going to be a birth, there is first going to have to be a kind of death. One way or another, every new life born out of our old life, every flesh through which God speaks his Word, looks a little like raw beefsteak before it's through. If we are not afraid of it, then we do not know what it involves.

We labor to be born. All what little we have in us of holiness labors for breath, strains to be delivered of darkness into light. It is the secret, inner battle of every one of us. And through all our laboring, God also labors: to deliver what is whole in us from what is broken, to deliver what is true in us from what is false, until in the end we reach the measure of the stature of the fullness of Christ, Paul says—until in the end we become Christ ourselves, no less than that: Christs to each other and Christs to God.

No one ever said it was going to be easy to turn a sow's ear into a silk purse. "Be perfect, as your heavenly Father is perfect," the great voice sings (Matt. 5:48). Be holy. Be healed. Be human. Because the light shines forth in the darkness, giving power to us all to become children of God. But every time that voice rings out, we answer with the voice of our own littleness, our own earthboundness, that such things are too wonderful for us, that the spirit is willing but the flesh is weak, that we can will what is right but cannot bring it about. It is no easy matter to save us when half the time we don't even want to be saved because we are so at home in the darkness that is home. We none of us come to the end of our days with the saving more than a fraction done at best. But, praise God, the end of our days is not the end of us.

"The light shines in the darkness, and the darkness has not overcome it," the great voice calls out; and with this life behind us, we move on through realms of mystery and mercy and new life beyond our power to imagine until at last, through the cloddish and reluctant flesh of all of us, Almighty God of his grace will speak again in a different tongue and to a lesser but unthinkably significant end the word that was once made flesh and dwelt among us, from whose fullness we have all received.

Behold the Lamb of God who takes away, who gives.

17.

The Clown in the Belfry

The Lord is my shepherd; I shall not want. He maketh me to lie
down in green pastures: he leadeth me beside the still waters. He restoreth my soul: he leadeth me in the paths of righteousness for his
name's sake. Yea, though I walk through the valley of the shadow of
death, I will fear no evil: for thou art with me; thy rod and thy staff
they comfort me. Thou preparest a table before me in the presence of
my enemies: thou anointest my head with oil; my cup runneth over.
Surely goodness and mercy shall follow me all the days of my life: and
I will dwell in the house of the Lord forever.

—PSALM 23, KJV

Happy Birthday! Happy Birthday to this old church, which was first organized two hundred years ago day before yesterday with seven members
and a pastor who bore the somewhat less than promising name of Increase
Graves. Happy Birthday to this old building, which has seen many a howling blizzard in its time and many a scorching summer day before the road it
stands on ever dreamed of being paved and the air was thick with the dust
of horses' hooves and wagon wheels. Happy Birthday to all of you because
more than an organization, more than a building, a church is the people
who come to it to pray and sing and fidget and dream, to shed a tear or two

if some word strikes home, and to try to keep a straight face if the soloist strikes a sour note or somebody's hearing aid starts to buzz. Happy Birthday to all of you, who listen to some sermons and doze through other sermons and do all the other things people do that make them a church and make them human.

And Happy Birthday to Jesus too, I guess it's proper to say, because before this is a Congregational church, or Rupert's church, or your church, it is after all *his* church. If it hadn't been for Jesus, who knows what other kind of building might have stood on this spot, or what other line of work Increase Graves might have gone into, or where you and I might be to-day—not just where we might be geographically, but where we might be humanly, inside ourselves, if it hadn't been for Jesus and all the things he said and did and all the things people have kept on saying and doing be-cause of him ever since.

What do you do on a birthday? You get together with your friends, of course. You put on your best clothes. You sing songs. You bring offerings. You whoop it up. You do a lot of the same things, in other words, that we're doing here today, and it seems to me that that's just as it should be. But there's one thing I propose to do that is usually not done on birthdays. Just for a moment or two I suggest we set aside our snappers and party hats and give at least one quick look at what it is that we're whooping it up about, what it is that really makes people into a church in the first place.

Since 1786 people have been coming here the way you and I came here today. Men who fought in the American Revolution and the widows of men who never got back from it. Civil War veterans. Two centuries' worth of farmers, dairymen, mill workers, an occasional traveler. Old men and old women with most of their lives behind them, and young men and young women with most of their lives ahead of them. People who made a go of it and are remembered still, and people who somehow never left their mark in any way the world noticed and aren't remembered anymore by anybody. Despite the enormous differences between them, all these men and women entered this building just the way you and I entered it a few minutes ago because of one thing they had in common.

What they had in common was that, like us, they believed (or some-times believed and sometimes didn't believe; or wanted to believe; or liked to think they believed) that the universe, that everything there is, didn't come about by chance, but was created by God. Like us, they believed, on their best days anyway, that, all appearances to the contrary notwithstanding, this God was a God like Jesus, which is to say a God of love. That, I think, is the crux of the matter. In 1786 and 1886 and 1986 and all the years between, that is at the heart of what has made this place a church. That is what all the whooping has been about. In the beginning it was not some vast cosmic explosion that made the heavens and the earth. It was a loving God who did. That is our faith and the faith of all the ones who came before us.

The question is, is it true? If the answer is no, then what we're celebrating today is at best a happy and comforting illusion. If the answer is yes, then we have something to celebrate that makes even a two-hundredth birthday look pale by comparison.

I don't suppose there is any passage in either the Old Testament or the New that sums up the faith this church was founded on more eloquently and movingly than the Twenty-third Psalm. "The Lord is my shepherd; I shall not want." How many times would you guess those words have been spoken here over the years, especially at dark moments when people needed all the faith they could muster? How many times have we spoken them ourselves at our own dark moments? But for all their power to bring comfort, do the words hold water? This faith in God that they affirm, is it borne out by our own experience of life on this planet? That is a hard and painful question to raise, but let us honor the occasion by raising it anyway. Does this ancient and beautiful psalm set forth a faith that in the secrecy of our hearts we can still honestly subscribe to? And what exactly is that faith it sets forth? The music of the psalm is so lovely that it's hard sometimes to hear through it to what the psalm is saying.

"God's in his heaven, all's right with the world," Robert Browning wrote, and the psalm is certainly not saying that any more than you or I can say it either. Whoever wrote it had walked through the valley of the shadow the way one way or another you and I have walked there too. He says so himself. He believed that God was in his heaven despite the fact that he knew as well as we do that all was far from right with the world. And he believed that God was like a shepherd.

When I think of shepherds, I think of my friend Vernon Beebe, who used to keep sheep here in Rupert a few years back. Some of them he gave names to, and some of them he didn't, but he knew them equally well either way. If one of them got lost, he didn't have a moment's peace till he found it again. If one of them got sick or hurt, he would move heaven and earth to get it well again. He would feed them out of a bottle when they were new-born lambs if for some reason the mother wasn't around or wouldn't "own" them, as he put it. He always called them in at the end of the day so the wild dogs wouldn't get them. I've seen him wade through snow up to his knees with a bale of hay in each hand to feed them on bitter cold winter evenings, shaking it out and putting it in the manger. I've stood with him in their shed with a forty-watt bulb hanging down from the low ceiling to light up their timid, greedy, foolish, half holy faces as they pushed and butted each other to get at it, because if God is like a shepherd, there are more than just a few ways, needless to say, that people like you and me are like sheep. Being timid, greedy, foolish, and half holy is only part of it.

Like sheep we get hungry, and hungry for more than just food. We get thirsty for more than just drink. Our *souls* get hungry and thirsty; in fact it is often that sense of inner emptiness that makes us know we have souls in the first place. There is nothing that the world has to give us, there is nothing that we have to give to each other even that ever quite fills them. But once in a while that inner emptiness is filled even so. That is part of what the psalm means by saying that God is like a shepherd, I think. It means that, like a shepherd, he feeds us. He feeds that part of us which is hungriest and most in need of feeding.

There is richer, more profitable land in the world certainly than what we have in this small corner of the state of Vermont, but it's hard to believe there is any lovelier land. There are the sloping hillside pastures and meadows we live among—green pastures, then golden pastures, then pastures whiter than white, blue-shadowed. There are still waters—the looking-glass waters of pasture ponds filled with sky and clouds—and there are waters that aren't still at all, but overflow their banks when the melting snow swells them and they go rattling and roaring and chuckling through the woods in a way that makes you understand how human beings must have first learned what music is. Most of the time we forget to notice this place where we live—because we're so used to it, because we get so caught up in whatever our work is, whatever our lives are—but every once and so often maybe we notice and are filled. "He restoreth my soul," is the way the psalm says it. For a little while the scales fall from our eyes and we actually see the beauty and holiness and mystery of the world around us, and then from deeper down even than our hunger, restoring comes, nourishment comes. You can't make it happen. You can't make it last. But it is a glimpse, a whisper. Maybe it is all we can handle.

"I shall not want," the psalm says. Is that true? There are lots of things we go on wanting, go on lacking, whether we believe in God or not. They are not just material things like a new roof or a better-paying job, but things like good health, things like happiness for our children, things like being understood and appreciated, like relief from pain, like some measure of inner peace not just for ourselves but for the people we love and for whom we pray. Believers and unbelievers alike, we go on wanting plenty our whole lives through. We long for what never seems to come. We pray for what never seems to be clearly given. But when the psalm says "I shall not want," maybe it is speaking the utter truth anyhow. Maybe it means that if we keep our eyes open, if we keep our hearts and lives open, we will at least never be in want of the one thing we want more than anything else. Maybe it means that, whatever else is withheld, the shepherd never withholds himself, and he is what we want more than anything else.

Not at every moment of our lives, heaven knows, but at certain rare moments of greenness and stillness, we are shepherded by the knowledge that, though all is far from right with any world you and I know anything about, all is right deep down. All will be right at last. I suspect that is at least part of what "He leadeth me in the paths of righteousness" is all about. It means righteousness not just in the sense of *doing* right, but in the sense of *being* right—being right with God, trusting the deep-down rightness of the life God has created for us and in us, and riding that trust the way a red-tailed hawk rides the currents of the air in this valley where we live. I suspect that the paths of righteousness he leads us in are more than anything else the paths of trust like that and the kind of life that grows out of that trust. I think that is the shelter he calls us to with a bale in either hand when the wind blows bitter and the shadows are dark.

"Yea, though I walk through the valley of the shadow of death, I will fear no evil." The psalm does not pretend that evil and death do not exist. Terrible things happen, and they happen to good people as well as to bad people. Even the paths of righteousness lead through the valley of the shadow. Death lies ahead for all of us, saints and sinners alike, and for all the ones we love. The psalmist doesn't try to explain evil. He doesn't try to minimize evil. He simply says he will not fear evil. For all the power that evil has, it doesn't have the power to make him afraid.

And why? Here at the very center of the psalm comes the very center of the psalmist's faith. Suddenly he stops speaking about God as "he," because you don't speak that way when the person is right there with you. Suddenly he speaks *to* God instead of about him, and he speaks to him as "thou." "I will fear no evil," he says, "for thou art with me." That is the center of faith. Thou. That is where faith comes from.

When somebody takes your hand in the dark, you're not afraid of the dark anymore. The power of dark is a great power, but the power of light is greater still. It is the shepherd of light himself who reaches out a hand, who is "Thou" to us. Death and dark are not the end. Life and light are the end. It is what the cross means, of course. The cross means that out of death came, of all things, birth. Happy Birthday indeed! The birth we are here to celebrate is not just the birth of this old church in this old town, but the birth of new life, including our own new life—hope coming out of hopelessness, joy coming out of sorrow, comfort and strength coming out of fear. Thanks be to all that the cross means and is, we need never be afraid again. That is the faith that has kept bringing people to this place from Increase Graves's time to our time. That is what has brought me here. Unless I miss my guess, that is what has brought you here.

The psalmist stops speaking of God as a shepherd then. God becomes instead the host at a great feast. He prepares a table for us the way the table of Holy Communion is prepared for us, and "in the presence of our enemies" he prepares it because there is no other place. Our enemies are always present. All the old enemies are always gathered around us everywhere. I mean the enemies that come at us from within—doubt and self-doubt, anxiety, boredom, loneliness, failure, temptation. Let each of us name our special enemies for ourselves. How well we know them. How long we have done battle with them, and how long we will doubtless have to go on battling. But no matter. The table is prepared. Our cups are filled to running over. We are anointed with this occasion itself—with the sense it gives us of how much we need each other, you and I, and how the party wouldn't be complete without every last one of us; the sense we have of being not just strangers, acquaintances, friends, momentarily gathered under the same roof, but fellow pilgrims traveling the same long and bewildering road in search of the same far city. It is a rare glimpse that we catch at this enchanted table. The feast that is laid for us here is only a foretaste of the feast to come. The old enemies will be vanquished at last. "Surely goodness and mercy shall follow us all the days of our lives," as goodness and mercy have followed us our whole lives through even when we thought they were farthest from us. "And we will dwell in the house of the Lord forever," a house that is older than Eden and dearer than home.

Something like that is the faith this psalm sings. In the secrecy of our hearts can we say Yes to it? We must each of us answer for ourselves, of course. Some days it's easier to say Yes than other days. And even when we say Yes, there's always a no lurking somewhere in the shadows, just as when we say no there's always a Yes. That's the way faith breathes in and breathes out, I think, the way it stays alive and grows. But a birthday is a Yes day if ever there was one. So pick up the snappers and party hats again. Let the feast continue. And just one final, festal image to grace it with.

In the year 1831, it seems, this church was repaired and several new additions were made. One of them was a new steeple with a bell in it, and once it was set in place and painted, apparently, an extraordinary event took place. "When the steeple was added," Howard Mudgett writes in his history, "one agile Lyman Woodard stood on his head in the belfry with his feet toward heaven."

That's the one and only thing I've been able to find out about Lyman Woodard, whoever he was, but it is enough. I love him for doing what he did. It was a crazy thing to do. It was a risky thing to do. It ran counter to all standards of New England practicality and prudence. It stood the whole idea that you're supposed to be nothing but solemn in church on its head just like Lyman himself standing upside down on his. And it was also a magical and magnificent and Mozartian thing to do.

If the Lord is indeed our shepherd, then everything goes topsy-turvy. Losing becomes finding and crying becomes laughing. The last become first and the weak become strong. Instead of life being done in by death in the end as we always supposed, death is done in finally by life in the end. If the Lord is our host at the great feast, then the sky is the limit.

There is plenty of work to be done down here, God knows. To struggle each day to walk the paths of righteousness is no pushover, and struggle we must, because just as we are fed like sheep in green pastures, we must also feed his sheep, which are each other. Jesus, our shepherd, tells us that. We must help bear each other's burdens. We must pray for each other. We must nourish each other, weep with each other, rejoice with each other. Sometimes we must just learn to let each other alone. In short, we must love each other. We must never forget that. But let us never forget Lyman Woodard either, silhouetted up there against the blue Rupert sky. Let us join him in the belfry with our feet toward heaven like his, because heaven is where we are heading. That is our faith and what better image of faith could there be? It is a little crazy. It is a little risky. It sets many a level head wagging. And it is also our richest treasure and the source of our deepest joy and highest hope.

18.
The Truth of Stories

Give ear, O my people, to my teaching; incline your ears to the words of my mouth! I will open my mouth in a parable; I will utter dark sayings from of old, things that we have heard and known, that our fathers have told us. We will not hide them from their children, but tell to the coming generation the glorious deeds of the Lord, and his might, and the wonders which he has wrought.

—PSALM 78:1–4

All this Jesus said to the crowd in parables; indeed he said nothing to them without a parable. This was to fulfill what was spoken by the prophet: "I will open my mouth in parables, I will utter what has been hidden since the foundation of the world."

—MATTHEW 13:34

Somebody should write a book someday about the silences in Scripture. Maybe somebody already has. "For God alone my soul waits in silence," the psalmist says (62:1), which is the silence of waiting. Or "Be not silent, O God of my praise," which is the silence of the God we wait for (109:1). "And when the Lamb opened the seventh seal," says the book of Revelation, "there was silence in heaven" (8:1)—the silence of creation itself coming to an end and of a new creation about to begin. But the silence that has always most haunted me is the silence of Jesus before Pilate. Pilate asks his famous question, "What is truth?" (John 18:38), and Jesus answers him with a silence that is overwhelming in its eloquence. In case there should be any question as to what that silence meant, on another occasion Jesus put it into words for his disciple Thomas. "I," he said, "I am the truth" (14:6).

Jesus did not say that religion was the truth, or that his own teachings were the truth, or that what people taught about him was the truth, or that the Bible was the truth, or the church, or any system of ethics or theological doctrine. There are individual truths in all of them, we hope and believe, but individual truths were not what Pilate was after, or what you and I are after either, unless I miss my guess. Truths about this or that are a dime a dozen, including religious truths. THE truth is what Pilate is after: the truth about who we are and who God is if there is a God, the truth about life, the truth about death, the truth about truth itself. That is the truth we are all of us after.

It is a truth that can never be put into words because no words can contain it. It is a truth that can never be caught in any doctrine or creed including our own because it will never stay still long enough but is always moving and shifting like air. It is a truth that is always beckoning us in different ways and coming at us from different directions. And I think that is precisely why whenever Jesus tries to put that ultimate and inexpressible truth into words (instead of into silence as he did with Pilate), the form of words he uses is a form that itself moves and shifts and beckons us in different ways and comes at us from different directions. That is to say he tells stories.

Jesus does not sound like Saint Paul or Thomas Aquinas or John Calvin when we hear him teaching in the Gospels. "Once upon a time" is what he says. Once upon a time somebody went out to plant some seeds. Once upon a time somebody stubbed a toe on a great treasure. Once upon a time somebody lost a precious coin. The Gospels are full of the stories Jesus tells, stories that are alive in somewhat the way the truth is alive, the way he himself is alive when Pilate asks him about truth and his silence is a way of saying, "Look at my aliveness if you want to know! Listen to my life!" Matthew goes so far as to tell us that "he said nothing to them without a parable," that is to say without a story, and then quotes the words, "I will open my mouth in parables, I will utter what has been hidden since the foundation of the world." In stories the hiddenness and the utterance are both present, and that is another reason why they are a good way of talking about God's truth, which is part hidden and part uttered too.

It is too bad we know Jesus's stories so well, or think we do. We have read them so often and heard them expounded in so many sermons that we have all but lost the capacity for hearing them even, let alone for hearing what they are really about. His stories are like photographs that have been exposed to the light so long they have faded almost beyond recognition. They are like family anecdotes so ancient and time-honored we groan at their approach. And what a pity that is when you think what rich stories they are till preachers start making a homiletic shambles of them—so full of surprises and sudden reversals and sad Jewish comedy before people start delivering sermons about them.

The worst of it, of course, is the way we think we know what Jesus's stories mean. Heaven knows people like me who ought to know better have explained the life out of them often enough, have tried so hard to pound the point in that more often than not all you can hear is the pounding. The story about the good Samaritan, for instance. Is the point of it that our neighbor is anybody who needs us and that loving our neighbor means doing whatever needs to be done even if it costs an arm and a leg to do it? That is a good point as points go, but does getting it mean that now we can move on to the next story? How about the one about the wise women who fill their lamps with oil and the foolish ones who forget to, so that when Love himself looms up out of the night with vine leaves in his hair and his eyes aflame, they are left in the dark while the others go in to the marriage supper to have the time of their lives. Having gotten whatever the point of that one is, can we move on again and suck the next one dry?

If we think the purpose of Jesus's stories is essentially to make a point as extractable as the moral at the end of a fable, then the inevitable conclusion is that once you get the point, you can throw the story itself away like the rind of an orange when you have squeezed out the juice. Is that true? How about other people's stories? What is the point of *A Midsummer Night's Dream* or the *Iliad* or *For Whom the Bell Tolls*? Can we extract the point in each case and frame it on the living-room wall for our perpetual edification?

Or is the story itself the point and truth of the story? Is the point of Jesus's stories that they point to the truth about you and me and our stories? We are the ones who have been mugged, and we are also the ones who pass by pretending we don't notice. Hard as it is to believe, maybe every once in a while we are even the ones who pay an arm and a leg to help. The truth of the story is not a motto suitable for framing. It is a truth that one way or another, God help us, we live out every day of our lives. It is a truth as complicated and sad as you and I ourselves are complicated and sad, and as joyous and as simple as we are too. The stories that Jesus tells are about us. Once upon a time is *our* time, in other words.

Once upon a time, for instance, I got fed up and left home, got the hell out, no matter why. I bought a one-way ticket for as far as there was to go and got off at the last stop. I spent myself down to where I didn't have the price of a cup of coffee, and that was not the worst of it. The worst of it was I didn't give a damn because there wasn't anything else I wanted even if I'd had the price. There wasn't anything to see I hadn't seen. There wasn't anything to do I hadn't done. There wasn't anything to lose I hadn't lost. The only thing worse than being fed up with the world is being fed up with yourself. I envied the pigs their slops because at least they knew what they were hungry for whereas I was starving to death and had no idea why. All I knew was that the emptiness inside me was bigger than I was. So I went back. As I might have guessed, the old man was waiting for me. I was ready to crawl to him, say anything he wanted. He looked smaller than I remembered him. He looked small and breakable against the tall sky. His coat didn't look warm enough. It flapped around his shins. We ran the last length between us, if you could call the way he did it running. I couldn't get a word out. My mouth was pushed crooked against his chest, he held me so tight. I was blinded by whatever blinded me. I could still hear, though. I could hear the thump of his old ticker through the skimpy coat. I could hear his voice break.

Once upon a time again—and as far as I'm concerned, being brother to the one who in his own sweet time came back, it was only right he should hear the breaking of the old man's voice, because he was the one who broke it as sure as if he'd taken a stick to it. Yet you'd have thought he was the golden-haired darling of the world the way the old man carried on. More to the point, you'd have thought the old man was senile, pathetic. I have been faithful. I have been dutiful. I have given him the best years of my life and asked nothing in return. And I think he hardly sees me sometimes when he passes me in the field with those watery old eyes. I would sooner gnaw the hand off my wrist than make merry with an ass over the triumphal return of a pig.

Once upon a time, and at this time now, and for as far beyond time as east is beyond west, I that am the ass, laboring under my holy and appalling burden, love them both. I love the pig and I also love the fox, if foxes are the ones that gnaw off their hands. I love them both because the great feast wouldn't be complete without either of them. I love them to the point where, if either of them had to suffer some awful pain, I would suffer it in either of their places if that meant they didn't have to. I think I would even be willing to die for them if by some unthinkable chain of events it should ever come down to that.

These stories Jesus tells. Every once in a while it is not just the point that we see, but ourselves that we see and each other that we see and God that we see—the whole great landscape of things lit up for a moment as if by lightning on a dark night. And there is more to it than that, of course. Jesus doesn't just tell stories. He himself is a story.

Jesus is the Word made flesh, the truth narrated in bone and bowel, space and time. That is the story he is. He is the one who tells the waves of the sea to stop their raging and throws the money-changers out of the Temple in a rage. He is the one who says the only way to make it to the Kingdom of Heaven is to be like little children who don't care beans about making it to the Kingdom of Heaven, but just let heaven happen the way they let everything else happen. He is the one who scandalizes decent people with his eating and drinking and blasphemies, not to mention with the company he keeps, and who weeps when the friend dies he might have saved if only he had been there. He is the one who tells us we must love our enemies and then tells his own enemies that they are vipers and stink of death underneath their whitewash and tells them that exactly *because* he loves them. He is also the one who is hauled up before Pilate looking as if he had been run over by a truck, that part of his story too as it converges briefly with Pilate's story. Pilate wants Jesus to tell him what truth is so he can put it in his pocket and go his way just that much the wiser but otherwise the same old Pilate. But Jesus will not give him the words he wants any more than God would give them to Job when Job wanted them, because words are not the point. Jesus himself is the point.

You can hardly blame Pilate for washing his hands of him. He asks so bloody much, this Jesus. Bloody is the word for it. How religious people do treasure all their doctrines and theologies and creeds and catchphrases. How we love moving them around like checkers on a checkerboard just the way Pilate would have loved Jesus to give him some religious truth or another he could play around with and even maybe make his own. But Jesus goes farther than that. What he calls us to is the terrifying game of letting *him* enormously move us as the story of him lives and breathes and converges on us beyond all our ideas of him; as it bids us, moves us, to do and to be God only knows what, which can be a very bloody business indeed if we do it right. When we put crosses up in our Protestant churches, we take the body off first as if once the resurrection happens, we somehow no longer have to worry about the crucifixion anymore—as if once we have gotten the message of Jesus's life, grasped the point of it (whatever that means), we can set the life itself aside along with the death like the rind of the squeezed orange again. It becomes merely something we can draw on for moral guidance perhaps or spiritual comfort or religious truth.

Only Jesus himself is the truth, the whole story of him. He will not let us settle for any truth less than that, tidier than that, easier than that. And the truth seems to be that if he is indeed everybody's best friend the way the old Jesus hymns proclaim, he is at the same time everybody's worst enemy. He is the enemy, at least, of everything in us that keeps us from giving him what he is really after. And what he is really after is our heart's blood, our treasure, our selves themselves. It is the cross he is inviting us to, not a Sunday school picnic, and therefore if it is proper to rejoice in his presence, it is proper also to be scared stiff in his presence.

He tells us not to be this or to be that, but to be his. Not to follow this way or that way, but to follow him. He promises to give us everything and in return asks us to give up everything the way he himself gave up everything—that is his story. And only then the miracle that not even all our tragic and befuddled history has ever quite managed to destroy. Only then the miracle of you and me not just talking about him two thousand years later but holding on to him for dear life, believing from time to time that he is indeed the one we draw dear life from, dearest life. That is his story too, and of course it is also our story.

So in the long run the stories all overlap and mingle like searchlights in the dark. The stories Jesus tells are part of the story Jesus is, and the other way round. And the story Jesus is is part of the story you and I are because Jesus has become so much a part of the world's story that it is impossible to imagine how any of our stories would have turned out without him, even the stories of people who don't believe in him or even know who he is or care about knowing. And my story and your story are all part of each other too if only because we have sung together and prayed together and seen each other's faces so that we are at least a footnote at the bottom of each other's stories.

In other words, all our stories are in the end one story, one vast story about being human, being together, being here. Does the story point beyond itself? Does it mean something? What is the truth of this interminable, sprawling story we all of us are? Or is it as absurd to ask about the truth of it as it is to ask about the truth of the wind howling through a crack under the door?

Either life is holy with meaning, or life doesn't mean a damn thing. You pay your money and you take your choice. Only never take your choice too easily, of course. Never assume that because you have taken it one way today, you may not take it another way tomorrow.

One choice is this. It is to choose to believe that the truth of our story is contained in Jesus's story, which is a love story. Jesus's story is the truth about who we are and who the God is who Jesus says loves us. It is the truth about where we are going and how we are going to get there, if we get there at all, and what we are going to find if we finally do. Only for once let us not betray the richness and depth and mystery of that truth by trying to explain it.

Let us instead tell a story that is the story about every one of us. It is a story about a pig, and a fox, and an ass under his holy and appalling burden. It is a story about a mouth pushed crooked, about a voice breaking. Let the rest be Christ's silence.

19

Growing Up

And Moses went up unto God, and the Lord called unto him out of the mountain, saying, Thus shalt thou say to the house of Jacob, and tell the children of Israel: Ye have seen what I did unto the Egyptians, and how I bore you on eagles' wings, and brought you unto myself. Now therefore, if ye will obey my voice indeed, and keep my covenant, then ye shall be a peculiar treasure unto me above all people; for all the earth is mine; and ye shall be unto me a kingdom of priests, and an holy nation. These are the words which thou shalt speak unto the children of Israel.

—Exodus 19:3–6, kjv

So put away all malice and all guile and insincerity and envy and all slander. Like newborn babes, long for the pure spiritual milk, that by it you may grow up to salvation; for you have tasted the kindness of the Lord. You are a chosen race, a royal priesthood, a holy nation, God's own people, that you may declare the wonderful deeds of him who called you out of darkness into his marvelous light.

—1 Peter 2:1–3, 9

"Rich man, poor man, beggar man, thief, doctor, lawyer, merchant chief," or "Indian chief" sometimes if that is how you happened to be feeling that day. That was how the rhyme went in my time anyway, and you used it when you were counting the cherry pits on your plate or the petals on a daisy or the buttons on your shirt or blouse. The one you ended up counting was, of course, the one you ended up being. Rich? Poor? Standing on a street corner with a tin cup in your hand? Or maybe a career in organized crime?

What in the world, what in heaven's name, were you going to be when you grew up? It was not just another question. It was the great question. In fact everything I want to say here is based on the belief that it is the great question still. What are you going to be? What am I going to be? I have been in more or less the same trade now for some thirty years and contemplate no immediate change, but I like to think of it still as a question that is wide open. For God's sake, what do you suppose we are going to be, you and I? When we grow up.

Something in us rears back in indignation, of course. We are not children anymore, most of us. Surely we have our growing up behind us. We have come many a long mile and thought many a long thought. We have taken on serious responsibilities, made hard decisions, weathered many a crisis. Surely the question is, rather, what are we now and how well are we doing at it? If not doctors, lawyers, merchant chiefs, we are whatever we are—computer analysts, businesswomen, schoolteachers, artists, ecologists, ministers even. We like to think that one way or another we have already made our mark on the world. So isn't the question not "What are we going to be?" but "What are we now?" We don't have to count cherry pits to find out what we are going to do with our lives because, for better or worse, those dice have already been cast. Now we simply get on with the game, whatever is left of it for us. That is what life is all about from here on out.

But then. Then maybe we have to listen—listen back farther than the rhymes of our childhood even, thousands of years farther back than that. A thick cloud gathers on the mountain as the book of Exodus describes it. There are flickers of lightning, jagged and dangerous. A clap of thunder shakes the earth and sets the leaves of the trees trembling, sets even you and me trembling a little if we have our wits about us. Suddenly the great *shophar* sounds, the ram's horn—a long-drawn, pulsing note louder than thunder, more dangerous than lightning—and out of the darkness, out of the mystery, out of some cavernous part of who we are, a voice calls: "Now therefore, if ye will obey my voice indeed, and keep my covenant, then ye shall be a peculiar treasure unto me above all people"—my *segullah* the Hebrew word is, my precious ones, my darlings—"and ye shall be unto me a kingdom of priests, and an holy nation."

Then, thousands of years later but still thousands of years ago, there is another voice to listen to. It is the voice of an old man dictating a letter. There is reason to believe that he may actually have been the one who up till almost the end was the best friend that Jesus had: Peter himself. "So put away all malice and all guile and insincerity and envy and all slander," he says. "Like newborn babes, long for the pure spiritual milk, that by it you may grow up to salvation; for you have tasted the kindness of the Lord." And then he echoes the great cry out of the thunderclouds with a cry of his own. "You are a chosen race, a royal priesthood, a holy nation, God's own people," he says, "that you may declare the wonderful deeds of him who called you out of darkness into his marvelous light."

What are we going to *be* when we grow up? Not what are we going to do, what profession are we going to follow or keep on following, what niche are we going to occupy in the order of things. But what are we going to *be*—inside ourselves and among ourselves? That is the question that God answers with the Torah at Sinai. That is the question that the old saint answers in his letter from Rome.

Holy. That is what we are going to be if God gets his way with us. It is wildly unreasonable because it makes a shambles out of all our reasonable ambitions to be this or to be that. It is not really a human possibility at all because holiness is Godness and only God makes holiness possible. But being holy is what growing up in the full sense means, Peter suggests. No matter how old we are or how much we have achieved or dream of achieving still, we are not truly grown up until this extraordinary thing happens. Holiness is what is to happen. Out of darkness we are called into "his marvelous light," Peter writes, who knew more about darkness than most of us, if you stop to think about it, and had looked into the very face itself of Light. We are called to have faces like that—to be filled with light so that we can be bearers of light. I have seen a few such faces in my day, and so have you, unless I miss my guess. Are we going to be rich, poor, beggars, thieves, or in the case of most of us a little of each? Who knows? In the long run, who even cares? Only one thing is worth really caring about, and it is this: "Ye shall be unto me a kingdom of priests, and an holy nation."

Israel herself was never much good at it, God knows. That is what most of the Old Testament is mostly about. Israel did not want to be a holy nation. Israel wanted to be a nation like all the other nations, a nation like Egypt, like Syria. She wanted clout. She wanted security. She wanted a place in the sun. It was her own way she wanted, not God's way; and when the prophets got after her for it, she got rid of the prophets, and when God's demands seemed too exorbitant, God's promises too remote, she took up with all the other gods who still get our votes and our money and our nine-to-five energies, because they are gods who could not care less whether we are holy or not and promise absolutely everything we really want and absolutely nothing we really need.

We cannot very well blame Israel because of course we are Israel. Who wants to be holy? The very word has fallen into disrepute—holier-than-thou, holy Joe, holy mess. And "saint" comes to mean plaster saint, somebody of such stifling moral perfection that we would run screaming in the other direction if our paths ever crossed. We are such children, you and I, the way we do such terrible things with such wonderful words. We are such babes in the woods the way we keep getting lost.

And yet we have our moments. Every once in a while, I think, we actually long to be what out of darkness and mystery we are called to be; when we hunger for holiness even so, even if we would never dream of using the word. There come moments, I think, even in the midst of all our cynicism and worldliness and childishness, maybe especially then, when there is something about the saints of the earth that bowls us over a little. I mean real saints. I mean saints as men and women who are made not out of plaster and platitude and moral perfection but out of human flesh. I mean saints who have their rough edges and their blind spots like everybody else but whose lives are transparent to something so extraordinary that every so often it stops us dead in our tracks. Light-bearers. Life-bearers.

I remember once going to see the movie *Gandhi* when it first came out, for instance. We were the usual kind of noisy, restless Saturday night crowd as we sat there waiting for the lights to dim with our popcorn and soda pop, girlfriends and boyfriends, legs draped over the backs of the empty seats in front of us. But by the time the movie came to a close with the flames of Gandhi's funeral pyre filling the entire wide screen, there was not a sound or a movement in that whole theater, and we filed out of there—teenagers and senior citizens, blacks and whites, swingers and squares—in as deep and telling a silence as I have ever been part of.

"You have tasted of the kindness of the Lord," Peter wrote. We had tasted it. In the life of that little bandy-legged, bespectacled man with his spinning wheel and his bare feet and whatever he had in the way of selfless passion for peace and passionate opposition to every form of violence, we had all of us tasted something that at least for a few moments that Saturday night made every other kind of life seem empty, something that at least for the moment I think every last one of us yearned for the way in a far country you yearn for home.

"Ye shall be unto me a kingdom of priests, an holy nation." Can a nation be holy? It is hard to imagine it. Some element of a nation maybe, some remnant or root—"A shoot coming forth from the stump of Jesse," as Isaiah put it, "that with righteousness shall judge the poor and decide with equity for the meek of the earth" (11:1, 4). The eighteenth-century men and women who founded this nation dreamed just such a high and holy dream for us too and gave their first settlements over here names to match. New Haven, New Hope, they called them—names that almost bring tears to your eyes if you listen to what they are saying, or once said. Providence. Concord. Salem, which is *shalom*, the peace of God. Dreams like that die hard, and please God there is still some echo of them in the air around us. But for years now, the meek of the earth have been scared stiff at the power we have to blow the earth to smithereens a thousand times over and at our failure year after year to work out with our enemies a way of significantly limiting that hideous power. In this richest of all nations, the poor go to bed hungry, if they are lucky enough to have a bed, because after the staggering amounts we continue to spend on defending ourselves, there is not enough left over to feed the ones we are defending, to help give them decent roofs over their heads, decent schools for their children, decent care when they are sick and old.

The nation that once dreamed of being a new hope, a new haven, for the world has become the number one bully of the world, blundering and blustering and bombing its way, convinced that it is right and that everyone who disagrees with it is wrong. Maybe that is the way it inevitably is with nations. They are so huge and complex. By definition they are so exclusively concerned with their own self-interest conceived in the narrowest terms that they have no eye for holiness, of all things, no ears to hear the great command to be saints, no heart to break at the thought of what this world could be—the friends we could be as nations if we could learn to listen to each other instead of just shouting at each other, the common problems we could help each other solve, all the human anguish we could join together to heal.

You and I are the eyes and ears. You and I are the heart. It is to us that Peter's Letter is addressed. "So put away all malice and all guile and insincerity and envy and all slander," he says. No *shophar* sounds or has to sound. It is as quiet as the scratching of a pen, as familiar as the sight of our own faces in the mirror. We have always known what was wrong with us. The malice in us even at our most civilized. Our insincerity, the masks we do our real business behind. The envy, the way other people's luck can sting like wasps. And all slander, making such caricatures of each other that we treat each other like caricatures, even when we love each other. All this infantile nonsense and ugliness. "Put it away!" Peter says. "Grow up to salvation!" For Christ's sake, grow up.

Grow up? For old people isn't it a little too late? For young people isn't it a little too early? I do not think so. Never too late, never too early to grow up, to be holy. We have already tasted it after all—tasted the kindness of the Lord, Peter says. That is a haunting thought. I believe you can see it in our eyes sometimes. Just the way you can see something more than animal in animals' eyes, I think you can sometimes see something more than human in human eyes, even yours and mine. I think we belong to holiness even when we cannot believe it exists anywhere, let alone in ourselves. That is why everybody left that crowded shopping-mall theater in such unearthly silence. It is why it is hard not to be haunted by that famous photograph of the only things that Gandhi owned at the time of his death: his glasses and his watch, his sandals, a bowl and spoon, a book of songs. What does any of us own to match such riches as that?

Children that we are, even you and I, who have given up so little, know in our hearts not only that it is more blessed to give than to receive, but that it is also more fun—the kind of holy fun that wells up like tears in the eyes of saints, the kind of blessed fun in which we lose ourselves and at the same time begin to find ourselves, to grow up into the selves we were created to become.

When Henry James, of all people, was saying good-bye once to his young nephew Billy, his brother William's son, he said something that the boy never forgot. And of all the labyrinthine and impenetrably subtle things that that most labyrinthine and impenetrable old romancer could have said, what he did say was this: "There are three things that are important in human life. The first is to be kind. The second is to be kind. The third is to be kind."

Be kind because although kindness is not by a long shot the same thing as holiness, kindness is one of the doors that holiness enters the world through, enters us through—not just gently kind but sometimes fiercely kind.

Be kind enough to yourselves not just to play it safe with your lives for your own sakes, but to spend at least part of your lives like drunken sailors—for God's sake, if you believe in God, for the world's sake, if you believe in the world—and thus to come alive truly.

Be kind enough to others to listen, beneath all the words they speak, for that usually unspoken hunger for holiness that I believe is part of even the unlikeliest of us because by listening to it and cherishing it maybe we can help bring it to birth both in them and in ourselves.

Be kind to this nation of ours by remembering that New Haven, New Hope, Shalom are the names not just of our oldest towns but of our holiest dreams, which most of the time are threatened by the madness of no enemy without as dangerously as they are threatened by our own madness within.

"You have tasted of the kindness of the Lord," Peter wrote in his Letter, and ultimately that, of course, is the kindness, the holiness, the sainthood and sanity we are all of us called to. So that by God's grace we may "grow up to salvation" at last.

The way the light falls through the windows. The sounds our silence makes when we come together like this. The sense we have of each other's presence. The feeling in the air that one way or another we are all of us here to give each other our love, and to give God our love. This kind moment itself is a door that holiness enters through. May it enter you. May it enter me. To the world's saving.

20.

The Church

And he called to him his twelve disciples and gave them authority over unclean spirits, to cast them out, and to heal every disease and every infirmity. The names of the twelve apostles are these: first, Simon, who is called Peter, and Andrew his brother; James the son of Zebedee, and John his brother; Philip and Bartholomew; Thomas and Matthew the tax collector; James the son of Alphaeus, and Thaddeus; Simon the Cananaean, and Judas Iscariot, who betrayed him.

These twelve Jesus sent out, charging them, "Go nowhere among the Gentiles, and enter no town of the Samaritans, but go rather to the lost sheep of the house of Israel. And preach as you go, saying, 'The kingdom of heaven is at hand.' Heal the sick, raise the dead, cleanse lepers, cast out demons."

—MATTHEW 10:1–8

I suppose the most famous of the twelve disciples was Simon Peter, who was the one who seems to have been the first to realize who Jesus actually was. He was also the one who occasioned the only pun Jesus is on record as having made, when he said that Peter, whose name means "rock" in Greek, was the rock he was going to found his church on. There were also Peter's brother Andrew, and Zebedee's two sons, James and John, plus another James and another Simon known as the Cananaean. Thaddeus and Bartholomew were among them too, whoever they were, and Matthew the tax collector and Philip, who was from Peter's hometown of Bethsaida, and Thomas the doubter, and finally Judas Iscariot, of course, who in the garden, by moonlight, betrayed his friend by kissing him and was thus the last human being to touch him except for those who did so for the purpose of inflicting pain.

Those were the people Jesus started his church with, as Matthew names them anyway. We know so little about them and would give so much to know more. If they weren't all of them Jews, presumably most of them were. They've had a pretty bad press over the centuries, and by and large they seem to have deserved it. On the night of the arrest, for instance, not one of them apparently so much as raised a finger to defend their friend except Peter, who cut the ear off one of the high priest's slaves with his sword, which can hardly have made matters anything but worse and might have led to worse still if Jesus hadn't told him in effect to cool it, adding that those who live by the sword usually end up dying by the sword, which is a point so close to the heart of his message in general that you'd think they'd have gotten it by then.

But of course the other reason for their bad press is that they never seem to have gotten *any* of his points very well, or if and when they did get them, never seem to have lived by them very well, which makes them people very much like you, if I may say so, and also, if I may say so, very much like me. That is to say, they were *human beings*. Jesus made his church out of human beings with more or less the same mixture in them of cowardice and guts, of intelligence and stupidity, of selfishness and generosity, of openness of heart and sheer cussedness as you would be apt to find in any of us. The reason he made his church out of human beings is that human beings were all there was to make it out of. In fact, as far as I know, human beings are all there is to make it out of still. It's a point worth remembering.

It is also a point worth remembering that even after Jesus made these human beings into a church, they seem to have gone right on being human beings. They actually knew Jesus as their friend. They sat at his feet and listened to him speak; they ate with him and tramped the countryside with him; they witnessed his miracles; but not even all of that turned them into heroes. They kept on being as human as they'd always been with most of the same strengths and most of the same weaknesses.

And finally when it comes to remembering things, we do well to keep in mind that the idea of becoming the church wasn't their idea. It was Jesus's idea. It was Jesus who made them a church. They didn't come together the way like-minded people come together to make a club. They didn't come together the way a group of men might come together to form a baseball team or the way a group of women might come together to lobby for higher teachers' salaries. They came together because Jesus called them to come together. That is what the Greek word *ekklesia* means, from which we get our word "church." It means those who have been *called out,* the way the original twelve were called out of fishing or tax collecting or running a kosher restaurant or a Laundromat or whatever else they happened to be involved in at the time.

Somebody appears on your front stoop speaking your name, say, and you go down to open the door to see what's up. Sometimes while it's still raining, the sun comes out from behind the clouds, and suddenly, arching against the gray sky, there is a rainbow, which people stop doing whatever they're doing to look at. They lay down their fishing nets, their tax forms, their bridge hands, their golf clubs, their newspapers to gaze at the sky because what is happening up there is so marvelous they can't help themselves. Something like that, I think, is the way those twelve men Matthew names were called to become a church, plus Mary, Martha, Joanna, and all the other women and men who one way or another became part of it too. One way or another Christ called them. That's how it happened. They saw the marvel of him arch across the grayness of things—the grayness of their own lives perhaps, of life itself. They heard his voice calling their names. And they went.

They seem to have gone right on working at pretty much whatever they'd been working at before, which means that he didn't so much call them out of their ordinary lives as he called them out of believing that ordinary life is ordinary. He called them to see that no matter how ordinary it may seem to us as we live it, life is extraordinary. "The Kingdom of God is at hand" is the way he put it to them, and the way he told them to put it to others. Life even at its most monotonous and backbreaking and heart-numbing has the Kingdom buried in it the way a field has treasure buried in it, he said. The Kingdom of God is as close to us as some precious keepsake we've been looking for for years, which is lying just in the next room under the rug all but crying out to us to come find it. If we only had eyes to see and ears to hear and wits to understand, we would know that the Kingdom of God in the sense of holiness, goodness, beauty is as close as breathing and is crying out to be born both within ourselves and within the world; we would know that the Kingdom of God is what we all of us hunger for above all other things even when we don't know its name or realize that it's what we're starving to death for. The Kingdom of God is where our best dreams come from and our truest prayers. We glimpse it at those moments when we find ourselves being better than we are and wiser than we know. We catch sight of it when at some moment of crisis a strength seems to come to us that is greater than our own strength. The Kingdom of God is where we belong. It is home, and whether we realize it or not, I think we are all of us homesick for it.

A fat man drives by in his Chevy pickup with a cigarette in his mouth and on his rear bumper a sticker that says *Jesus Loves You.* There's a shotgun slung across the back window. He is not a stranger we've never seen before and couldn't care less if we ever see again. He is our brother, our father. He is our son. It is true that we have never seen him before and that we will probably never see him again—just that one quick glimpse as he goes by at twenty-five miles an hour because it is a school zone—but if we can some-how fully realize the truth of that, fully understand that this is the one and only time we will ever see him, we will treasure that one and only time the way we treasure the rainbow in the sky or the ring we finally found under the rug after years of looking for it. The old woman with thick glasses who sits in front of us at the movies eating popcorn is our mother, our sister, our child grown old, and once we know that, once we see her for who she truly is, everything about her becomes precious—the skinny back of her neck, the way she puts her hand over her mouth when she laughs.

These are not ordinary people any more than life is ordinary. They are extraordinary people. Life is extraordinary, and the extraordinariness of it is what Jesus calls the Kingdom of God. The extraordinariness of it is that in the Kingdom of God we all belong to each other the way families do. We are all of us brothers and sisters in it. We are all of us mothers and fathers and children of each other in it because that is what we are called together as the church to be. That is what being the church means. We are called by God to love each other the way Jesus says that God has loved us. That is the good news about God—the gospel—which he came to proclaim. Loving each other and loving God and being loved by God is what the Kingdom is. No scientific truth or philosophic truth, no truth of art or music or literature is as important as that Kingdom truth.

Loving God means rejoicing in him. It means trusting him when you can think of a hundred reasons not to trust anything. It means praying to him even when you don't feel like it. It means watching for him in the beauty and sadness and gladness and mystery of your own life and of life around you. Loving each other doesn't mean loving each other in some sentimental, unrealistic, greeting-card kind of way but the way families love each other even though they may fight tooth and nail and get fed up to the teeth with each other and drive each other crazy, yet all the time know deep down in their hearts that they belong to each other and need each other and can't imagine what life would be without each other—even the ones they often wish had never been born.

Matthew the tax collector and Thomas the doubter. Peter the rock and Judas the traitor. Mary Magdalene and Lazarus's sister Martha. And the popcorn-eating old woman. And the fat man in the pickup. They are all our family, and you and I are their family and each other's family, because that is what Jesus has called us as the church to be. Our happiness is all mixed up with each other's happiness and our peace with each other's peace. Our own happiness, our own peace can never be complete until we find some way of sharing it with people who, the way things are now, have no happiness and know no peace. Jesus calls us to show this truth forth, live this truth forth. Be the light of the world, he says. Where there are dark places, be the light especially there. Be the salt of the earth. Bring out the true flavor of what it is to be alive truly. Be truly alive. Be life-givers to others. That is what Jesus tells the disciples to be. That is what Jesus tells his church, tells us, to be and do. Love each other. Heal the sick, he says. Raise the dead. Cleanse lepers. Cast out demons. That is what loving each other means. If the church is doing things like that, then it is being what Jesus told it to be. If it is not doing things like that—no matter how many other good and useful things it may be doing instead—then it is not being what Jesus told it to be. It is as simple as that.

The old woman has gone to the movies to help take her mind off the fact that she has cancer. Cancer is a sickness that you and I don't know how to heal, more's the pity, but it is not her only sickness. Her other sickness is being lonely and scared, and in some ways that sickness is the worse of the two. Sometimes she wakes up in the middle of the night and thinks about it—wishes she had somebody she could talk to about it or just somebody she could go to the movies with once in a while and share her popcorn with. Heal her, Jesus says.

The fat man in the pickup has a son who is dying. He is dying of AIDS. It was his wife who put the *Jesus Loves You* sticker on his bumper. The way he sees it, if you do not believe in God anymore, it doesn't make much difference whether Jesus loves you or not. If God lets things happen to people like what has happened to his son, then what is the point of believing in God. Raise him, Jesus says.

"Heal the sick, raise the dead, cleanse lepers, cast out demons," Jesus tells the disciples. That is the work he sets us. In other words, we are to be above all else healers, and that means of course that we are also to be healed because God knows you and I are in as much need of healing as anybody else, and being healed and healing go hand in hand. God knows we have our own demons to be cast out, our own uncleanness to be cleansed. Neurotic anxiety happens to be my own particular demon, a floating sense of doom that has ruined many of what could have been, should have been, the happiest days of my life, and more than a few times in my life I have been raised from such ruins, which is another way of saying that more than a few times in my life I have been raised from death—death of the spirit anyway, death of the heart—by the healing power that Jesus calls us both to heal with and to be healed by.

I remember an especially dark time of my life. One of my children was sick, and in my anxiety for her I was in my own way as sick as she was. Then one day the phone rang, and it was a man named Lou Patrick, whom I didn't know very well then though he has become a great friend since, a minister from Charlotte, North Carolina, which is about eight hundred miles or so from Rupert, Vermont, where I live. I assumed he was calling from home and asked him how things were going down there only to hear him say that, no, he wasn't in Charlotte. He was at an inn about twenty minutes away from my house in Rupert. He knew something about what was going on in my family and in me, and he said he thought maybe it would be some help to have an extra friend around for a day or two. The reason he didn't tell me in advance that he was coming was that he knew I would tell him for heaven's sake not to do anything so crazy, so for heaven's sake he did something crazier still, which was to come those eight hundred miles without telling me he was coming so that for all he knew I might not even have been there. But as luck had it, I was there, and for a day or two he was there with me. He was there for me. I don't think anything we found to say to each other amounted to very much. There was nothing particularly religious about it. I don't remember even spending much time talking about my troubles with him. We just took a couple of walks, had a meal or two together, and smoked our pipes. I drove him around to see some of the countryside, and that was about it.

I have never forgotten how he came all that distance just for that, and I'm sure he has never forgotten it either. I also believe that, although as far as I can remember we never so much as mentioned the name of Christ, Christ was as much in the air we breathed those few days as the fragrance of our pipes was in the air or the dappled light of the woods we walked through. I believe that for a little time we both of us touched the hem of Christ's garment. I know that for a little time we both of us were healed.

We are called to be Christs to each other like that, I think. Like Peter, like Thomas, the Marys, Joanna, we are called to be not just human beings but human beings open to the possibility of being transformed by the grace of God as it comes to us who knows how or when—in the fragrance of pipe smoke in the air, the band of a rainbow arched against the gray sky. Somebody calling on the phone: "Just twenty minutes down the road did you say? Good God, you must be crazy!" And that is just it, of course. We are called to be crazy exactly like that. We are called by the good God to be the hands and feet and heart of Christ to each other.

The church buildings and budgets came later. The forms of church government, the priests and pastors, Baptists and Protestants. The Sunday services with everybody in their best clothes, the Sunday schools and choirs all came later. So did the Bible study groups and the rummage sales. So did the preachers, the ones on TV who make you sick to your stomach with their phoniness and vulgarity, and the ones closer to home who so often, when I listen to them, seem to proclaim a faith that rarely seems to have much to do either with their own real day-to-day lives in this world or with mine, and the ones also through whose words every once in a while the Word itself touches your heart. They all came later. Maybe the best thing that could happen to the church would be for some great tidal wave of history to wash all that away—the church buildings tumbling, the church money all lost, the church bulletins blowing through the air like dead leaves, the differences between preachers and congregations all lost too. Then all we would have left would be each other and Christ, which was all there was in the first place.

"Truly, I say to you, as you did it to one of the least of these my brethren, you did it to me," Jesus said (Matt. 25:40), which means that in this world now Jesus is each other. Heal the sick and be healed. Raise the dead and be raised. Everything that matters comes out of doing those things. Doing those things is what the church is, and when it doesn't do those things, it doesn't matter much what else it does. Preach as you go, saying "The kingdom of heaven is at hand," Jesus told the disciples. *Be* the Kingdom of Heaven.

The Kingdom of Heaven is only twenty minutes down the road, for Christ's sake. The Kingdom of Heaven is in the movie theater as the old woman gets up to leave, shaking popcorn crumbs out of her lap. The Kingdom of Heaven is there as the fat man goes driving by in his pickup with the bumper sticker he can't believe in. The Kingdom of Heaven is in the eyes of love and longing and blessing that we raise to look at him as though he is a rainbow in the sky.

21.

The Kingdom of God

The beginning of the gospel of Jesus Christ, the Son of God.

As it is written in Isaiah the prophet, "Behold, I send my messenger before thy face, who shall prepare thy way; the voice of one crying in the wilderness: Prepare the way of the Lord, make his paths straight—" John the baptizer appeared in the wilderness, preaching a baptism of repentance for the forgiveness of sins. And there went out to him all the country of Judea, and all the people of Jerusalem; and they were baptized by him in the river Jordan, confessing their sins. Now John was clothed with camel's hair, and had a leather girdle around his waist, and ate locusts and wild honey. And he preached, saying, "After me comes he who is mightier than I, the thong of whose sandals I am not worthy to stoop down and untie. I have baptized you with water; but he will baptize you with the Holy Spirit."

In those days Jesus came from Nazareth of Galilee and was baptized by John in the Jordan. And when he came up out of the water, immediately he saw the heavens opened and the Spirit descending upon him like a dove; and a voice came from heaven, "Thou art my beloved Son; with thee I am well pleased."

The Spirit immediately drove him out into the wilderness. And he was in the wilderness forty days, tempted by Satan; and he was with the wild beasts; and the angels ministered to him.

Now after John was arrested, Jesus came into Galilee, preaching
the gospel of God, and saying, "The time is fulfilled, and the kingdom
of God is at hand; repent, and believe in the gospel."

—MARK 1:1–15

I always get the feeling as I read the opening verses of the Gospel of Mark
that he is in a terrible rush, that he can't wait to reach the place where
he feels the Gospel really begins. He says absolutely nothing about how
Jesus was born. He gets through the baptism in no time flat. He barely
mentions the temptation in the wilderness. And only then, after racing
through those first fourteen verses, does he get where he seems to have
been racing to—the real beginning as he sees it—and that is the opening
words of Jesus himself. Up to that point it has all gone so fast that hardly
anybody except John the Baptist knows who Jesus really is yet, just as it
might be said that most of the time hardly any of us knows who Jesus
really is yet either.

He is destined to have a greater impact on the next two thousand years
of human history than anybody else in history—we know that now—but
here at the beginning of Mark nobody knows it yet. Not a single syllable has
escaped his lips yet, as Mark tells it. The ant lays down her crumb to listen.
The very stars in the sky hold their breath. Nobody in the world knows
what Jesus is going to say yet, and maybe it's worthwhile pretending we
don't know either—pretending we've never heard him yet ourselves, which
may be closer to the truth than we think.

"The time is fulfilled," he says, "and the kingdom of God is at hand;
repent, and believe in the gospel." That is how he launches the gospel—his
first recorded words. There is a kind of breathlessness in those three short,
urgent sentences. The question is, what do they urgently mean to us who
know them so well that we hardly hear them anymore? If they mean anything to us at all, urgent or otherwise, what in God's name is it?

At least there is no great mystery about what "the time is fulfilled"
means, I think. "The time is fulfilled" means the time is up. That is the dark
side of it anyway, saving the bright side of it till later. It means that it is possible we are living in the last days. There was a time when you could laugh

that kind of message off if you saw some bearded crazy parading through the city streets with it painted on a sandwich board, but you have to be crazy yourself to laugh at it in our nuclear age. The world is still a powder keg and the danger of the so-called war on terrorism recklessly spreading even farther and more disastrously may not be the worst of it. There is AIDS. There are drugs, and more to the point the darkness of our time that makes people seek escape in drugs. There is the slow poisoning of what we call "the environment" of all things, as if with that antiseptic term we can conceal from ourselves that what we are really poisoning is home, is here, is us.

It is no wonder that the books and newspapers we read, the movies and TV we watch, are obsessed with the dark and demonic, are full of death and violence. It is as if the reason we wallow in them is that they help us keep our minds off the real death, the real violence. And God knows the Christian faith has its darkness and demons too, so discredited by religious crooks and phonies, so distorted for political purposes, and in thousands of respectable pulpits proclaimed so blandly and shallowly and without passion, that you wonder sometimes not only if it will survive but if it even deserves to survive. As a character in Woody Allen's *Hannah and Her Sisters* puts it, "If Jesus came back and saw what was going on in his name, he'd never stop throwing up."

In other words, a lot of the kinds of things that happen at the ends of civilizations are happening today in our civilization, and there are moments when it is hard to avoid feeling not only that our time is up, but that it is high time for our time to be up. That we're ready to fall from the branch like overripe fruit under the weight of our own decay. Something like that, I think, is the shadow side of what Jesus means when he says that the time is fulfilled.

If he meant that the world was literally coming to an end back there in the first century A.D., then insofar as he was a human, he was humanly wrong. But if he meant that the world is always coming to an end, if he meant that we carry within us the seeds of our own destruction no less than the Roman and Jewish worlds of his day carried them within them, if he meant that in the long run we are always in danger of one way or another destroying ourselves utterly, then of course he was absolutely right.

But Jesus says something else too. Thank God for that. He says our time is up, but he also says that the Kingdom of God is at hand. The Kingdom of God is so close we can almost reach out our hands and touch it. It is so close that sometimes it almost reaches out and takes us by the hand. The Kingdom of God, that is. Not a human kingdom. Not Saddam Hussein's kingdom, not Bush's kingdom, not Osama bin Laden's kingdom. Not any of the kingdoms that worry like us about counting calories while hundreds of thousands starve to death. But God's Kingdom. Jesus says it is the Kingdom of God that is at hand. If anybody else said it, we would hoot him off the stage. But it is Jesus who says it. Even people who don't believe in him can't quite hoot him off the stage. Even people who have long since written him off can't help listening to him.

The Kingdom of God? Time after time Jesus tries to drum into our heads what he means by it. He heaps parable upon parable like a madman. He tries shouting it. He tries whispering it. The Kingdom of God is like a treasure, like a pearl, like a seed buried in the ground. It is like a great feast that everybody is invited to and nobody wants to attend.

What he seems to be saying is that the Kingdom of God is the time, or a time beyond time, when it will no longer be humans in their lunacy who are in charge of the world but God in his mercy who will be in charge of the world. It's the time above all else for wild rejoicing—like getting out of jail, like being cured of cancer, like finally, at long last, coming home. And it is at hand, Jesus says.

Can we take such a message seriously, knowing all that we know and having seen all that we've seen? Can we take it any more seriously than the Land of Oz? It's not so hard to believe in a day of wrath and a last judgment—just read the newspapers—but is the Kingdom of God any more than a good dream? Has anybody ever seen it—if not the full glory of it, then at least a glimpse of it off in the shimmering distance somewhere?

It was a couple of springs ago. I was driving into New York City from New Jersey on one of those crowded, fast-moving turnpikes you enter it by. It was very warm. There was brilliant sunshine, and the cars glittered in it as they went tearing by. The sky was cloudless and blue. Around Newark a huge silver plane traveling in the same direction as I was made its descent in a slow diagonal and touched down soft as a bird on the airstrip just a few hundred yards away from me as I went driving by. I had music on the radio, but I didn't need it. The day made its own music—the hot spring sun and the hum of the road, the roar of the great trucks passing and of my own engine, the hum of my own thoughts. When I came out of the Lincoln Tunnel, the city was snarled and seething with traffic as usual; but at the same time there was something about it that was not usual.

It was gorgeous traffic, it was beautiful traffic—that's what was not usual. It was a beauty to see, to hear, to smell, even to be part of. It was so dazzlingly alive it all but took my breath away. It rattled and honked and chattered with life—the people, the colors of their clothes, the marvelous hodgepodge of their faces, all of it; the taxis, the shops, the blinding sidewalks. The spring day made everybody a celebrity—blacks, whites, Hispanics, every last one of them. It made even the litter and clamor and turmoil of it a kind of miracle.

There was construction going on as I inched my way east along Fifty-Fourth Street, and some wino, some bum, was stretched out on his back in the sun on a pile of lumber as if it was an alpine meadow he was stretched out on and he was made of money. From the garage where I left the car, I continued my way on foot. In the high-ceilinged public atrium on the ground floor of a large office building there were people on benches eating their sandwiches. Some of them were dressed to kill. Some of them were in jeans and sneakers. There were young ones and old ones. Daylight was flooding in on them, and there were green plants growing and a sense of deep peace as they ate their lunches mostly in silence. A big man in a clown costume and whiteface took out a tubular yellow balloon big around as a noodle, blew it up, and twisted it squeakily into a dove of peace, which he handed to the bug-eyed child watching him. I am not making this up. It all happened.

In some ways it was like a dream and in other ways as if I had woken up from a dream. I had the feeling that I had never seen the city so *real* before in all my life. I was walking along Central Park South near Columbus Circle at the foot of the park when a middle-aged black woman came toward me going the other way. Just as she passed me, she spoke. What she said was, "Jesus loves you." That is what she said: "Jesus loves you," just like that. She said it in as everyday a voice as if she had been saying good morning, and I was so caught off guard that it wasn't till she was lost in the crowd that I realized what she had said and wondered if I could possibly ever find her again and thank her, if I could ever catch up with her and say, "Yes. If I believe anything worth believing in this whole world, I believe that. He loves me. He loves you. He loves the whole doomed, damned pack of us."

For the rest of the way I was going, the streets I walked on were paved with gold. Nothing was different. Everything was different. The city was transfigured. I was transfigured. It was a new New York coming down out of heaven adorned like a bride prepared for her husband. "The dwelling of God is with men. He will dwell with them, and they shall be his people.... He will wipe away every tear from their eyes, and death shall be no more, neither shall there be mourning nor crying nor pain any more, for the former things have passed away" (Rev. 21:3–4). That is the city that for a moment I saw.

For a moment it was not the world as it is that I saw but the world as it *might* be, as something deep within the world wants to be and is preparing to be, the way in darkness a seed prepares for growth, the way leaven works in bread.

Buried beneath the surface of all the dirt and noise and crime and poverty and pollution of that terrifying city, I glimpsed the treasure that waits to make it a holy city—a city where human beings dwell in love and peace with each other and with God and where the only tears there are are tears of joy and reunion. Jesus said that as soon as the fig tree "becomes tender and puts forth its leaves, you know that summer is near. So also, when you see all these things, you know that [the Son of man] is near, at the very gates" (Matt. 24:32–33). For a few very brief and enormously moving minutes that day, the city itself became tender, put out leaves, and I knew beyond all doubt that more than summer was near, that something extraordinary was at the gates, something extraordinary was at least at the gates inside me. "The kingdom of God is within you"—or "among you"—Jesus said (Luke 17:21), and for a little while it was so.

All over the world you can hear it stirring if you stop to listen, I think. Good things are happening in and through all sorts of people. They don't speak with a single voice, these people. No one person has emerged yet as their leader. They are divided into many groups pulling in many different directions. Some are pressing for an end to the war. Some are pressing for women's rights, some for civil rights, or gay rights, or human rights. Some are concerned primarily with world hunger or with the way we are little by little destroying the oceans, the rain forests, the air we breathe. There are lots of different people saying lots of different things, and some of them put us off with their craziness and there are lots of points to argue with them about, but at their best they seem to be acting out of a single profound impulse, which is best described with words like tolerance, compassion, sanity, hope, justice. It is an impulse that has always been part of the human heart, but it seems to be welling up into the world with new power in our age now even as the forces of darkness are welling up with new power in our age now too. That is the bright side, I think, the glad and hopeful side, of what Jesus means by "The time is fulfilled." He means the time is ripe.

Humanly speaking, if we have any chance to survive, I suspect it is men and women who act out of that deep impulse who are our chance. By no means will they themselves bring about the Kingdom of God. It is God alone who brings about his Kingdom. Even with the best will in the world and out of our noblest impulses, we can't do that. But there is something that we can do and must do, Jesus says, and that is *repent*. Biblically speaking, to repent doesn't mean to feel sorry about, to regret. It means to turn, to turn around 180 degrees. It means to undergo a complete change of mind, heart, direction. To individuals and to nations both, Jesus says the same thing. Turn *away from* madness, cruelty, shallowness, blindness. Turn *toward* that tolerance, compassion, sanity, hope, justice that we all have in us at our best.

We cannot make the Kingdom of God happen, but we can put out leaves as it draws near. We can be kind to each other. We can be kind to ourselves. We can drive back the darkness a little. We can make green places within ourselves and among ourselves where God can make his Kingdom happen. That transfigured city. Those people of every color, class, condition, eating their sandwiches together in that quiet place. The clown and the child. The sunlight that made everybody in those teeming streets a superstar. The bum napping like a millionaire on his pile of two-by-fours. The beautiful traffic surging all around me and the beautiful things that I could feel surging inside myself, in that holy place that is inside all of us. Turn *that* way. Everybody. While there is still time. Pray for the Kingdom. Watch for signs of it. Live as though it is here already because there are moments when it almost is, such as those moments in Tiananmen Square before the massacre started when the students were gentle and the soldiers were gentle and something so holy and human was trying to happen there that it was hard to see pictures of it without having tears come to your eyes.

And "Believe in the gospel." That's the last of those first words that Jesus speaks. Believe in the good news. Believe in what that black woman said. Hurrying along Central Park South, she didn't even stop as she said it. It was as if she didn't have time to stop. She said it on the run the way Mark's Gospel says it. "Jesus loves you," she said. It was a corny thing for her to say, of course. Embarrassing. A screwball thing to blurt out to a total stranger on a crowded sidewalk. But, "Jesus loves you." She said it anyway. And that is the good news of the gospel, exactly that.

The power that is in Jesus, and before which all other powers on earth and in heaven give way, the power that holds all things in existence from the sparrow's eye to the farthest star, is above all else a loving power. That means we are loved even in our lostness. That means we are precious, every one of us, even as we pass on the street without so much as noticing each other's faces. Every city is precious. The world is precious. Someday the precious time will be up for each of us. But the Kingdom of God is at hand. Nothing is different and everything is different. It reaches out to each of our precious hands while there's still time.

Repent and believe in the gospel, Jesus says. Turn around and believe that the good news that we are loved is gooder than we ever dared hope, and that to believe in that good news, to live out of it and toward it, to be in love with that good news, is of all glad things in this world the gladdest thing of all.

Amen, and come, Lord Jesus.

22.
Two Narrow Words

Then Job answered: "Today also my complaint is bitter; his hand is heavy despite my groaning. Oh, that I knew where I might find him, ... and fill my mouth with arguments.... If I go forward, he is not there; or backward, I cannot perceive him; on the left he hides, and I cannot behold him; I turn to the right, but I cannot see him.... If only I could vanish in darkness, and thick darkness would cover my face!"

—JOB 23:1–17 PASSIM, NRSV

We do not want you to be unaware, brothers and sisters, of the affliction we experienced in Asia; for we were so utterly, unbearably crushed that we despaired of life itself. Indeed, we felt that we had received the sentence of death so that we would rely not on ourselves but on God who raises the dead. He who rescued us from so deadly a peril will continue to rescue us; on him we have set our hope that he will rescue us again.

—2 CORINTHIANS 1:8–10, NRSV

O eloquent, just and mightie Death! Whom none could advise, thou hast persuaded; what none hath dared, thou hast done; and whom all the world hath flattered, thou only hast cast out of the world and despised. Thou hast drawn together all the far-stretched greatness, all the pride, cruelty, and ambition of man, and covered it all over with these two narrow words: *hic jacet.*

—SIR WALTER RALEIGH

So wrote the brilliant and ill-starred Sir Walter Raleigh at the end of his *History of the World,* and you cannot enter the ancient building of Westminster Abbey, I think, without some echo of his words sounding deep within you and making you catch your breath. *Hic jacet.* "Here lies." And there they all lie indeed, including Edward the Confessor, who was a holy saint, and many of his successors who were holy terrors; and both twelve-year-old Edward V and, not far away, his uncle Richard of Gloucester, who, if he didn't actually have him murdered as Tudor historians contend, at least had him declared a bastard and usurped his throne. Charles Dickens lies there too, the champion of the poor and dispossessed, and in unmarked graves beneath visitors' feet who knows how many of the poor and dispossessed themselves.

If their ghosts were to arise and stand there in the Abbey now, nowhere in Christendom would there be a richer assemblage of great ones and obscure ones, wise ones and foolish ones, proud ones and humble ones, saints and scoundrels; and in our own way you and I are just such a rich and miscellaneous assemblage within our single selves.

We are wise, and we are also foolish. In some ways we are rich and powerful and in other ways poor and helpless. To some we are friends but to others, or even to the same ones, we are enemies, enemies sometimes even to ourselves. There are days when our faith in God is strong and sustaining, and there are days when it is hard to believe that God exists at all. It is this inner complexity we share that makes each one of us a kind of walking Westminster Abbey and that unites us not only with each other, but also with the fabled ghosts who haunt its shadows. And we are united with them too in that we, like them, will one day be covered by those same two narrow words.

There they lie, and if not in the Abbey, the chances are then most surely somewhere else, we too will someday lie because just as they all came to face at last that eloquent, just, and mightie foe, so we also will come to face him, and in the meantime—although we have much to rejoice in and much to hold fast to and many days, we hope, still left ahead of us to live—we must somehow come to terms with the darkness not just of death, but also of life. And that is of course the darkness that our two scriptural texts speak to and confront us with.

Where can we look for hope then? To what, to whom, can we turn when the shadows gather around us and within us? These are the questions that Job and Saint Paul ask. They are the questions that Richard of Gloucester must have asked, no less than the two little princes in the Tower. It is the question that we all of us must ask and go on asking. "Whom none could advise, thou hast persuaded; what none hath dared, thou hast done." Is there anything in our faith to strengthen us against such an adversary as that—not just against death, but against the whole deadly side of things like suffering and sorrow and loss and growing old that foreshadow death's coming?

Everybody knows Job's story. He was a man "blameless and upright, one who feared God and turned away from evil" (1:1), we are told, and he was also a very rich man with great quantities of cattle and land and servants and children to carry on his name. Then came the famous wager in which Satan, the adversary, bet God that if Job were ever to fall on evil times, his faith would be destroyed and, instead of worshiping God, he would curse him to his face. God accepted the wager and little by little allowed Satan to make terrible things happen to this blameless and upright man. His cattle died, his servants were put to the sword, and his children were all killed, so that in the end he had nothing left to sustain him except for his all but devastated faith in a God who his whole life long he had thought rewarded the righteous with prosperity and visited only the wicked with horrors such as had befallen him. If God was just, how could he permit such unspeakable injustice? That was the question he addressed to God, and in the meanwhile how could he even get God to listen to him, to hear his case? It is an ancient folk tale that goes back a thousand years or more before the author of the book of Job used it as the basis for his great poem, but it has survived all these tens of centuries because of course the question itself has survived to become also our question. If God is all he's cracked up to be, then for God's sake, for Christ's sweet sake, where is he?

It is God alone who can answer the question, but where is God when our need for him is most desperate? "If I go forward, he is not there; or backward, I cannot perceive him," Job cries out. "On the left he hides, and I cannot behold him; I turn to the right, but I cannot see him." Is there anyone who at one dark time or another has not echoed Job's cry from the depths—a cry to the Creator to enter the creation and make all things right? But is such a thing possible even for God? In what conceivable way could God, as God, enter the world he has made in love without destroying it with his overwhelming presence?

By way of analogy, I think of William Shakespeare as creator and god of the plays he wrote trying to make himself known somehow to Cymbeline, say, or to Juliet, whose only reality is the plays that contain them and who know no more of true reality than they know what a midsummer night is truly, or a tempest, because all they have to go by is what Shakespeare scratched down about them with a quill. I think of the great playwright shouting out the devastating truth about who he is and about who they are to Lady Macbeth, for instance, who can hear only the raven croaking himself hoarse at the fatal entrance of Duncan under her battlements, or to Hamlet, who has ears only for his father's ghost. I think of him pounding his Elizabethan fist down on the crabbed manuscript before him to make himself heard and not a single one of them so much as turning a hair.

The characters in the world of Shakespeare's plays cannot hear Shakespeare or see him or know him directly any more than we can know God in God's world directly because even though there is nothing in the world of the plays, including themselves, that does not draw its only life from his life, his ways are not their ways, and whereas Shakespeare dwells in what amounts to eternity by contrast with anything they can imagine, they dwell only in the five acts' worth of make-believe time allotted to them on the printed page.

So how else could Shakespeare reach them then? If he were able somehow actually to enter the world of the plays as himself in all his multidimensional richness and fullness, if he were able somehow to thrust himself bodily into their fictive and derivative world, leap down feet foremost into their midst with a terrible ripping and scattering of parchment, how could it do anything less than blow the whole show sky-high?

Maybe the best he could manage would be to write himself into the plays as yet another character, into the fourth act of *King Lear,* for instance, where the Duke of Gloucester, betrayed by his bastard and blinded by his enemies, cries out, "As flies to wanton boys are we to the gods. They kill us for their sport." Let us say that Shakespeare, hearing Gloucester's anguish, appears at his side in the role of a shepherd, perhaps, or some homeless wanderer, takes him by the arm and tells him that his suffering is not the work of wanton gods at all but a precious and holy suffering that, before it kills him, will confer on him a strength and self-knowledge he would never have attained in any other way, one that will add to the depth and beauty of the whole world he inhabits as well as to his own depth and beauty. Would Gloucester believe him? Would he find comfort and healing in his words? Would he recognize him as the great Author himself, incarnate in the little world of the drama whose author he is? My guess is that he would not. My guess is that he would take him only for another half-crazed Tom O'Bedlam in a world gone mad.

Suppose then that Shakespeare went further still and decided to take Gloucester's suffering from him altogether. Suppose he reworked the entire play so that Edmund would never betray him and Cornwall and Regan never put out his eyes. Could he do such a thing without not only destroying the whole magnificent drama as he conceived it but also in a sense destroying Gloucester himself by so high-handedly altering his destiny? Part of an author's genius, which one might say is also part of God's genius, is never to manipulate his people like puppets to be what he wants them to be but to leave them continually free to become whatever they have it in them to become in the world he has created for them, so that they may rise out of his creating heart and spirit with their own rich measure of his truth the way you and I rise out of God's heart and become forever part of it.

When Job, like Gloucester, cries out to God to enter his world and deliver him from the darkness that has befallen him, we know in detail just what that darkness is, but in his Second Letter to the Corinthians, St. Paul, on the other hand, leaves his darkness for us to imagine. He speaks only of "the affliction we experienced in Asia," says only, "we were so utterly, unbearably crushed that we despaired of life itself." Who knows what affliction he is referring to, but at the same time who does not know well what it means to be afflicted like that? Who of us, looking back at our lives, cannot remember moments of such nearly unbearable sadness?

In my case, I have found that often such moments occur in conjunction with moments of nearly unbearable joy. Two years ago, for instance, I met the first of my grandchildren for the first time, and it was on a staircase that I met him. My daughter Dinah, his mother, was coming down carrying him in her arms, and I was going up with my heart in my mouth to meet him—this very small boy named Oliver with the blood in his veins of so many people I have loved, this fragile bit of a two-month-old child who, God willing, will carry some fragment of who I am into a future I will never see. He was on his way down into the world, and I was on my way up out of it into God only knows what unimaginable world awaits every one of us, if indeed any world beyond this one awaits us at all. On the one hand, there was my joy at seeing him for the first time, which brought tears to my eyes, but on the other hand, part of where those tears came from was the realization that the world he was entering was full of great sorrow as well as of great gladness, the realization that he will one day die even as I also will one day die before I can ever know what becomes of him. That is a far cry from the anguish of Job and the despair of Paul—maybe only the saints are strong enough to look into the abyss—but it is of the same texture and substance, I think, and leads something deep in me to call out in Job's words, "Oh, that I knew where I might find him!" Oh, that we all of us knew where we might find the One who beyond any world we can imagine wipes every tear from our eyes and death from our hearts and creates all things new.

Job and Paul both found him before they were through although it was only Paul who knew him by name. God never answered Job's question as to why it is that bad things happen to good people and why, as Sir Walter Raleigh knew, those two narrow words, *hic jacet,* in the long run will cover us all, good and bad alike. But my guess is that it was not an answer that Job was really after, not some sort of theological explanation of the problem of suffering, which would have left him wiser than he was before but suffering still. I believe, instead, that what Job was really after was not God's answer, but God's presence. And of course that was what Job finally found because the way God entered the world without destroying it was to enter Job's heart even as from the depths of his heart Job cried out to him. And that is the way he makes himself present to all of us.

In the greatest aria that God sings in the entire Bible, he sets forth in gorgeous poetry all the mystery and grandeur of creation as a way of showing Job that the mystery is ultimately unfathomable, and it is then that Job finally says, "I had heard of you by the hearing of the ear, but now my eye sees you" (42:5). And that was what Job needed above all else—not an explanation of suffering, but the revelation that even in the midst of suffering there is a God who is with us and for us and will never let us go.

It was a few miles outside the city of Damascus that Paul made the same overwhelming discovery. He was on his way to bring back to Jerusalem for punishment members of the heretical sect who called themselves Christians when Christ himself appeared to him and called him by name and gave him a new faith to live for and die for, a faith that led him to write years later, "I am convinced that neither death, nor life,... nor things present, nor things to come,... nor anything else is all creation, will be able to separate us from the love of God in Christ Jesus our Lord" (Rom. 8:38–39).

So Job, the rich man, and Paul, the tent-maker, both of them in their darkest moments, found, or were found by, the light that shines in the darkness and that not even the darkness can ever finally be overcome. And may it prove so also for you and for me, as I believe it proved so too for all the great ones lying in Westminster Abbey at whose names the world once trembled as well as for all the others whose names have been all but forgotten. I believe that if their ghosts were to rise before us now and their long-stilled tongues were able to speak once more, they would tell us with one voice of the unimaginable grace and mercy of God.

23.

Faith and Fiction

A year or so ago, a friend of mine died. He was an Englishman—witty, elegant, multifaceted. One morning in his sixty-eighth year he simply didn't wake up. It was about as easy a way as he could possibly have done it, but it was not easy for the people he left behind because it gave us no chance to start getting used to the idea beforehand or to say good-bye either in words, if we turned out to be up to it, or in some awkward, unspoken way if we weren't. He died in March, and in May my wife and I were staying with his widow overnight when I had a short dream about him. I dreamed he was standing there in the dark guest room where we were asleep, looking very much himself in the navy blue jersey and white slacks he often wore. I told him how much we had missed him and how glad I was to see him again. He acknowledged that somehow. Then I said, "Are you really there, Dudley?" I meant was he there in fact, in truth, or was I merely dreaming he was. His answer was that he was really there. "Can you prove it?" I asked him. "Of course," he said. Then he plucked a strand of wool out of his jersey and tossed it to me. I caught it between my thumb and forefinger, and the feel of it was so palpably real that it woke me up. That's all there was to it. It was as if he'd come on purpose to do what he'd done and then left. I told the dream at breakfast the next morning, and I'd hardly finished when my wife spoke. She said that she'd seen the strand on the carpet as she was getting dressed. She was sure it hadn't been there the night before. I rushed upstairs to see for myself, and there it was—a little tangle of navy blue wool.

Another event. I went into a bar in an airport not long ago to fortify myself against my least favorite means of transportation. It was an off hour, so I was the only customer and had a choice of the whole row of empty bar stools. On the counter in front of each of them was a holder with a card stuck in it advertising the drink of the day or something like that. I noticed that the one in front of me had a small metal piece on top of the card that wasn't on the others, so I took a look at it. It turned out to be a tie clip that somebody must have stuck there. It had three letters engraved on it, and the letters were C.F.B. Those are my initials.

Lastly this. I was receiving Communion in an Episcopal church early one morning. The priest was an acquaintance of mine. I could hear him moving along the rail from person to person as I knelt there waiting my turn. The body of Christ, he said, the bread of heaven. The body of Christ, the bread of heaven. When he got to me, he put in another word. The word was my name. "The body of Christ, Freddy, the bread of heaven."

The dream about my friend may well have been just another dream, and you certainly don't have to invoke the supernatural to account for the thread on the carpet. The tie clip I find harder to explain away. It seems to me that, mathematically speaking, the odds against its having not just one or two but all three of my initials on it in the right order must be astronomical, but I suppose that could be just a coincidence too. On the other hand, in both cases there is the other possibility too. Far-out or not, I don't see how any open-minded person can a priori deny it, and in a way it is that other possibility, as a possibility, that is at the heart of everything I want to say here.

Maybe my friend really did come to me in my dream and the thread was his sign to me that he had. Maybe it is true that by God's grace the dead are given back their lives again and that the doctrine of the resurrection of the body is not just a doctrine. He couldn't have looked more substantial and less ectoplasmic standing there in the dark, and it was such a crisp, no-nonsense exchange we had, with nothing surreal or wispy about it. It was so much like him. As to the tie clip, it seemed so extraordinary that for a moment I almost refused to believe it had happened at all. I think that's worth marking. Even though I had the thing right there in my hand, my first inclination was to deny it for the simple reason, I suspect, that it was so unsettling to my whole commonsense view of the way the world works that it was easier and less confusing just to shrug it off as a crazy fluke. I think we are all inclined to do that. But maybe it wasn't a fluke. Maybe it was a crazy little peek behind the curtain, a dim little whisper of providence from the wings. I had been expected. I was on schedule. I was taking the right journey at the right time. I was not alone.

What happened at the Communion rail was rather different. There was nothing extraordinary about the priest's knowing my name—I knew he knew it—and there was nothing extraordinary about his using it in the service either, I learned later, because it was a practice he not infrequently followed. But its effect upon me was extraordinary. It caught me off guard. It moved me deeply. For the first time in my life perhaps it struck me that when Jesus picked up the bread at his last meal and said, "This is my body, which is for you," he was doing it not just in a ritual way for humankind in general but in an unthinkably personal way for every particular man, woman, child who ever existed or someday would exist. Most unthinkable of all, as far as I was concerned, maybe he was doing it for me. At that holiest of feasts, we are known not just by our official names but by the names people use who have known us longest and most intimately. We are welcomed not as the solid citizens that our Sunday best suggests we are, but in all our inner tackiness and tatteredness that no one in the world knows better than we each of us know it about ourselves—the bitterness, the phoniness, the confusion, the irritability, the prurience, the half-heartedness. The bread of heaven, *Freddy*, of all people? Molly? Bill? Ridiculous little What's-her-name? Boring old So-and-so? Extraordinary. It seemed a revelation from on high. Was it?

All that's extraordinary about these three minor events is the fuss I've made about them. Things like that happen every day to everybody. They are a dime a dozen. They mean absolutely nothing. Or things like that are momentary glimpses into a Mystery of such depth, power, and beauty that if we were to see it head-on, we would be annihilated.

If I had to bet my life on one possibility or the other, which one would I bet it on? If you had to bet your life, which one would you bet it on? On

Yes, there is God in the highest, or, if such language is no longer viable, there is Mystery and Meaning in the deepest? On No, there is whatever happens to happen, and it means whatever you choose it to mean, and that is all there is?

We may bet Yes this evening and No tomorrow morning. We may know we are betting or we may not know. We may bet one way with our lips, our minds, our hearts even, and another way with our feet. But we all of us bet, and it's our lives themselves we're betting with in the sense that the betting is what shapes our lives. And we can never be sure we've bet right, of course. The evidence both ways is fragmentary, fragile, ambiguous. A coincidence can be, as somebody has said, God's way of remaining anonymous, or it can be just a coincidence. Is the dream that brings healing and hope just a product of wishful thinking? Or is it a message from another world? Whether we bet Yes or No, it is equally an act of faith.

Religious faith, the Letter to the Hebrews says in a famous chapter, "is the assurance of things hoped for, the conviction of things not seen" (11:1). Noah, Abraham, Sarah, and the rest of them it goes on to say, "all died in faith, not having received what was promised, but having seen it and greeted it from afar, and having acknowledged that they were strangers and exiles on the earth. For people [like that] make it clear that they are seeking a homeland" (11:13–14).

Faith, therefore, is distinctly different from other aspects of the religious life and not to be confused with them even though we sometimes use the word to mean religious belief in general, as in phrases like "the Christian faith" or "the faith of Islam." Faith is different from theology because theology is reasoned, systematic, and orderly, whereas faith is disorderly, intermittent, and full of surprises. Faith is different from mysticism because mystics in their ecstasy become one with what faith can at most see only from afar. Faith is different from ethics because ethics is primarily concerned not, like faith, with our relationship to God but with our relationship to each other. Faith is closest perhaps to worship because like worship it is essentially a response to God and involves the emotions and the physical senses as well as the mind, but worship is consistent, structured, single-minded and seems to know what it's doing while faith is a stranger and exile on the earth and doesn't know for certain about anything. Faith is homesickness. Faith is a lump in the throat. Faith is less a position *on* than a movement *toward,* less a sure thing than a hunch. Faith is waiting. Faith is journeying through space and through time.

If someone were to come up and ask me to talk about my faith, it is exactly that journey that I would eventually have to talk about—the ups and downs of the years, the dreams, the odd moments, the intuitions. I would have to talk about the occasional sense I have that life is not just a series of events causing other events as haphazardly as a break shot in pool causes the billiard balls to career off in all directions but that life has a plot the way a novel has a plot, that events are somehow or other leading somewhere. Whatever your faith may be or my faith may be, it seems to me inseparable from the story of what has happened to us, and that is why I believe that no literary form is better adapted to the subject than the form of fiction.

Faith and fiction both journey forward in time and space and draw their life from the journey, *are* in fact the journey. Faith and fiction both involve the concrete, the earthen, the particular more than they do the abstract and cerebral. In both, the people you meet along the way, the things that happen, the places—the airport bar, the room where you have your last supper with a friend—count for more than ideas do. Fiction can hold opposites together simultaneously like love and hate, laughter and tears, despair and hope, and so of course does faith, which by its very nature both sees and does not see and whose most characteristic utterance, perhaps, is "Lord, I believe; help thou my unbelief" (Mark 9:24, kjv). Faith and fiction both start once upon a time and are continually changing and growing in mood, intensity, and direction. When faith stops changing and growing, it dies on its feet. So does fiction. And they have more in common than that.

They both start with a leap in the dark, for one. How can Noah, Abraham, Sarah, or anyone else know for sure that the promise they die without receiving will ever be kept and that their journey in search of a homeland will ever get them there? How can anybody writing a novel or a story know for sure where it will lead and just how and with what effect it will end or even if it is a story worth telling? Let writers beware who from the start know too much about what they are doing and keep too heavy a hand on the reins. They leave too little room for luck as they tell their stories, just the way Abraham and Sarah, if they know too much about what they are doing as they *live* their stories, leave too little room for grace.

The word *fiction* comes from a Latin verb meaning "to shape, fashion, feign." That is what fiction does, and in many ways it is what faith does too. You fashion your story, as you fashion your faith, out of the great hodge-podge of your life—the things that have happened to you and the things you have dreamed of happening. They are the raw material of both. Then, if you're a writer like me, you try less to impose a shape on the hodgepodge than to see what shape emerges from it, is hidden in it. You try to sense what direction it is moving in. You listen to it. You avoid forcing your characters to march too steadily to the drumbeat of your artistic purpose, but leave them some measure of real freedom to be themselves. If minor characters show signs of becoming major characters, you at least give them a shot at it because in the world of fiction it may take many pages before you find out who the major characters really are just as in the real world it may take you many years to find out that the stranger you talked to for half an hour once in a railway station may have done more to point you to where your true homeland lies than your closest friend or your psychiatrist.

As a writer I use such craft as I have at my command, of course. I figure out what scenes to put in and, just as important, what scenes to leave out. I decide when to use dialogue and spend hours trying to make it sound like human beings talking to each other instead of just me talking to myself. I labor to find the right tone of voice to tell my story in, which is to say the right style, ultimately the right word, which is the most demanding part of it all—sentence after sentence, page after page, looking for the word that has freshness and power and life in it. But I try not to let my own voice be the dominant one. The limitation of the great stylists, of course—of a James, say, or a Hemingway—is that it is their voices you remember long after you have forgotten the voices of any of their characters. "Be still, and know that I am God," is the advice of the psalmist (46:10), and I've always taken it to be good literary advice too. Be still the way Tolstoy is still, or Anthony Trollope is still, so your characters can speak for themselves and come alive in their own way.

In faith and fiction both you *fashion* out of the raw stuff of your experience. If you want to remain open to the luck and grace of things anyway, you *shape* that stuff in the sense less of imposing a shape on it than of discovering the shape. And in both you *feign*—feigning as imagining, as making visible images for invisible things. Fiction can't be true the way a photograph is true, but at its best it can feign truth the way a good portrait does, inward and invisible truth. Fiction at its best can be true to the experience of being a human in this world, and the fiction you write depends, needless to say, on the part of that experience you choose. The part that has always most interested me is best illustrated by such incidents as the three I described at the outset. The moment that unaccountably brings tears to your eyes, that takes you by crazy surprise, that sends a shiver down your spine, that haunts you with what is just possibly a glimpse of something far beyond or deep within itself. That is the part of the human experience I choose to write about in my fiction. It is the part I am most concerned to feign, that is, make images for. In that sense I can live with the label of religious novelist. In any other sense, it is a label that makes my flesh crawl.

I lean over backwards not to preach or propagandize in my fiction. I don't dream up plots and characters to illustrate some homiletic message. I am not bent on driving home some theological point. I am simply trying to conjure up stories in which people are touched with what may or may not be the presence of God in their lives as I believe we all of us are even though we might sooner be shot dead than use that kind of language to describe it. In my own experience, the ways God appears in our lives are elusive and ambiguous always. There is always room for doubt in order, perhaps, that there will always be room to breathe. There is so much in life that hides God and denies the very possibility of God that there are times when it is hard not to deny God altogether. Yet it is possible to have faith nonetheless. Faith is that Nonetheless. That is the experience I am trying to be true to in the same way that other novelists try to be true to the experience of being a woman, say, or an infantryman in World War II. In all of them, there is perhaps nothing more crucial than honesty.

If you are going to be a religious novelist, you have got to be honest not just about the times that glimmer with God's presence but also about the ones that are dark with his absence, because needless to say you have had your dark times like everybody else. Terrible things happen in the four novels (*Lion Country, Open Heart, Love Feast,* and *Treasure Hunt*) I wrote about

Leo Bebb. In a drunken fit, Bebb's wife, Lucille, kills her own baby, and when Bebb tells her long afterwards that she has been washed clean in the blood of the Lamb, she answers him by saying, "Bebb, the only thing I've been washed in is the shit of the horse," and dies a suicide. Poor Brownie, reeking of aftershave, decides in the end that his rose-colored faith in the goodness of things is as false as his china choppers and loses it. Miriam Parr dies of cancer wondering if she is "going someplace," as she puts it, or "just out like a match." The narrator is a rather feckless, rootless young man named Antonio Parr, who starts out in the first book with no sense of commitment to anything or anybody but who, through his relationship with Leo Bebb, gradually comes alive to at least the possibility of something like religious faith. He has learned to listen for God in the things that happen to him anyway, just in case there happens to be a God to listen for. Maybe all he can hear, he says, is "Time's winged chariot hurrying near." Or, if there is more to it than that, the most he can say of it constitutes the passage with which the last of the four novels ends, in which he uses the Lone Ranger as an image for Christ: "To be honest, I must say that on occasion I hear something else too—not the thundering of distant hoofs, maybe, or *Hi-yo, Silver. Away!* echoing across the lonely sage, but the faint chunk-chunk of my own moccasin heart, of the Tonto afoot in the dusk of me somewhere who, not because he ought to but because he can't help himself, whispers *Kemo Sabe* every once in a while to what may or may not be only a silvery trick of the failing light."[*]

Terrible things as well as wonderful things happen in those books, but it's not so much that I have to cook them up in order to give a balanced view of the way life is as it is that they have a way of happening as much on their own in the fictional world as in the real world. If you're preaching or otherwise grinding an axe, you let happen, of course, only the things you want to have happen; but insofar as fiction, like faith, is a journey not only forward in space and time, but a journey inward, it is full of surprises. Even the wonderful things—the things that religious writers in the propagandist sense would presumably orchestrate and control most of all—tend at their

[*]*The Book of Bebb* (New York: Atheneum, 1979; San Francisco: HarperSanFrancisco, 1990), p. 530.

best to come as a surprise, and that is what is most wonderful about them. In the case of the Bebb books again, for instance, I was well along into *Lion Country*, the first of them, before I came to the surprising conclusion that Bebb himself was, wonderfully, a saint.

Imagine setting out consciously to write a novel about a saint. How could you avoid falling flat on your face? Nothing is harder to make real than holiness. Certainly nothing is harder to make appealing and attractive. The danger, I suppose, is that you start out with the idea that sainthood is something people achieve, that you get to be holy more or less the way you get to be an Eagle Scout. To create a saint from that point of view would be to end up with something on the order of Little Nell.

The truth, of course, is that holiness is not a human quality like virtue. If there is such a thing at all, holiness is Godness and as such is not something people do but something God does in them, if there is such a thing as God. It is something God seems especially apt to do in people who are not virtuous at all, at least not to start with. Think of Francis of Assisi or Mary Magdalene. Quite the contrary. If you're too virtuous, the chances are you think you are a saint already under your own steam, and therefore the real thing can never happen to you. Leo Bebb was not an Eagle Scout. He ran a religious diploma mill and ordained people through the mail for a fee. He did five years in the pen on a charge of indecent exposure involving children. He had a child by the wife of his twin brother. But he was a risk-taker. He was as round and fat and as full of bounce as a rubber ball. He was without pretense. He was good company. Above all else, he was extraordinarily alive—so much so for me anyway that when I was writing about him I could hardly wait to get back to my study every morning. That's when I began not only to see that he was a saint, but to see also what a saint is.

A saint is a life-giver. I hadn't known that before. A saint is a human being with the same sorts of hang-ups and abysses as the rest of us, but if a saint touches your life, you become alive in a new way. Even aimless, involuted Antonio Parr came more alive through knowing Bebb though at first he was out to expose him as a charlatan. So did the theosophist Gertrude Conover, Bebb's blue-haired octogenarian paramour. More extraordinary yet, I came more alive myself. I am a bookish, private sort of man, but in my old age I find myself doing and saying all sorts of outrageous things that, before Bebb came into my life and my fiction, I would have never even considered. I didn't think Bebb up at all the way he finally emerged as a character—sometimes I wonder if he was the one who thought me up. I had another kind of character in mind entirely when I started. In his tight-fitting raincoat and Tyrolean hat, he simply turned out to be the person he was in the journey of writing those books. I didn't expect him. I didn't deserve him. He came making no conditions. There were no strings attached. He was a free gift.

That is also what grace is—to use the religious word for it. Grace is God in his givenness. Faith is not *sui generis*. It is a response to the givenness of grace. Faith is given a glimpse of *something*, however dimly. Men and women of faith know they are strangers and exiles on the earth because somehow and somewhere along the line they have been given a glimpse of home. Maybe the little tangle of navy blue wool on the carpet was grace, even if it could be proved that it had only come from my own sweater. By grace we see what we see. To have faith is to respond to what we see by longing for it the rest of our days; by trying to live up to it and toward it through all the wonderful and terrible things; by breathing it in like air and growing strong on it; by looking to see it again and see it better. To lose faith is to stop looking. To lose faith is to decide, like Brownie, that all you ever saw from afar was your own best dreams.

The whole idea of the Muse is another way of speaking of this same matter of course, the goddess who inspires. And the word "in-spiration" itself as a *breathing into* is another. In fiction as in faith something from outside ourselves is breathed into us if we're lucky, if we're open enough to inhale it. I think writers of religious fiction especially have to stay open in that way. They've got to play their hunches more and take risks more. They shouldn't try to keep too tight a rein on what they're doing. They should be willing to be less professional and literary and more eccentric, antic, disheveled—less like John Updike or Walker Percy, maybe, and more like Kurt Vonnegut, or Peter de Vries, or G. K. Chesterton. In the stories of Flannery O'Connor, for instance, I have a sense of the author herself being caught off guard by a flash of insight here, a stab of feeling there. She is making discoveries about holy things and human things in a way that I think would never have been possible if she had known too well where she was going and how she was going to get there; and as her readers we share in the freshness and wonder of her surprise. I suppose *The Brothers Karamazov* would be the classic example of what I'm talking about—that great seething bouillabaisse of a book. It is digressive and sprawling, with many too many characters in it and much too long, and yet it is a book that, just because Dostoevsky leaves room in it for whatever comes up to enter, is entered here and there by maybe no less than the Holy Spirit itself, thereby becoming, as far as I am concerned, what at its best a religious novel can be—that is to say a novel less *about* the religious experience than a novel the reading of which itself *is* a religious experience—of God both in his subterranean presence and in his appalling absence.

Is it the Holy Spirit? Is it the Muse? Is it just a lucky break? Who dares say without crossing the fingers. But as in the journey of faith it is possible every once and a while to be better than you are—"Do you not know that ... God's Spirit dwells within you?" Paul asks (1 Cor. 3:16)—in the journey of fiction-making it is possible to write more than you know. Bebb was a saint—a kind of saint anyway—and when I finally finished with him, or he with me, I found that it was very hard to write a novel about any other kind of person. I tried a fifteenth-century alchemist, a twentieth-century woman novelist, a dishwasher in a New England restaurant, an old lady in a nursing home, and one by one they failed to come to life for me. They were all in their own ways too much like me, I suppose, and after so many years I have come to be a little tired of me. And too many other authors were writing novels about people like that, many of them better than I could do it, so why add to the number? Then I realized that, more even than those reasons, the basic reason none of them worked for me was that, after Bebb, only saints really interest me as a writer.

There is so much life in them. They are so in touch with, so transparent to, the mystery of things that you never know what to expect from them. Anything is possible for a saint. They won't stay put or be led around by the nose no matter how hard you try. And then entirely by accident one day—or by grace, or by luck—I came across a historical saint whom I'd never heard of before even by name. He was born in England in 1065 and died there in 1170. His name was Godric.

If, like me, you don't happen to be a saint yourself, I don't know how you write about one without being given something from somewhere. That is especially true if you try, as I did, to make the saint himself your narrator so that you have his whole interior life on your hands as well as his career. Add to that, Godric was a man who was born close to a thousand years ago—lived in a different world, spoke a different language, saw things in a different way. I did some research, needless to say—not of the thoroughgoing sort that I assume a real historical novelist undertakes, because it wasn't primarily the historical period that I was interested in but, rather, Godric himself. Nonetheless I read enough to give myself some idea of roughly what was going on in Europe at the time, especially in England. Largely through the ineffable *Dictionary of National Biography,* I found out what I could about such historical figures who played parts in Godric's life as Abbot Ailred of Rievaulx Abbey and Ranulf Flambard, bishop of Durham and former chancellor to William II. I tried with meager success to find out what Rome and Jerusalem looked like when Godric made his pilgrimages there. I dug a little into the First Crusade because Godric was briefly involved with it apparently. The principal source on Godric himself is a contemporary biography written by a monk known as Reginald of Durham, who knew him and who figures as a character in the novel.

The book has never been translated from medieval Latin, and in that regard something rather remarkable happened comparable to the discovery of the tie clip with my initials on it. My own Latin came to an end with Caesar's *Commentaries* some fifty years ago, so the best I could do was to look up promising references in the English index and then try to get at least the gist of them with the help of a dictionary. Then, just as I was getting started on that, one of my daughters, who was off at boarding school, phoned to ask if she could bring some friends home for the weekend, and one of the friends turned out to be chairman of the school's classics department. I suppose he was the only person within a radius of a hundred miles or more who could have done the job, and both evenings he was with us he gave me sight translations of the passages I was after.

But I am talking about something even odder than that and more precious. I am talking about how, by something like grace, you are given every once in a while to be better than you are and to write more than you know. Less because of the research I did than in spite of it, Godric came alive for me—that is what I was given: the way he thought, the way he spoke, the humanness of him, the holiness of him. I don't believe any writer can do that just by taking thought and effort and using the customary tools of the craft. Something else has to happen more mysterious than that. Godric not only came alive for me, but he came speaking words that had a life and a twist to them that I can't feel entirely responsible for. I don't want to make it sound spookier than it was. I was the one who wrote his words, of course. In some sense I invented them, dredged them up out of some subbasement of who I am. But the words were more like him than they were like me, and without him I feel certain I could never have found them and written them.

Year after year as a hermit in the north of England, the old man used to chasten his flesh in all seasons by bathing in the river Wear a few miles out of Durham. When he got too feeble to do that, he had a servant dig a hole in the chapel he had built for the Virgin Mary and fill it with water from the river so he could still bathe in it there. Here is a passage from the novel in which he describes what it was like both to bathe in the river in midwinter and, later, to bathe in the little pool of it in the chapel:

First there's the fiery sting of cold that almost stops my breath, the aching torment in my limbs. I think I may go mad, my wits so out-raged that they seek to flee my skull like rats a ship that's going down. I puff. I gasp. Then inch by inch a blessed numbness comes. I have no legs, no arms. My very heart grows still. These floating hands are not my hands. This ancient flesh I wear is rags for all I feel of it.

"Praise, praise!" I croak. Praise God for all that's holy, cold, and dark. Praise him for all we lose, for all the river of the years bears off. Praise him for stillness in the wake of pain. Praise him for emptiness. And as you race to spill into the sea, praise him yourself, old Wear. Praise him for dying and the peace of death.

In the little church I built of wood for Mary, I hollowed out a place for him. Perkin brings him by the pail and pours him in. Now that I can hardly walk, I crawl to meet him there. He takes me in his chilly lap to wash me of my sins. Or I kneel down beside him till within his depths I see a star.

Sometimes this star is still. Sometimes she dances. She is Mary's star. Within that little pool of Wear she winks at me. I wink at her. The secret that we share I cannot tell in full. But this much I will tell. What's lost is nothing to what's found, and all the death that ever was, set next to life, would scarcely fill a cup.*

Feigning is part of it. Imagining, image-making. Reaching deep. But it feels like more than that. Godric told me things I didn't know. He revealed something of himself to me and something of the distant past. He also revealed something of myself to me and something of the not so distant future. I will grow old. I will die. I think it was through his eyes that I first saw beyond the inevitability of it to the mercy of it. "All's lost. All's found." I have faith that that is true, or someday will turn out to be true, but on the old saint's lips the words have a ring of certitude and benediction from which I draw courage as I think I could not from any words merely of my own.

Is that why we write, people like me—to keep our courage up? Are novels such as mine a kind of whistling in the dark? I think so. To whistle in the dark is more than just to try to *convince* yourself that dark is not all there is. It is also to *remind* yourself that dark is not all there is or the end of all there is because even in the dark there is hope. Even in the dark you have the power to whistle, and sometimes that seems more than just your own power, because it is powerful enough to hold the dark back. The tunes you whistle in the dark are the images you make of that hope, that power. They are the books you write.

In just the same way faith could be called a kind of whistling in the dark too, of course. The living out of faith. The writing out of fiction. In both you shape, you fashion, you feign. Maybe what they have most richly in common is a way of paying attention. Page by page, chapter by chapter, the story unfolds. Day by day, year by year, your own story unfolds, your

---

Godric (New York: Atheneum, 1980; San Francisco: Harper & Row, 1983), pp. 95–96.

life's story. Things happen. People come and go. The scene shifts. Time runs by, runs out. Maybe it is all utterly meaningless. Maybe it is all unutterably meaningful. If you want to know which, pay attention. What it means to be truly human in a world that half the time we are in love with and half the time scares the hell out of us—any fiction that helps us pay attention to that is as far as I am concerned religious fiction.

The unexpected sound of your name on somebody's lips. The good dream. The odd coincidence. The moment that brings tears to your eyes. The person who brings life to your life. Maybe even the smallest events hold the greatest clues. If it is God we are looking for, as I suspect we all of us are even if we don't think of it that way and wouldn't use such language on a bet, maybe the reason we haven't found him is that we are not looking in the right places.

Pay attention. As a summation of all that I have had to say as a writer, I would settle for that. And as a talisman or motto for that journey in search of a homeland, which is what faith is, I would settle for that too.

24.
The Good Book as a Good Book

As an occasional writer of novels, I have always thought that the most appealing aspect of the form is that it allows you to do anything you can get away with. I think of *Moby Dick*, with its endless excursions into the minutiae of whaledom, or *Ulysses*, *Tristram Shandy*, and *The Countesse of Pembroke's Arcadia*, with their endless excursions into everything else. Or I think of the later novels of Henry James—*The Golden Bowl*, for instance—where the star of the show is not the story it tells or the characters it tells about but the sheer madness of the style, or of Anthony Trollope's *The Warden*, which has virtually no style at all, but like a clear window pane allows you to watch the dance old Septimus Harding's delicate conscience leads him in without the sound of anyone's voice in your ears except his own. The Bible is not a novel, needless to say, but like a novel there is almost nothing it does not attempt and by and large not much that it fails to get away with. In that sense it is not only the Good Book but a book that, except for a few notorious *longueurs*, is a remarkably good one. You might better say that it is not really a book at all but a library of some sixty-six of them written over the course of centuries by heaven only knows whom, or for how many divergent purposes, or from how many variegated points of view, yet in some sense it manages to be one book even so. Something holds it together. When we think of it, we think of it somehow as a whole.

A novelist, for example, might well envy the way the opening chapters of Genesis set the stage for everything that is to follow and foreshadow all the great biblical themes. Creation is one of them. "In the beginning God *created,*" the opening words proclaim, and from there right on to the book of Revelation it is proclaimed again and again. More almost than anything else he does, as the Bible depicts him, God makes things. He makes the world in all its splendor, and the psalms never stop stammering out their wonder at it—"Praise him, sun and moon, praise him, all you shining stars! Praise him, you highest heavens, and all you waters above the heavens! Let them praise the name of the Lord! For he commanded and they were created" (Ps. 148:3–5).

When God presents his credentials to Job in what is perhaps the greatest of all his soliloquies, it is the creation that he himself points to—the springs of the sea and the storehouses of the snow are his, he says; the young lions crouch in their dens, the ostrich waves her proud wings, Behemoth makes the deep boil like a pot, because with his fathomless ingenuity he made them that way. Men and women he made too, of course, and perhaps because he loved them most, perhaps to make it up to them for all the trouble he saw in store for them because they were so bad at loving him back, he made them a little like himself. Even after their fall and the terrible sentence pronounced upon them, "he made for Adam and for his wife garments of skins, and clothed them," Genesis says (3:21), and in a way the entire remainder of the Bible is about how history itself is the record of the Creator's endless efforts to restore his creation to himself, to clothe it again in the glory for which he created it in the first place.

He also made a people, Israel, to be a blessing to all peoples. He raised up prophets to bring them to heel when they strayed. Somewhat reluctantly he anointed kings to rule over them. When his people abandoned him to go wantoning after other gods, he made a people within a people out of the faithful few who were left—he brought forth "a shoot from the stump of Jesse" (Isa. 11:1)—and when those few fell away also, he came down finally to making one single person, a second Adam, who was like no other because "in him all the fullness of God was pleased to dwell," as St. Paul tried to explain the mystery of it to the Colossians (1:19). Finally, having funneled down to that single person, the whole vast creative process starts funneling out again through the twelve disciples to, little by little, a new people altogether—a new Israel, the church—which, ragged and inadequate as it must always be in its humanness, in its holiness is yet another garment that the Creator has fashioned for the sheltering of the creation, which for better or worse, as Genesis suggests, he can never stop loving because he made it and it is his. Being what it is, the human race will go on failing till the end of time, but even at the end of time God is there again, as John finally tells it. "Behold, I make all things new!" he calls forth (Rev. 21:5), and while the words are still on his lips, the new Jerusalem he has created comes down out of heaven like a bride.

Creation is perhaps the greatest of the themes adumbrated in the opening chapters of this extraordinary book of books, but of course all the other great themes are implicit in those chapters too. The old covenant of law grows out of God's telling Adam and Eve that all Eden is theirs if only they will not eat of that one fatal tree; and the whole tragic history of Israel, not to mention of the rest of us, stems from their eating it anyway; and out of those garments of skins as emblematic of the love that will not let them go grows the new covenant of grace where nothing is asked of them except that they allow themselves to be clothed. As St. Paul understood it, in the face of Adam, who went wrong, are already faintly visible the features of Jesus, who went right, was right, lived and died to make all things finally right and whole. "Happy families are all alike; every unhappy family is unhappy in its own way," is how Tolstoy wonderfully and unforgettably sets the stage for all eight hundred pages or more of the *Anna Karenina* to come. The opening pages of Genesis do much the same for the whole great library that they unlock.

Genesis sets the stage for the drama, and then of course there is the cast of characters. Who can count their number? Who can describe their variety? Patriarchs and judges, kings and courtesans, peasants and priests; in short, men and women of every possible sort, heroes and scoundrels and some, like ourselves, who from time to time manage to be something of both. The central character, of course—the one who dominates everything and around whom all the others revolve—is God himself. The Bible is God's book. It is as unimaginable without him as *Moby Dick* would be without the great white whale, yet like the great white whale, he is scarcely to be seen. He appears briefly walking in Eden in the cool of the day, but there is no description of him there, nor is there one anywhere else in all those thousand pages and more that come later. Such is his holiness that to look upon him is death, and the commandment to make no graven image of him or of anything else in the heaven above or the earth beneath that might be supposed to be like him is basic to the faith of Israel. When Moses is allowed to take refuge in the cleft of a rock so that he may see his glory passing by, God tells him, "You shall see my back; but my face shall not be seen" (Exodus 33:23), and when Moses comes down from talking with God on Mount Sinai, his own face shines with such an unearthly light that the people are afraid to come near him until he puts on a veil (Exodus 34:29–35). God is not to be seen in this book that is his except as he is reflected in the faces and lives of people who have encountered him, and the whole New Testament grows out of the experience of those who, like St. Paul, encountered "the glory of God in the face of Christ" (2 Cor. 4:6).

God is not to be seen in space because in space he is not seeable any more than in *La Comédie Humaine* Balzac is seeable. But he can be heard. God's words can be heard because words move forward not through space but through time, and although time cannot be inhabited by eternity, it can be impinged upon by eternity the way the horizontal can be impinged upon by the vertical. God is known in the Bible as he speaks—speaks to and through the prophets and patriarchs, the priests and poets, speaks through the mighty acts he works both in the history of Israel and in the small histories of men and women when their ears and lives are in some measure attuned to him, or sometimes even when they are not. The Bible is the Word of God—the word about God and God's word about himself—and it is also the endless words of God, the unanticipatable and elusive self-disclosures of God to countless numbers of people through the medium of what in Hebrew is called *dabhar,* which means both *word* and *deed*—the word that is also a deed because it makes things happen, and the deed that is also a word because, through it, is revealed meaning.

How remote, inaccessible, amorphous all this makes God sound, yet as the Bible depicts him, he is anything but that. God is now wrathful, now loving. He is jealous. He laughs. He cries out like a woman in labor. He is Abraham's friend. He destroys cities. He speaks in the still, small voice that Elijah heard and answers Moses in thunder. He makes himself known to thousands through the cataclysms of history and hides himself from thousands of others, hides himself—inexplicably, horrifyingly—even from Christ in his dying. It is God himself who says what he ultimately is, the only one who can do it. "I the Lord your God am holy," he says to Moses (Lev. 19:2), which is another way of saying, "I am who I am" (Exod. 3:14). Mystery, power, righteousness, love even—all the words that we use to describe him are in the end as crude as the behavior the Bible ascribes to him. He is none of them. He is all of them. He is who he is experienced to be by Eve, by Rachel, by Ahab, by Hannah, by Bathsheba, by Judas. He is who he is experienced to be by each one of us. He is holy. He is God.

As to the Eves and Hannahs, the Judases and Ahabs themselves—the rest of the cast—we wish we could know what they looked liked, but for the most part the Bible is interested much less in seeing than in hearing and tells us as little about these matters as it does in the case of God. We are told that David was a handsome redhead with beautiful eyes. We are told that Joseph had a coat that was the envy of his brothers, that the bride in Solomon's song had breasts like two fawns, twins of a gazelle, that feed among the lilies. We are told that when Jesus fell asleep in the stern of the boat, he had a pillow under his head, and that Paul was weak in his bodily presence and his speech of no account. But how much we would give to see more—especially when it comes to the leading characters, the ones who not only loomed large in their time but have continued to do so ever since. Abraham and Sarah, for instance. Just one glimpse of their ancient, sand-blasted faces when the angel told them they were to have a child at last would be as precious almost as to them the child was. Or the way Moses looked as he stood on Mount Pisgah letting his gaze wander from the lands of Dan and Naphtali in the north to the Negeb and the Jordan Valley in the south, knowing that he would not live to set foot on any of it. Or Solomon in all his glory, or Mary when the angel came upon her with his troubling word. We are allowed to see that pillow under Jesus's head where he lay sleeping in the stern as the storm came up, but his head we never see. We know nothing of how he sounded when he talked, how he looked when he was asleep or awake, the slope of his shoulders when he was tired. Yet we know much without seeing, of course. We know him as we know all of them, as we know God, through their *dabharim*—through the words they speak which are also their deeds.

The Bible is full of their marvelous words. Isaac, hoodwinked into thinking that it is Esau who is kneeling before him instead of Jacob dressed up in Esau's clothes, sniffs the air as he blesses him and says, "See, the smell of my son is as the smell of the field that the Lord has blessed" (Gen. 27:27), and suddenly the blind old man is there before us in chiaroscuro as rich and moving as even Rembrandt could have managed it. "O my son Absalom, my son, my son Absalom! Would I had died instead of you, O Absalom, my son, my son!"—we see, without seeing, all that is most kingly about David as well as all that is most human about him in those words he speaks when he learns that the son who betrayed him has fallen in battle (2 Sam. 18:333). And we see Elijah's face in an ecstasy of derision as with scalding words he taunts the rival prophets whose frenzied efforts have all failed to persuade Baal to touch off the sacrificial pyre. "Cry aloud, for he is a god," Elijah says, his voice shrill with mockery. "Either he is musing, or he has gone aside, or he is on a journey, or perhaps he is asleep and must be awakened" (1 Kings 18:27). A camera could capture the scene no better.

There are also dialogues that not only evoke the character of the speakers, but bring them alive before our eyes. Guiltily and in disguise King Saul goes at night to ask the witch of Endor to summon from the dead old Samuel, who in life had been his friend, his conscience, his most implacable enemy:

"Divine for me by a spirit, and bring up for me whomever I shall name to you."

The woman said to him, "Surely you know what Saul has done, how he has cut off the mediums and the wizards from the land. Why then are you laying a snare for my life to bring about my death?"

But Saul swore to her by the Lord, "As the Lord lives, no punishment shall come upon you for this thing."

Then the woman said, "Whom shall I bring up for you?"

He said, "Bring up Samuel for me."

When the woman saw Samuel, she cried out with a loud voice; and the woman said to Saul, "Why have you deceived me? You are Saul."

The king said to her, "Have no fear; what do you see?"

And the woman said to Saul, "I see a god coming up out of the earth."

He said to her, "What is his appearance?"

And she said, "An old man is coming up, and he is wrapped in a robe."

And Saul knew that it was Samuel, and he bowed with his face to the ground, and did obeisance. (1 Sam. 28:8–14)

Or take the words that Pilate and Jesus speak to each other when they come face-to-face for the first time:

"Are you the King of the Jews?"

"Do you say this of your own accord, or did others say it to you about me?"

"Am I a Jew? Your own nation and the chief priests have handed you over to me; what have you done?"

"My kingship is not of this world; if my kingship were of this world, my servants would fight, that I might not be handed over to the Jews; but my kingship is not from the world."

"So you are a king?"

"You say that I am a king. For this I was born, and for this I have come into the world, to bear witness to the truth. Every one who is of the truth hears my voice."

"What is truth?" (John 18:33–38)

It was by speaking his creative word into the primordial darkness that God on the first day brought forth light, and it is by speaking and listening to each other that out of the darkness of our separate mysteries is brought to light the truth of who we are.

They speak, this huge gathering of people who crowd the pages of the Bible. They listen. They emerge, if we in turn listen to them, not as allegorical embodiments of Goodness and Badness but as flesh-and-blood men and women who no less ambiguously than the rest of us are good one day, bad the next, and occasionally both at once. Of all people in the world, Noah is the one who found favor with God, but Noah is also the one who quaffs so deeply of the fruit of his own vines that he passes out cold. No less a one than Father Abraham himself—the exemplar of faith, God's friend—willingly abandons the wife of his bosom to Pharaoh's harem rather than risk his neck trying to save her. Jacob is a schemer and a crook, but he is also the one whom God visits with holy dreams and chooses over his blameless twin, Esau, to be Israel, the father of the twelve tribes and bearer of the promise. In religious art, the disciples of Jesus appear wearing halos, but in the Gospel story they are largely indistinguishable from everybody else—vying with each other for first place, continually missing the point, and, when the going gets rough, interested in nothing so much as saving their own skins down to the last man. Even Jesus himself comes through as far more complex and human than generations of piety have portrayed him. His fellow townspeople at Nazareth are so offended by him that they all but throw him headlong off a cliff. He speaks sharply if not downright heartlessly to his mother. When the full horror of what lies ahead comes through to him at Gethsemane, he sweats blood and pleads with God to let him off. As Mark tells it, the last words he ever spoke were not a ringing affirmation of faith but a cry of dereliction and despair.

Whatever else they may be, they are real human beings, in other words, and it is not the world of the Sunday school tract that they move through but a Dostoevskian world of darkness and light commingled, where suffering is sometimes redemptive and sometimes turns the heart to stone. It is a world where, although God is sometimes to be known through his life-giving presence, there are other times when he is known only by his appalling absence. The Bible is a compilation of stories of what happened to these human beings in such a world, and the stories are not only as different from one another as the people they are about but are told in almost as many different ways. Side by side in the opening pages of Genesis, for instance, there are two stories of the creation, one of them as stately and rhythmic as plainsong, the other as homely and human as the way you might tell it to your grandchildren. The groups of stories about Jacob and his son Joseph, told in as unpretentious a style as the second creation story, are nonetheless complex, full of psychological motivation and rich with detail; and in the case of Jacob in particular, no character in fiction is more multifaceted, fascinating, or believable.

In a different style altogether is, say, the story of Nebuchadnezzar's golden idol as it appears in the book of Daniel:

> King Nebuchadnezzar made an image of gold, whose height was sixty cubits and its breadth six cubits. He set it up on the plain of Dura, in the province of Babylon. Then King Nebuchadnezzar sent to assemble the satraps, the prefects, and the governors, the counselors, the treasurers, the justices, the magistrates, and all the officials of the provinces to come to the dedication of the image which King Nebuchadnezzar had set up. Then the satraps, the prefects, and the governors, the counselors, the treasurers, the justices, the magistrates, and all the officials of the provinces, were assembled for the dedication of the image that King Nebuchadnezzar had set up; and they stood before the image that Nebuchadnezzar had set up. And the herald proclaimed aloud, "You are commanded, O peoples, nations, and languages, that when you hear the sound of the horn, pipe, lyre, trigon, harp, bagpipe, and every kind of music, you are to fall down and worship the golden image that King Nebuchadnezzar has set up; and whoever does not fall down and worship shall immediately be cast into a burning fiery furnace." Therefore, as soon as all the peoples heard the sound of the horn, pipe, lyre, trigon, harp, bagpipe, and every kind of music, all the peoples, nations, and languages fell down and worshiped the golden image which King Nebuchadnezzar had set up. (Dan. 3:1–7)

Here all is sophisticated artistry—the wondrously satiric effect of those sonorous, deadpan repetitions of musical instruments and officials that continue to occur throughout the story, for example, and the way each time the words "the image which King Nebuchadnezzar set up" appear, they manage to convey again not only that all the setting up in the world will fail to prevent the golden image from someday tumbling down but that even on a Babylonian scale all human glory in general is a vain and transitory thing. Not even the book of Ecclesiastes conveys it better.

The author of the book of Job takes an ancient folktale and with a different kind of artistry entirely uses it as the frame for his fathomless poem, which comes closer to classic drama than any other work that Israel produced. The mission of Israel is to preach God's mercy to all nations, and to dramatize that point the author of the book of Jonah tells a story that seems to me to come closer than anything else in the Bible to high comedy—the recalcitrant prophet preaching salvation to the heathen while grumbling all the way, and God at the end pretending to mistake Jonah's anger at the sun for scorching him as pity for the shriveled vine that no longer gives him shade.

In the realm of historical as distinct from fictional narrative, the apparently eyewitness account in 2 Samuel 9–20 and 1 Kings 1–2 of the intrigues of David's court is as psychologically convincing, thorough, and full of life as any history the ancient world produced. One thinks also of the unforgettable portrait it provides of the ruthless, emotional, vulnerable character of David himself, who could order Uriah's murder without batting an eye yet give sanctuary to the crippled son of his dead friend Jonathan, and of the particularly vivid account of the last years of his reign when Bathsheba was nagging him about the succession and not even having the beautiful young Abishag for a bedmate was able to drive the chill of approaching death out of his old bones.

There could hardly be a greater miscellany of stories, characters, and styles than are contained in this massive volume. There could hardly be a greater divergence among the ways God is portrayed—vindictive and bellicose, loving and merciful—or the ways human beings are portrayed either and the ways God is shown as wanting them to be related to him and to each other. Yet for all of that, the whole great drama somehow holds together.

Genesis is part of what does it—the prologue in which the stage is set and all the major themes first introduced. And the major themes themselves are part—creation, covenant, law, sin, grace, weaving in and out through all the histories and stories, all the poems, psalms, prophecies. And the leading characters are part: God in his holiness pervading every page, and such heroes of the faith as the Letter to the Hebrews lists—Abraham and Sarah, Moses and Rahab, David and Samuel, and the prophets—who both appear in their places and then keep on reappearing in the long memory of their people. And for Christians, of course, Jesus holds it together because it is both his Bible and the Bible about him.

Finally I think it is possible to say that in spite of all its extraordinary variety, the Bible is held together by having a single plot. It is one that can be simply stated: God creates the world, the world gets lost; God seeks to restore the world to the glory for which he created it. That means that the Bible is a book about you and me, whom he also made and lost and continually seeks, so you might say that what holds it together more than anything else is us. You might add to that, of course, that of all the books that humanity has produced, it is the one that more than any other—and in more senses than one—also holds us together.

25.
Paul Sends His Love

The Greek rhetorician Alciphron wrote in his memoirs, "Never yet have I been to Corinth, for I know pretty well the beastly kind of life the rich enjoy there and the wretchedness of the poor," and—from the time of Aristophanes on—the city could even claim the distinction of having its name made into a verb. To "corinthianize" meant to go to the dogs. Situated on the narrow isthmus that connects Greece proper with the Peloponnesus, it was a major center for trade and shipping. Its population was largely immigrant, and sailors from everywhere under the sun prowled its streets bringing their gods with them—Isis and Serapis from Egypt, Astarte from Syria, Artemis from Ephesus, to name just a few. The most striking geographical feature of the place was a steeply rising peak known as Acrocorinth, and on its summit—to symbolize her ascendancy both over all rivals and in the hearts of the citizenry—there stood a temple to the goddess Aphrodite, which according to the Greek historian Strabo employed the services of some one thousand sacred prostitutes. "Not every man should go to Corinth" was an ancient byword whose reasonableness seems beyond challenge.

Saint Paul should have taken it to heart. Around A.D. 50 he arrived there for the first time, and the book of Acts gives a brief but vivid account of the consequences. He went to live with a Jewish couple named Priscilla and Aquila—leather workers like him—who had left Rome when the emperor Claudius ordered all Jews out. They introduced him to the local synagogue, and as a distinguished guest he was invited to address the congregation. His zealous promotion of the claim that a Nazarene named Jesus, only some twenty years earlier crucified in Jerusalem, was the Messiah and Lord of life of ancient Jewish expectation so horrified some of the synagogue leaders that they told him, a blasphemer and heretic, to leave and never show his face again. This he did, but not before taking with him a number of Jews he had converted to the new faith including a man named Crispus, the synagogue's ruler. In the house of one Titus Justus, who to add insult to injury was the synagogue's next-door neighbor, he set up a Christian church where for a year and a half he preached the gospel until he decided to continue his missionary activities elsewhere. This journey eventually landed him across the Aegean in the city of Ephesus, and it was there a few years later that he received from the converts he had left behind in Corinth a letter that First Corinthians is in part an answer to.

Paul's responses to the specific questions they posed and to the local problems they asked him to advise them on by no means constitute the most important or interesting part of the Letter, but they give a rich sense of the kind of document it was written to be. Paul was not primarily concerned with setting forth religious doctrine as he did in Romans and Galatians. He made no attempt to present an orderly résumé of the Christian faith. He was simply trying to set his Corinthian friends straight on the concrete matters that immediately concerned them and only in the process of doing that got sidetracked into some of the most eloquent, moving, and self-revelatory passages he ever wrote.

You can't help wishing you knew more about those concrete matters. There is just enough here to tantalize. Was the Sosthenes he mentions in his opening salutation the same Sosthenes whom the Corinthian Jews beat up after their unsuccessful attempt to get Paul into trouble with the Roman proconsul Gallio, who threw the whole pack of them out of court saying in so many words that the internecine squabbles of the Jews bored him to death? And how about Chloe, whose "people"—slaves? household members?—brought Paul news in Ephesus of certain goings-on that the Corinthians themselves had apparently chosen not to mention in their letter? She seems to have been one of the few well-heeled members of a congregation, which otherwise, Paul tells us, consisted mainly of the lower orders, the more or less down and out. It would be especially interesting to know more about Apollos, an Alexandrian Jew who preached in Corinth after Paul's departure. Is it possible that Paul's disparagement of philosophical eloquence and, in Second Corinthians, his acerbic reference to "super-apostles" are allusions to him? Is it conceivable that Luther was right in identifying him, not Paul, as the one who wrote the eloquent Letter to the Hebrews? Or, as others have believed, was it Priscilla, Paul's hostess, who wrote it? Her name is mentioned ahead of her husband's in the passage in Acts that describes them as the ones who took Apollos aside and "expounded to him the way of God more accurately" (18:26), suggesting perhaps that, theologically speaking anyway, she was the one who called the shots in the family. In any case they were both of them with Paul in Ephesus when he wrote his Letter, and he sends their greetings back home along with his own.

But if Paul gives us only a fragmentary picture of the dramatis personae, he leaves us in no doubt as to the general situation they were involved in. It is clear that one way or another all hell had broken loose. Foreshadowing the fate of Christendom from then on, the small church had already split up into a number of factions. One of them followed Paul himself, another his successor Apollos, another the apostle Peter, and a fourth Christ, whoever these last could have been, possibly a group of Christian Gnostics who denied the humanity of Jesus. There had also sprung up a group of charismatics, or *pneumatikoi,* who claimed to have such spiritual gifts as speaking in tongues and "prophecy" and who seem to have been given not only to playing at spiritual one-upmanship with each other but to looking down their noses at pretty much everybody else. One member of the congregation and his stepmother were living together as man and wife despite the fact that Roman as well as Jewish law condemned such a relationship. Others were gorging themselves and getting drunk at the Lord's Supper, which at this early point was not the ritual wafer and sip of wine that it later became but still a full meal that the whole church ate together presumably in the house of one of its members. And so on. Things couldn't have been much worse. Paul wrote to them: "But I, brethren, could not address you as spiritual men, but as men of the flesh, as babes in Christ.... For while there is jealousy and strife among you, are you not of the flesh and behaving like ordinary men?" (3:1–3).

Jealousy and strife were almost the least of it. The church in Corinth, and everywhere else for that matter, was indeed made up of ordinary men and women who, spiritually speaking, hadn't cut their first teeth yet. It was slaves, dock hands, shopkeepers, potters, housewives, bronze workers, leather workers, and what have you. They were no better than anybody else and at least in one sense worse because, "sanctified in Christ Jesus" as Paul believed them to be, so much more was expected of them and should have been forthcoming. They were in fact Christ's body, as he wrote them using one of his most enduring metaphors—Christ's eyes, ears, hands—but the way they were carrying on could only leave Christ bloodshot, ass-eared, and all thumbs to carry on God's work in a fallen world. What came forth from them was just the kind of wretched tangle they were in at the moment and, harder still for him to deal with, the wretchedness it gave rise to within himself. It is this that is in many ways what First Corinthians is essentially about—his sense of futility and despair at war with his exultant hope, the terrible tension between the *in spite of* and the *because of* of his restless and often anguished faith.

He fielded their questions as best he could—questions about sex and marriage, about the role of women in church, about whether or not it was proper to eat meat, which in a Gentile city like Corinth had probably all been dedicated to some godling or other down to the last lamb chop. His answers tend to be pedagogic, avuncular, appealing more to tradition than to theology. It was better to marry than to burn, he told them in a phrase that has echoed down the centuries. Women should be veiled in church and not speak. It couldn't matter less that the meat they ate had already been offered up to Serapis or Astarte—that was just the sort of religious pedantry that Christ had set them free from—but if by eating it they shook the faith of some Christian friend to whom it did matter, then of course they should abstain for the friend's sake. But there is no mistaking that for Paul the real question lay deeper down than any of these. "The word of the cross is folly to those who are perishing," he wrote (1:18). Was it possible that it was folly, period? It seems clear enough that in his heart of hearts that was the question that haunted him above all others.

The message that a convicted felon was the bearer of God's forgiving and transforming love was hard enough for anybody to swallow and for some especially so. For hellenized sophisticates—the Greeks, as Paul puts it—it could only seem absurd. What uglier, more supremely inappropriate symbol of, say, Plato's Beautiful and Good could there be than a crucified Jew? And for the devout Jew, what more scandalous image of the Davidic king-messiah, before whose majesty all the nations were at last to come to heel? Paul understood both reactions well. "The folly of what we preach," he called it (1:21), and he knew it was folly not just to the intellectually and religiously inclined but to the garden variety Corinthians who had no particular pretensions in either direction but simply wanted some reasonably plausible god who would stand by them when the going got rough. Paul's God didn't look much like what they were after, and Paul was the first to admit it. Who stood by Jesus when the going got rough, after all? He even goes so far as to speak of "the foolishness of God" (1:25). What other way could you describe a deity who chose as his followers not the movers and shakers who could build him a temple to make Aphrodite's look like two cents but the weak, the despised, the ones who were foolish even as their God was and poor as church mice?

To pray for your enemies, to worry about the poor when you have worries enough of your own, to start becoming yourself fully by giving of yourself prodigally to whoever needs you, to love your neighbors when an intelligent fourth-grader could tell you that the way to get ahead in the world is to beat your neighbors to the draw every chance you get—that was what this God asked, Paul wrote. That was who this God was. That was who Jesus was. Paul is passionate in his assertion, of course, that in the long run it is such worldly wisdom as the intelligent fourth-grader's that is foolish and the sublime foolishness of God that is ultimately wise, and nobody heard him better than William Shakespeare did when he wove the rich fabric of *King Lear* around precisely this paradox. It is the Fool, Edgar, Kent, Cordelia, Gloucester—the foolish, weak, despised ones—who in their fatal loyalty to the ruined king triumph, humanly speaking, over the powerful cunning of Regan, Goneril, Edmund, and the rest of them. "Upon such sacrifices, my Cordelia, the gods themselves throw incense," Lear says to Cordelia—that is their triumph—just as, before him, Paul quoted Isaiah's: "What no eye has seen, nor ear heard, nor the heart of man conceived, [that is] what God has prepared for those who love him" (2:9).

But Paul was as aware, as Shakespeare was, that when the final curtain rings down, the ones who loved this God of love end up just as dead as the ones who never gave him the time of day, and he was aware that any Corinthians shopping around for a new religion were aware of it too. So it was a matter of not only what could look more foolish than the gospel he preached but perhaps even of what could actually *be* more foolish. Terrible as that possibility was, he did not flinch from putting it down in black and white. "If for this life only we have hoped in Christ," he wrote, "we are of all men most to be pitied" (15:19).

He must have considered the possibility that, as Edmund believed, the only God worth a hoot is the god of raw Nature, that it is the fittest not the fairest who survive longest, and that in the long run the only law that matters is the law of the jungle. "If Christ has not been raised," he flatly said, "then our preaching is in vain and your faith is in vain.... If the dead are not raised, 'Let us eat and drink, for tomorrow we die'" (15:14, 32). It is impossible to read these words without having the sense that he is speaking here not just theologically, apodictically, but personally, out of his own darkest misgivings. "We are fools for Christ's sake," he wrote (4:10), meaning fools as holy as Christ himself was holy. But if Christ ended up as dead as everybody else, then he knew they were also damned fools and Christ himself had been fooled most tragically. "To the present hour we hunger and thirst, we are ill-clad and buffeted and homeless.... We have become, and are now, as the refuse of the world, the offscouring of all things" (4:11–13). That is how he described his life as apostle to the Gentiles, but it was the inner buffeting and homelessness that were the worst of it.

Paul was no beauty if the description of him in the apocryphal *Acts of Paul and Thecla* is to be believed: "Bald-headed, bowlegged, strongly built, a man small in size, with meeting eyebrows, with a rather large nose. His letters are strong, but his bodily presence is weak." You see those meeting eyebrows knotted, see the way he holds his bald head in his hands, his rather large nose lost in shadow, as he writes out of his grimness. But something extraordinary keeps him going on those bowlegs of his anyway, in spite of everything. He has himself seen Christ after the crucifixion. That is what keeps him going through thick and thin. That is what keeps him firing off his letters like rockets.

In this Letter he does not describe what it was like to see Christ; he simply states it as a fact, but it is described elsewhere, and doubtless he told them about it in Corinth when he was there, about the light that blinded him for days afterward, the voice calling him by name. He never forgot the sheer and giddy grace of it, of Christ appearing to him of all people, professional persecutor of Christians as he was at the time; of Christ not only forgiving him but enlisting him, signing him up as apostle to the Gentiles. Everything Paul ever did or wrote from that moment on flamed up out of that extraordinary encounter on the Damascus road. And there was something else if anything even more extraordinary. If death was not the end of Christ, then it was not to be the end of any of them. "For as in Adam all die, so also in Christ shall all be made alive" (15:22). They were all of them in Christ—one of his favorite phrases—as Christ was also in all of them, and thus life, not death, was to be the last thing for them too. Nor was it to be some disembodied life either, as the Greek dualists argued, with their dim view of bodies generally, but life as themselves, wearing some marvelous new version of corporeality, not of flesh and blood any longer, but of "spirit ... imperishable ... raised in glory" (15:42–44).

"Lo! I tell you a mystery." His tone becomes lyric, exultant. "We shall all be changed, in a moment, in the twinkling of an eye, at the last trumpet.... Thanks be to God, who gives us the victory.... Therefore, my beloved brethren, be steadfast, immovable, always abounding in the work of the Lord, knowing that in the Lord your labor is not in vain" (15:51, 57–58). The great nostrils swell.

That is the farthest and deepest his eyes have seen, farther even than the depths of the dark, the brightest thing he has to tell. Then in the next breath he is down to brass tacks again, explaining to them how the money for the Jerusalem church is to be collected, how it is to be sent there, where he plans to travel next and when. Who knows when the last trumpet will sound? In the meanwhile, for all of them, there is much work to be done. Yet in the meanwhile too—he has already written them of this—there is much to rejoice in on this side of the great Joy.

There is among other things the Lord's Supper, which some of the Corinthians have been turning into a three-ring circus. He berates them at first. The sentences are short and sharp. They have behaved outrageously. He is outraged. "What shall I say to you?" (11:22). Then abruptly the language changes and his tone with it. The words start to come with a kind of twilight hush to them. They have an almost dazed quality, as if he is so caught up in the scene he is describing that he is more there than here. He hadn't actually been there, of course, but he knew some who had been—like Peter, for instance, his old colleague and sometime adversary. Peter must have spoken of what he remembered about the last time they had all of them eaten together with Jesus, and it is such memories as his that Paul is presumably drawing on here though that is not what he says. He "received [it] from the Lord," is what he says (11:23). Who knows what he means—that it was the significance of that last meal, the full truth of those last words, that he received perhaps. In any case, he remembers details, remembers that the night of his betrayal was when it happened, remembers how the bread was taken, broken, thanked for, remembers the wine. It is the first time you realize fully how few years had gone by since it all happened. There were men and women around still who had eaten and drunk with Jesus if not at that final meal, who knew the sound of his voice, could have picked him out in a crowd. Paul remembers what he said. That the bread was his body. The wine was his blood. It was he himself they were eating and drinking, taking his life into their lives, into them. This meal was their proclamation of what his death had done and meant, and for anybody to make a drunken shambles of it was to risk sickness and death. It was their consolation and the Lord's great gift to them till he came back again in his glory. And there were other gifts.

Not even in the Gospels is there a more familiar passage than the thirteenth chapter of First Corinthians. "Though I speak with the tongues of men and of angels ... when I was a child, I spake as a child ... through a glass darkly ..." (KJV). Words as familiar as these are like coins worn smooth with long handling. After a while it is hard to tell where they came from or what they are worth. Paul has been speaking about spiritual gifts—prophecy, tongues, healing, miracles, and so on—and making the point that they should not be the cause of still further divisiveness, people gifted one way disparaging people gifted another. He sees all Christians as parts of Christ's body and each part in its own way as necessary as every other. "The eye cannot say to the hand, 'I have no need of you.'" Each gift is to be cherished.

"But," he says then, "earnestly desire the higher gifts" (12:21, 31) and at that point sets off into what turned out to be perhaps the most memorable words he ever wrote.

The highest gift of all is *agape,* he says. Without it even faith, almsgiving, martyrdom are mere busyness and even great wisdom doesn't amount to a hill of beans. The translators of the King James Version render the Greek word as "charity," which in seventeenth-century usage was a happy choice—charity as the beneficence of the rich to the poor, the lucky to the unlucky, the powerful to the weak, the lovely to the unlovely. But since to our age the word all too often suggests a cheerless and demeaning handout, modern translators have usually rendered it as "love." But *agape* love is not to be confused with *eros* love. That is what Paul is at such pains to make clear here.

Eros love is love that reaches upwards. It is love for what we need to fill our emptiness, love for what is lovely and lovable. It is Dante's love for Beatrice as well as Cleopatra's for Antony, the child's love for the parent, humankind's love for God. William Blake engraved the picture of a tiny human figure with a ladder pitched toward the moon and underneath, in block capitals, the words "I WANT! I WANT!" Those are the words that *eros* always speaks. Not so with *agape. Agape* does not want. It gives. It is not empty. It is full to overflowing. Paul strains to get the distinction right. *Agape* is patient; *eros* champs at the bit. *Agape* puts up with anything; *eros* insists on having things its own way. *Agape* is kind—never jealous, boastful, rude. It does not love because, but simply loves—the way the rain falls or the sun shines. It "bears all things," up to and including even its own crucifixion. And it has extraordinary power.

The power of *agape*—otherwise quite powerless—is perhaps nowhere better seen than in the tale of *Beauty and the Beast,* in which Beauty does not love the Beast because he is beautiful but makes him beautiful by loving him. Ultimately, in other words, *agape* is God's love for humankind, and only as God's gift are humans enabled at rare moments to love that way themselves—transformingly, unconditionally, no matter what. Thus when Paul says, "Love never ends," he is not being sentimental or merely rhetorical. There is no doubt that *eros* ends. Even in its noblest forms it ends when the desired becomes undesirable or when desire ends. *Agape,* on the other hand, is as without end as God is without end, because it is of the essence of God. That is what Paul experienced on the Damascus road, where he found that the One who had every cause to deplore him loved him. For as long as the moment lasted anyway, the beetle-browed, bowlegged Christian-baiter put away his own childish things and in an unutterable instant saw Truth itself not through a glass darkly for once but face-to-face; understood, as he put it, even as he was understood.

He himself was the first to admit that he remained in many ways as much of a mess as the rest of us—full of anguished doubts and depressions, hostilities, exaltations, hang-ups, whatever he meant by "the thorn in the flesh," which he interpreted in his Second Letter to Corinth as God's way of keeping him "from being too elated." The bitter and the better of him, it is all there in the words with which he closes his Letter, the words he tells us he is writing with his own hand.

"If any one has no love for the Lord, let him be accursed. Our Lord, come. The grace of the Lord be with you" (16:21). A malediction, a prayer, a benediction, in that order. They are all mixed up together as God knows they were all mixed up in Paul himself. But then, "My love be with you all in Christ Jesus. Amen" (16:24), so that the very last thing of all that he does is send them his love—*agape* is again the word he uses—the most precious thing he ever received, the most precious thing he ever had to give.

26

Adolescence and
the Stewardship of Pain

All the dictionaries agree that the word "adolescent" derives from the Latin verb *adolescere*, which is made up of *ad*, meaning "toward," and *alescere*, meaning "to grow." The word designates human beings who are in the process of growing up. It is as simple as that. Adolescents are the ones who are on their way to becoming what we call adults, from the past participle of *adolescere;* adults, in other words, are the having-grown-up ones, the ones who have the messy and complicated process behind them. Adolescents, that is to say, are on their way to becoming what adults by definition already are.

What I like about that etymology is that it gets us away from the sense of adolescent as a pejorative—"Don't be so adolescent," we say, or "That is a very adolescent way of looking at things"—and makes it a purely clinical term. As larva becomes pupa becomes adult in the insect world, so child becomes adolescent becomes adult, or grown-up, in the human world. It is healthy to be reminded that we are as much a part of the natural order of things as the caterpillar. It is reassuring to be told that for all the mysteries and ambiguities of the human condition, we can at a certain level be as clearly categorized as the common housefly.

What I don't like about it, of course, is that it makes everything sound too tidy. We are as much a part of the animal kingdom as any other animal, but we are also more mysterious and ambiguous than the rest of them, or at least that is the way we experience ourselves. Maybe the process of growing up is no messier or more complicated for us than it is for the dung beetle, but it feels messier and more complicated. Physiologically we leave adolescence behind for adulthood. We look like adults. We sound like adults. We move around through the world more or less like adults. But is the process as comprehensive as the Latin term indicates? Have we joined the ranks of the having-grown-up as conclusively as the past participle suggests? Have we put our growing up behind us as the butterfly puts behind the cocoon? Physiologically yes. Intellectually maybe. But how about psychologically, emotionally? How about sexually? How about spiritually? I will not try to answer for anybody else, but I have no hesitation about answering for myself.

Let me put it this way. My technical adolescence is many decades behind me, and the youngest of my three children is about forty, so that for me their adolescence is mostly a memory too. I taught at Lawrenceville for five years and at Phillips Exeter for nine, so that for a significant time I remained in fairly close touch with the adolescent world well after my own official exit from it. But I haven't taught in a secondary school since 1967, which is also a long time ago. In other words, I have no qualifications for speaking about adolescence with anything like authority except in one respect. I am in my eightieth year. I have fathered children and have ten grandchildren. I have written books. I have letters after my name and an ecclesiastical title before it. I can get into movies and motels at a reduced rate. But to call me an adult or grown-up is an oversimplification at best and a downright misnomer at worst. I am not a past participle but a present participle, even a dangling participle. I am not a having-grown-up one but a growing-up one, a groping-up one, not even sure much of the time just where my growing and groping are taking me or where they are supposed to be taking me. I am a verbal adjective in search of a noun to latch onto, a grower in search of a self to grow into. As far as the outer world is concerned, my acne cleared up around 1945, but in terms of my inner world, it is still with me to add to my general embarrassment and confusion about myself. I speak about adolescence with authority because in many ways I still am in the throes of it. That is my only qualification for addressing myself to the subject here. I am a hybrid, an adult adolescent to whom neither term alone does full justice. So much for the official etymology—useful up to a point and then to be laid aside, at least for me.

Let me put forth an alternate etymology—entirely spurious, but my own. It has no basis in linguistic fact, but seems truer to the essence of my own experience of adolescence than the official etymology. Let me suggest with total inaccuracy that the word adolescent is made up of the Latin preposition *ad*, meaning "toward," and the Latin noun *dolor*, meaning "pain." Thus "adolescent" becomes a term that designates human beings who are in above all else a painful process, more specifically those who are in the process of discovering pain itself, of trying somehow to come to terms with pain, to figure out how to deal with pain, not just how to survive pain but how to turn it to some human and creative use in their own encounters with it. Thus adolescents, as in the official etymology, are ones who are growing to be sure but who, in terms of my spurious etymology, are growing in this one specific area of human experience. Adolescents are Adam and Eve in the process of tasting the forbidden fruit and discovering that in addition to good, there is also evil, that in addition to the joy of being alive, there is also the sadness and hurt of being alive and being themselves. Adolescents are Gautama the Buddha as he recognizes the first of the Four Noble Truths, which is that life is suffering, that at any given moment life can be lots of happy things too, but that suffering is universal and inevitable and that to face that reality and to come to terms with that reality is the beginning of wisdom and at the heart of what human growing is all about.

There is no denying that pre-adolescent children know pain too. Abused children, abandoned children, starving or sick children, children who one way or another suffer at home or at school—the newspapers are full of horrors, and I doubt there is one of us who cannot point to the pain of our own childhood. But remembering myself as a child, I believe that at that early stage of our lives, we have a kind of natural immunity not to the painfulness of what is happening certainly, but to the realization that by its nature life itself is painful. The little boy is beaten up by the school bully. The little girl sees her kitten run over. The mother dies. But by the time the next day comes around or the next week, children seem somehow to have been able to cast it off. Psychiatry tells us that maybe the place they cast it is a place deep inside themselves where it will cause them all kinds of trouble in years to come, but at least for as long as the years of childhood last, it is as if it has gone away for good, and the battered child sits in front of the TV screen with a bag of popcorn in her lap as self-forgetful and enraptured by what she sees as if one of the eyes she sees it with is not bruised and swollen from where her father whaled her. Children seem to come into the world with a capacity for living a day at a time. A bad day comes. Then maybe a day that is not so bad or even a good day. Then maybe a bad one again. But by and large children do not seem to keep score. Adolescence, as I etymologize the term, starts when score keeping starts.

In a novel that I wrote close to twenty years ago, I described the following brief scene based on an incident that took place during my days as teacher at Lawrenceville in the 1950s. It is the teacher himself who is the narrator, a young man named Antonio Parr:

I remember going on at excessive length to a group of ninth-graders about what irony meant. I think most of them understood it well enough before I started, but just to keep the silence at bay I rattled on about it anyway. I talked about outer meaning and inner meaning. I said that an ironic statement was a statement where you said one thing but to people who had their ears open said another. I explained that when Mark Antony in his funeral oration called the Romans who had murdered Caesar honorable men, he was being ironic because his inner meaning was that they were a bunch of hoods, and when that remark didn't seem to get anything started, I waded in deeper still. I said that in addition to ironic statements, you also had ironic situations. Their silence deepened. I remember then a small, fat boy named Stephen Kulak. He was young for the ninth grade and looked it, with a round, pink face and the judicious gaze of a child. He said he saw how something you said could mean two things, but he didn't see how something that happened could, so I reached down into my own silence and pulled out the first example that came to hand. I said suppose you had a bride on her wedding day. Suppose she was all dressed up in her white dress and wedding veil, and then on her way to the church a car ran into her and she was killed. That was an ironic situation, I said. It was ironic because on the same day that she was starting out on a new life, her life stopped. Two things. Now did he see what ironic meant? I remember watching him as he sat there at his desk in a Red Baron sweatshirt trying to puzzle through my lugubrious illustration until finally in some dim and memorable way his pink face seemed to change and he said, "I get it now. It's a kind of joke," and I could see that he really had gotten it, that there in a classroom with the Pledge of Allegiance framed on the wall and Christmas wreaths made of red and green construction paper Scotch-taped to the window panes, Stephen Kulak had learned from kindly old Mr. Parr, who had a hard time keeping his mouth shut, what irony was, and jokes, and life itself if you made the mistake of keeping your ears open. Once you get the reading and writing out of the way, I suppose what you teach children in an English class is, God help you, yourself.*

Much as I remember doing myself, Antonio Parr, the narrator, feels guilty about having been the one to teach the little boy the first of the Buddha's Four Noble Truths, but he might have drawn comfort from the knowledge that life itself would have taught it to him soon enough anyway and maybe not so gently. Maybe the teacher's main business is to teach gently the inevitability of pain. Themselves adolescents in my sense of the word—scorekeepers of *dolor*—maybe teachers have no higher calling than to help the Stephen Kulaks who come their way not just to see what the score is—forewarned is forearmed—but to help them also to see pain as value, the possibility of their pain's becoming one of their richest treasures.

As the Chorus in Shakespeare's *Henry V* puts it, describing the eve of the battle of Agincourt: "Now entertain conjecture of a time / When creeping murmurs and the poring dark / Fills the wide vessel of the universe." Let us instead entertain conjecture of the murmuring dark of a more obscure but in its way no less momentous battle. The place is the house, that corner

---

The Book of Bebb (New York: Atheneum, 1979; San Francisco: HarperSanFrancisco, 1990), p. 313.

of the wide vessel of the universe, where at the age of eight or nine I lived with my parents and younger brother. Money was short as it was in many families in those days. My father was drinking too much, though in every other way he was a conscientious, caring young man, handsome and full of charm, who over the years had kept changing jobs in the effort to do better by his wife and two small sons. My mother was a beautiful, demanding, discontented young woman who was in many ways a good mother but in most ways not a very good wife.

After a good deal of drinking one evening, my father decided to take the car and go driving off with it somewhere. My mother told him that he was in no condition to drive and wouldn't let him have the keys. I had already gone to bed, and she came upstairs to give the keys to me. She told me that under no circumstances was I to let my father have them. Somehow or other my father found out that I had them—I can only assume that she told him—and came upstairs to ask me to give them to him. He sat down on one twin bed, and I was lying on the one next to it with the covers over my head and the keys in my hand under the pillow. For what seemed an endless time, he sat there pleading with me to let him have them, and I lay there under the covers not saying anything because I no more knew what to say than I knew what to do or to be. I believe that at one point my mother came into the room where we were and excoriated him for humiliating himself in front of his own son. I don't remember how the little domestic Agincourt ended, but I think I finally just went to sleep with the sound of my father's pleading in my ears and the keys, which I never gave him, still clenched tight in my fist under the pillow. The child that I was certainly felt the pain of it as attested to by the fact that I have so long remembered it, but at the time, with the resilience of a child, I simply cast it off together with many other painful scenes like it. Bad days happened and good days happened, and with the capacity of a child for letting life run off me like water off a duck's back, I took them as they came. I lived in the garden where the tree of the knowledge of good and evil grew, but I hadn't yet tasted it.

It wasn't until I was some fifty years deep into my adolescence that I described the scene in a short autobiographical novel called *The Wizard's Tide*, and one day a couple of summers ago I read those few pages out loud to a group of some sixty people or so at a religious retreat in western Texas. I could see that they were moved by it as I read it, not because I had written it with any particular eloquence, but because, as best I could, I had written it in the simple language of a child in a way that must have awakened in them similar painful memories of their own childhoods. When I finished reading, a man named Howard Butt came up and said a few words to me that opened my eyes to something I had never clearly seen before. He said, "You have had a good deal of pain in your life, and you have been a good steward of it."

I did not hear his words as a compliment, although I suppose that is the way he meant them. I could take no credit for being a good steward of my pain—whatever that might mean—because I had had no idea that that was what I was being and had had no intention of being it. But his words caught me off guard and have haunted me ever since. I had always thought of stewardship as a rather boring, churchy word that the minister trots out on Budget Sunday or when launching the Every Member Canvass. I knew that a steward is a caretaker of some kind or other, the person who takes care of, takes care with, money particularly, or real estate, or the stateroom of an ocean liner. But what did it mean to take care of, take care with, the hurtful things that happen to you? How do you go about being the steward of, of all things, your pain?

Suffering is the undercurrent and bedrock of life, the Buddha said. Life is adventure and challenge and community. To live is to taste and touch, to smell and see and listen to the good things of the earth and to rejoice in them. It is to make friends and to be a friend. It is to create. It is to search for God if you are religiously inclined and, if you are not, to search for something in place of God to give meaning and purpose and value to your scattered days. But you become an adolescent at the moment when you begin to understand that what the Buddha meant is that beneath all of this, inextricably woven into the rich fabric of all of this, there are not just the sad things that happen one by one as they do in childhood, but there is sadness itself—the *lachrymae rerum* as Lucretius puts it, the "tears of things," the tears that all things can bring to your eyes when you once realize that dissolution and loss are to be the end of all of them, including the happiest. Adolescents are the ones who, whether fourteen years old or eighty years old, are in the process of growing into that knowledge and, if they are ever to become more or less grown-up human beings at last, growing by means of it.

There are many ways of dealing with your pain, and perhaps the most tempting of them all is to forget about it, to hide it not just from the world but also from yourself. It is the way of the stoic, the stiff upper lip. It is the way that is characteristic maybe especially of white Anglo-Saxon Protestants, WASPs, who are taught from infancy that they are to keep their troubles to themselves and that the eighth deadly sin, and one of the deadliest, is self-pity: that it is perfectly proper to pity other people when sorrow strikes, but when you yourself are stricken, you are supposed to keep it under your hat. When the father drinks too much. When the mother in desperation turns into a terrible-tongued shrew. When the child lives in terror. When the marriage comes apart or the business fails or the exam is hopelessly flunked, the rule is not to let yourself feel it any more than you can help, not to trust anybody with the truth of how it hurts, and maybe most of all not to talk about it, certainly not outside of the family and eventually not even there, not even to yourself.

To bury your pain is a way of surviving your pain and therefore by no means to be dismissed out of hand. It is a way that I venture to say has at one time or another served and continues to serve all of us well. But it is not a way of growing. It is not a way of moving through adolescence into adulthood. If you manage to put behind you the painful things that happen to you as if they never really happened or didn't really matter all that much when they did, then the deepest and most human things you have in you to become are not apt to happen either. It was not for many years that the small boy with the keys in his fist came to understand something of the Agincourt that he and his parents and kid brother had long ago all been involved in, with all the chances there might have been for them to be brave, to be kind, to be wise, to be a family; maybe even, on the far side of the murmuring dark of anger and tears, to be reconciled and healed.

The alternative to ignoring your pain is of course to be trapped in it. One thinks of Miss Havisham in Dickens's *Great Expectations,* jilted by her lover and living the rest of her life in a darkened room with the wedding dress she was never married in turning to rags upon her and the wedding cake moldering uneaten among the cobwebs. Caricature as she is, she can stand for all those whose pain somewhere along the line stops them dead in their tracks, leaving them to feed endlessly on their own bitterness in a world of enemies, none of whom is as deadly as they are to themselves. Or, turning again to Dickens, we find the professional widow Mrs. Gummidge, in *David Copperfield,* sniveling into her old black silk handkerchief and croaking her endless dirge of "I'm a lone lorn creetur'" as the one way she thinks she has of winning attention and sympathy because after years of wallowing in her pain she believes she has no other way of winning it. We don't need Dickens to caricature the way we can all of us use pain also as an excuse for failure. If only the terrible thing hadn't happened—the unhappy childhood, the weak heart, the financial disaster—there's no telling what wonderful things we could have done with our lives. In such ways as these, and more, we do the best we can with the worst that happens to us, and insofar as such ways keep the worst from destroying us, there is no denying their usefulness. But although they may help us to survive, they do not help us to grow, to change, to be transformed into something more nearly approaching full personhood. Like the princess in the fairy tale, we take the straw we are given and thatch the roof with it to keep the weather out, but we do not do what we might do, which is to spin it into gold.

What does it mean to be a *steward* of your pain, as Howard Butt put it? It is at least one of the subjects I think Jesus himself is talking about in one of the strangest and in a way darkest of the parables he told—strange because it turns out so differently from the way we would have supposed, and dark because there is a note of such apparent harshness and unfairness in it. According to the Gospel of Matthew, he told it as follows:

> For it will be as when a man going on a journey called his servants and entrusted to them his property; to one he gave five talents, to another two, to another one, to each according to his ability. Then he went away. He who had received the five talents went at once and traded with them; and he made five talents more. So also, he who had the two talents made two talents more. But he who had received the one talent went and dug in the ground and hid his master's money. Now after a long time the master of those servants came and settled accounts with them. And he who had received the five talents came

forward, bringing five talents more, saying, "Master, you delivered to me five talents; here I have made five talents more." His master said to him, "Well done, good and faithful servant; you have been faithful over a little, I will set you over much; enter into the joy of your master." And he also who had the two talents came forward saying, "Master, you delivered to me two talents; here I have made two talents more." His master said to him, "Well done, good and faithful servant; you have been faithful over a little, I will set you over much; enter into the joy of your master." He also who had received the one talent came forward, saying, "Master, I knew you to be a hard man, reaping where you did not sow, and gathering where you did not winnow; so I was afraid, and I went and hid your talent in the ground. Here you have what is yours." But his master answered him, "You wicked and slothful servant! You knew that I reap where I have not sowed, and gather where I have not winnowed? Then you ought to have invested my money with the bankers, and at my coming I should have received what was my own with interest. So take the talent from him, and give it to him who has the ten talents. For to every one who has will more be given, and he will have abundance; but from him who has not, even what he has will be taken away. And cast the worthless servant into the outer darkness; there men will weep and gnash their teeth." (25:14–30)

Bad times happen, good times happen; life itself happens and happens to all of us in different ways and with different mixtures of good and bad, pain and pleasure, luck and unluck. As I read it, that is what the parable is essentially about, and the question the parable poses is, what do we do with these mixed lives we are given, these hands we are so unequally dealt by God, if we believe in God, or by circumstance or by our genes or by whatever you want to interpret the rich man as representing? To use the mercenary terms of the parable itself, how do we get the most out of what we are so variously and richly and hair-raisingly given? It is the pain we are given that interests me most here and that I suspect must have interested Jesus too, because God knows he was dealt plenty of it himself during his thirty years on this planet, give or take. Two of the servants do one thing with it, and the third servant does something very different with it and with radically different results. What happened to the third servant, of course, is where the harshness and darkness come in.

The third servant takes what he is given—for our purposes let us focus particularly on the pain he is given—and buries it. He takes it and hides it in a hole in the ground and thereby, I would suggest, becomes the blood brother and soul mate of virtually all of us at one time or another. The small boy buries his hand under the pillow. Miss Havisham buries herself in the darkened room. Mrs. Gummidge buries her face in her black lace handkerchief. We bury for years the tragic memory, the secret fear, the unspoken loneliness, the unspeakable desire. "I was afraid," is what the third servant says when the rich man confronts him years later, and he had good reason to be. We all of us have good reason to be afraid because life is scary as hell, and I do not use that term lightly. "I knew you to be a hard man," the servant says, "reaping where you did not sow, and gathering where you did not winnow," and he is speaking no more or less than the truth. God is hard as well as merciful. Life is hard as well as marvelous. Hard and terrible things happen to us in this world that call us to be strong and brave and wise, to be heroes, when it is all we can do just to keep our heads above water. So we dig the hole in the ground, in ourselves, in our busyness or wherever else we dig it, and hide the terrible things in it, which is another way of saying that we hide ourselves from the terrible things. It seems as unfair to blame us for doing it as it seems unfair to blame the third servant because it is a way of keeping afloat, of saving ourselves from drowning, and yet the words of the parable are devastating. "Wicked and slothful" is what the rich man calls the third servant, who in so many ways can stand for us all—wicked in burying what he should have held to the light and made something of; slothful because playing it safe is another way of not really playing it at all. And then the rich man takes away what little the servant was given in the first place and says he is to be cast "into the outer darkness where men weep and gnash their teeth." It is an extraordinary story to come from the one who has been called the Light of the World and Prince of Peace.

I think what the parable means is that the buried pain in particular and all the other things we tend to bury along with pain, including joy, which tends to get buried too when we start burying things, that the buried life is itself darkness and weeping and gnashing of teeth and the one who casts us into it is no one other than ourselves. To bury your life is to stop growing, as for years a deep part of the small boy with his hand under the pillow stopped growing and the two old women out of Dickens with him. To bury your life is to have it wither in the ground and diminish. It is to be deeply alone. It is to be less alive than you were to start with. That may sound harsh and dark and unfair, but it is the way things are. It is the truth.

The other two servants are the ones, according to the parable, who get it right and do what they should do with what they have been given. The rich man calls them "good and faithful servants," and what he means apparently is that their goodness is their faithfulness—their faith in him, in life itself, which enables them to take it as it comes, the pain of it with the rest of it, and instead of burying it, to live it fully with the faith that one way or another it will work out. Taking the various sums of money they had been given, they "went and traded with them," as the parable puts it, and the word *trade* seems to me the key to what Jesus is saying about them.

To trade is to give of what it is that we have in return for what it is that we need, and what we have is essentially what we are, and what we need is essentially each other. The good and faithful servants were not life-buriers. They were life-traders. They did not close themselves off in fear, but opened themselves up in risk and hope. The trading of joy comes naturally, because it is of the nature of joy to proclaim and share itself. Joy cannot contain itself, as we say. It overflows. And so it should properly be with pain as well, the parable seems to suggest. We are never more alive to life than when it hurts—never more aware both of our own powerlessness to save ourselves and of at least the possibility of a power beyond ourselves to save us and heal us if we can only open ourselves to it. We are never more aware of our need for each other, never more in reach of each other, if we can only bring ourselves to reach out and let ourselves be reached. If only the small boy had been able to say, "I am scared." If only the father had been able to say to the small boy, "I am scared too. I am lost." We are never more in touch with life than when life is painful, never more in touch with hope than we are then, if only the hope of another human presence to be with us and for us.

Being a good steward of your pain involves all those things, I think. It involves being alive to your life. It involves taking the risk of being open, of reaching out, of keeping in touch with the pain as well as the joy of what happens, because at no time more than at a painful time do we live out of the depths of who we are instead of out of the shallows. There is no guarantee that we will find a pearl in the depths, that our pain will have a happy end, or even any end at all, but at least we stand a chance of finding in those depths who we most deeply and humanly are and who others are. At least we stand a chance of finding that we needn't live alone in our pain like Miss Havisham in her darkened room because, perhaps more than anything else, the universal experience of pain is what makes us all the brothers and sisters, the parents and children, of each other, and the story of one of us is the story of all of us. And that in itself is a pearl of great price. It is a way of transmuting passion into compassion, of leaving the prison of selfhood for a landscape of selves, of spinning straw into gold. Howard Butt said that I had been a good steward of my pain because I had written a book about it that had moved him and in some measure opened him healingly to depths of his own, as the writing of it had opened me to a new dimension of mine. But you do not have to write books about your pain to be a good steward of it. The trouble with writing books about it is that you risk reducing it to just a book you have written. You do not have to go around talking about it. What is perhaps most precious about pain is that if it doesn't destroy us, it can confer on us a humanity that needs no words to tell of it and that can help others become human even as they can help us.

I think of adolescents in the ordinary sense of human beings in the process of growing up. I think particularly of the young men and young women who come to schools like this one and other schools not like this one at all. I think of what we teach them and how we teach them and to what end. Basically, I suppose, what we teach them is how to deal with the world. We teach them history so that they will know where the world is coming from, and science so they will know what the world is made of and how it works. We teach them languages, including their own language, so they will be able to communicate successfully with the world and understand what the world is saying when it communicates with them. We give them physical education to develop their sense of what the disciplined human body is capable of and teach them sports to increase their ability to excel and win or, if they must lose, how to lose with grace. Ideally, we teach them something at least about the arts and maybe even about world religions, so they will have some familiarity with the dreams the world has dreamed of the great intangibles of truth, beauty, holiness. Less directly than indirectly, less through books than through example, we teach them also, we hope, about certain moral values that will serve them in good stead as they make their way in the world, values like honesty, integrity, industry, prudence, self-confidence, courage, independence. In other words, the essence, I think, of what we teach them is control and competence. We say in effect that this is the world and these are the things that it is important to know in order to live controlled and competent lives in it. We teach these things for the students' sake and also, of course, for the world's sake. If the world is not to succumb to the chaos that continually threatens it, these are things that the young must know.

But I believe there is something else they should know and that as teachers we should know too. The biblical theologian Walter Brueggeman says it as well as anybody I have come across and says it in a short passage where he is speaking specifically about church education but in my view could just as well be speaking about education in general:

> If you ask almost any adult about the impact of church school on his or her growth, he or she will not tell you about books or curriculum or Bible stories or anything like that. The central memory is of the teacher, learning is *meeting*. That poses problems for the characteristically American way of thinking about education for competence even in the church. Meeting never made anybody competent. Surely we need competence, unless we mean to dismantle much of our made world. But our business is not competence. It is meeting. We are learning slowly and late that education for competence without education as meeting promises us deadly values and scary options. And anyway, one can't become "competent" in morality or in Bible stories. But one can have life-changing meetings that open one to new kinds of existence. And that surely is what church education must be about.... Our penchant for control and predictability, our commitment to quantity, our pursuit of stability and security—all this gives us a sense of priority and an agenda that is concerned to reduce the element of surprise and

newness in our lives. And when newness and surprise fail, there is not likely to be graciousness, healing, or joy. Enough critics have made the point that when experiences of surprise and newness are silenced in our lives, there is no amazement, and where there is no amazement, there cannot be the full coming to health, wholeness, and maturity.*

Education is meeting, Brueggeman says. Living right is trading with what you have been given, Jesus says in his parable. It is living out of your humanness in a way to call forth the humanness of the people with whom you are living and your own humanness. That is what trading and meeting both point to, and the amazing result can be that new life happens for you both—as Brueggeman puts it, new graciousness, healing, or joy. I have concentrated here on the pain that our humanness inevitably involves because I believe that is the experience we are most apt less to trade with than to bury. It is not just the Buddha who reminds us of that inevitability, but Jesus too if I hear him right; and when he says, "Come to me, all who labor and are heavy laden" (Matt. 11:28), I believe he is speaking to all of us. The young are no less heavy laden than the old, the lucky no less than the unlucky, the young woman in French heels teetering across the platform to receive her diploma no less than the old man watching TV in a nursing home. Life is not for sissies no matter who you are or where or how you are living it. I have conjured up a fake etymology that makes *adolescent* mean not just growing up, but growing particularly into the experience of pain and growing by means of that experience. I have spoken of coming out from under the covers and unclenching the fist that holds the keys. I have spoken of opening, and reaching out of, and keeping in touch with your pain because that is the way it can become one of the richest of your treasures. But humanness involves joy as well as pain, and it is of course that experience too that we are bidden to live out of and to trade with and to meet on the ground of if we are to be good stewards not just of our most hurtful times, but of our most blessed times as well.

I don't know what all this means, practically speaking, for educators, but I suspect it means less a change in curriculum or basic pedagogic technique—

---

* Walter Brueggeman, *Living Toward a Vision* (New York: United Church Press, 1987), pp. 167–71.

though both of these may be involved—than maybe just a small but significant change of heart. I think it means that, although distinctions cannot be denied, teacher and student, preacher and congregation, parent and child do well not to stand always at the distance from each other that those terms suggest but, as often as they can, to meet on the ground of their common aliveness, where each has much to learn not just from the other but from whatever you call the mystery that life itself comes from. I don't think it is always necessary to talk *about* the deepest and most private dimension of who we are, but I think we are called to talk to each other *out of* it, and just as importantly to listen to each other out of it, to live out of our depths as well as our shallows. We are all of us adolescents, painfully growing and groping our way toward something like true adulthood, and maybe the greatest value we have both to teach and to learn as we go is the value of what Walter Brueggeman calls amazement—the capacity to be amazed at the unending power that can be generated by the meeting and trading of lives, which is a power to heal us and bless us and in the end maybe even to transform us into truly *human* beings at last.

27.
The Longing for Home

Home sweet home. There's no place like home. Home is where you hang your hat, or, as a waggish friend of mine once said, *Home is where you hang yourself.* "Home is the sailor, home from sea, / And the hunter home from the hill." What the word home brings to mind before anything else, I believe, is a place, and in its fullest sense not just the place where you happen to be living at the time, but a very special place with very special attributes that make it clearly distinguishable from all other places. The word *home* summons up a place—more specifically a house within that place—that you have rich and complex feelings about, a place where you feel, or did feel once, uniquely *at home*, which is to say a place where you feel you belong and that in some sense belongs to you, a place where you feel that all is somehow ultimately well even if things aren't going all that well at any given moment. To think about home eventually leads you to think back to your childhood home, the place where your life started, the place that off and on throughout your life you keep going back to, if only in dreams and memories, and that is apt to determine the kind of place, perhaps a place inside yourself, that you spend the rest of your life searching for even if you are not aware that you are searching. I suspect that those who as children never had such a place in actuality had instead some kind of dream of such a home, which for them played an equally crucial part.

I was born in 1926 and therefore most of my childhood took place during the years of the Great Depression of the 1930s. As economic considerations kept my father continually moving from job to job, we as a family kept moving from place to place, with the result that none of the many houses we lived in ever became home for me in the sense I have described. But there was one house that did become home for me in that sense and that for many years after the last time I saw it in 1938 or so I used to dream about and that I still often think about although by now I am old enough to be the grandfather of the small boy I was when I first knew it.

It was a large white clapboard house that belonged to my maternal grandparents and was located in a suburb of Pittsburgh, Pennsylvania, called East Liberty, more specifically in a private residential enclave in East Liberty called Woodland Road, which had a uniformed guard at the gate who checked you in and out to make sure you had good reason for being there. For about twenty years or so before he went more or less broke and moved away in his seventies with my grandmother to live out the rest of their days in North Carolina, my grandfather was a rich man and his house was a rich man's house, as were all the others in Woodland Road, including the one that belonged to Andrew Mellon, who lived nearby. It was built on a hill with a steep curving driveway and surrounded by green lawns and horse chestnut trees, which put out white blossoms in May and unbelievably sticky buds that my younger brother and I used to stir up with leaves and twigs in a sweetgrass basket, calling it witches' brew. It also produced glistening brown buckeyes that you had to split off the tough, thorny husks to find and could make tiny chairs out of with pins for legs or attach to a string and hurl into the air or crack other people's buckeyes with to see which would hold out the longest.

The house itself had a full-length brick terrace in front and lots of French windows on the ground floor and bay windows above and dormers on the third floor with a screened-in sleeping porch in the back under which was the kitchen porch, which had a zinc-lined, pre-electric icebox on it that the iceman delivered ice to and whose musty, cavelike smell I can smell to this day if I put my mind to it. To the right of the long entrance hall was the library lined with glassed-in shelves and books, some of which I can still remember like the slim, folio-sized picture books about French history with intricate full-page color plates by the great French illustrator Job, and my great-grandfather Golay's set of the works of Charles Dickens bound in calf-like law books with his name stamped on the front cover. To the left of the hall was the living room, which I remember best for a horsehair settee covered in cherry red damask that was very uncomfortable and prickly to sit on, and a Chinese vase almost large enough for a boy my size to hide in, and an English portrait done in the 1840s of a little girl named Lavinia Holt, who is wearing a dress of dotted white organdy with a slate blue sash and is holding in her left hand, her arm almost fully extended to the side, a spidery, pinkish flower that might be honeysuckle. In the basement there was a billiard room with a green baize table, which as far as I know was never used by anybody, and a moose head mounted on the wall that my brother and I and our cousin David Wick used to pretend to worship for reasons I have long since forgotten as the God of the Dirty Spittoon, and several tall bookcases full of yellow, paper-bound French novels that ladies of the French Alliance, of which my half French-Swiss grandmother was a leading light, used to come and borrow from time to time.

At the end of the entrance hall a broad white staircase ascended to a landing with a bench on it and then turned the corner and went up to the second floor where the grown-ups' bedrooms were, including my grand-parents', which had a bay window and a sun-drenched window seat where I used to count the pennies I emptied out of a little penny bank of my grandmother's made like the steel helmet of a World War I French *poilu*. The stairway then continued on up to the third floor, where you could look down through the banister railing to the carpeted hall, which seemed a dizzying distance below. The third floor was the part of the house that for many years I used to go back to in my dreams. My brother's and my bedroom was there, with a little gas fire that on winter mornings Ellen, the maid, used to light for us before we got out of bed, and the servants' rooms, and other rooms full of humpbacked trunks covered with steam-ship labels and tied-up cardboard boxes and round Parisian hatboxes and all sorts of other treasures my brother and I never fully explored—which is perhaps why for all those years my dreams kept taking me back for another look. The smell of the house that I remember best was the smell of cooking applesauce. Out in the kitchen paneled with dark matchboard, Williams, the cook, put cinnamon in it for flavoring, and the fragrance as it simmered and steamed on top of the stove was warm and blurred and dimly pungent and seemed somehow full of enormous comfort and kindness.

What was there about that house that made it home in a way that all the other houses of my childhood never even came close to being? The permanence of it was part of the answer—the sense I had that, whereas the other houses came and went, this one was there always and would go on being there for as far into the future as I could imagine, with Ellen bringing my grandmother her glass of buttermilk on a silver tray just at eleven every morning, and my grandfather going off to his downtown office and returning in time for a cocktail before dinner with the evening paper under his arm and maybe something he'd bought at the bakery on the way home, and the Saturday night suppers when the cook was out and the menu, in honor of the New England half of my grandmother's background, was always mahogany-colored beans baked with salt pork and molasses, steamed Boston brown bread with raisins in it, and strong black coffee boiled in a pot with an eggshell to settle the grounds and sweetened with lumps of sugar and cream heavy enough to whip.

And beauty was another part of the answer, beauty that I took in through my pores almost before I so much as knew the word *beauty*—the paintings and books and green lawns, the thunder of water falling in a long, silver braid from the gooseneck spigot into the pantry sink, the lighting of lamps with their fringed shades at dusk, the knee-length silk mandarin's coat with a coral lining and flowers and birds embroidered all over it that my grandmother sometimes wore in the evenings, and out behind the house by the grassed-over tennis court the white stables that were used to garage, among other cars, the elegant old Marmon upholstered in salmon-colored leather that had belonged to my mother in her flapper days and hadn't been used since.

But more than all of these things that made that house home, or at the heart of all those things, was my grandmother, whom for reasons lost to history I called Naya. How to evoke her? She loved books and music and the French language of her father, who had emigrated from Geneva to fight on the Union side in the Civil War and eventually died of a shoulder wound he received from a sniper's bullet at the siege of Petersburg. She loved Chesterfield cigarettes and the novels of Jean Ingelow and a daiquiri before dinner and crossword puzzles, and she spoke the English language with a wit and eloquence and style that I have never heard surpassed. She loved to talk about the past as much as I loved to listen to her bring it to life with her marvelous, Dickensian descriptions, and when she talked about the present, she made it seem like a richly entertaining play we both of us had leading roles in and at the same time were watching unfold from the safety and comfort of our seats side by side in the dress circle. The love she had for me was not born of desperate need for me like my mother's love, but had more to do simply with her interest in me as a person and with the pleasure she took in my interest in her as the one grandchild she had who was bookish the way she was and who sat endlessly enraptured by the spells she cast.

On my thirty-fourth birthday, when she was going on ninety-one, she wrote me a letter in which she said, "[This] is to wish you many and many a happy year to come. And to wish for you that along the way you may meet someone who will be to you the delight you have been to me. By which I mean someone of a younger generation." For all its other glories, the house on Woodland Road could never have become home without the extraordinary delight to me of her presence in it and the profound sense of serenity and well-being that her presence generated, which leads me to believe that if, as I started by saying, the first thing the word *home* brings to mind is a place, then the next and perhaps most crucial thing is people and maybe ultimately a single person.

Can it really, that home on Woodland Road, have been as wonderful as I make it sound, at least to myself, or has my memory reshaped it? The answer is that yes, of course, it was every bit that wonderful, and probably even more so in ways I have omitted from this account, and that is precisely why my memory has never let go of it as it has let go of so much else, but has continually reshaped it, the way the waves of the sea are continually reshaping the shimmering cliff, until anything scary and jagged is worn away, with the result that what has principally survived is a sense—how to put it right?—of charity and justice and order and peace that I have longed to find again ever since and have longed to establish inside myself.

All of this makes me wonder about the home that my wife and I created for ourselves and our three daughters, both of us coming from the homes of our childhood and consciously or unconsciously drawing on those memories as we went about making a new home for the family that we were becoming.

For thirty-odd years the five of us lived in the same house, at first just during vacations but eventually all year round, so that there was never any question as to where home was. It was a much smaller white clapboard house than my grandparents', but it was built on a much higher hill and surrounded not so much by lawns as by the meadows, pastures, and woods of our corner of southern Vermont. The house had a number of small bedrooms in it with a smallish, rather narrow living room, which all the other rooms more or less opened into, so that to sit there was to be aware of pretty much everything that was going on under our roof. For me as the ever watchful and ever anxious father, this had the advantage or disadvantage of letting me keep an eye on my children's comings and goings without, I hoped, giving them the sense that I was perpetually keeping tabs on them. But as they began to get bigger and noisier, there were times when I yearned for a place to escape to once in a while, so we built on a wing with a large living room paneled in the silvery gray siding of a couple of tumbledown prerevolutionary barns. I don't think that it was in conscious emulation of the Woodland Road library that I filled the new room with shelves full of wonderful books—a few of them copies of some of the same ones that Naya had had, like the Job-illustrated French histories—but I'm sure that the memory of it was in the back of my mind somewhere. Like Naya, and almost certainly because of her, I was fascinated by the past of my family—the mid-nineteenth-century German immigrants on my father's side and the mixture of English, French, Pennsylvania Dutch, old New England, and almost everything else on my mother's—and I became in a way the family archivist, the keeper of the family graves, and collected in the cupboards beneath the bookshelves as many old photograph albums, documents, letters, genealogies, and assorted family memorabilia as little by little came my way through various relatives who knew of my interest and sent them to me. It was in that silvery gray room too that for some twenty years I both read my books and wrote them. It was there that I listened to music and to what I could hear of the longings and fears and lusts and holiness of my own life. It was in that room that our best Christmases took place, with a nine-foot tree that we would all go out together and cut down in the woods and then trim with decorations of our own making.

What my wife brought to the home we were creating was entirely different. The chief delight of her childhood in New Jersey had been not indoor things, as with me, but outdoor things. She had loved horses and animals of all kinds and growing things in gardens and almost by nature knew as much about trees and birds and flowers as most people have to learn from books and then struggle to remember. She planted a fifty-by-hundred-foot vegetable garden and flowers all over the place. She saw to it that each of our children had not only horses to ride but other animals to love and take care of—for Sharmy, Aracana chickens, who laid eggs of three different colors; for Dinah, a pig who grew to the size of a large refrigerator and didn't suffer fools gladly; and for Katherine, some fawn-colored Toggenberg goats who skittered around the barnyard dropping their berries and gazing out at the hills through the inscrutable slits of their eyes.

Like everybody else, what we furnished home with was ourselves, in other words. We furnished it with the best that we knew and the best that we were, and we furnished it also with everything that we were not wise enough to know and the shadow side of who we were as well as the best side, because we were not self-aware enough to recognize those shadows and somehow both to learn from them and to disempower them.

It became home for us in a very full sense. It was the place where we did the best we knew how to do as father and mother and as wife and husband. It was the little world we created to be as safe as we knew how to make it for ourselves and for our children from the great world outside, which I more than my wife was afraid of especially for our children's sake, because I remembered so vividly the dark and dangerous times of my own childhood, which were very much part of me still and continue to be. In that Vermont house I found refuge from the dark, as I always had, mainly in books, which, unlike people, can always be depended upon to tell the same stories in the same way and are always there when you need them and can always be set aside when you need them no longer. I believe my wife would say that her refuge from the dark has always been the world of animals and growing things.

Did this home we made become for our children as richly home as my grandparents' home had been for me as a child? How would they answer that question if I were ever brave enough to ask it? Did I hold them too close with my supervigilance? Did my wife perhaps not hold them close enough? Were our lives in deep country away from any easy access to town or neighbors too intense and isolated for our own good? Did they find in our house on the hill anything like the same sense of charity, justice, order, and peace that I had found on Woodland Road? As they grow older, will they draw upon what was best about it as they make homes of their own with their husbands and children? I don't know any of these answers. Maybe they themselves don't entirely know them. Maybe even in their early thirties they are still too close to their childhood to be able to see it with the detachment with which I see mine in my late sixties. It was almost not until I found myself putting these thoughts together that I fully realized that my own true home had not been any of the places my brother and I had lived both before and after our father's suicide when I was ten years old, not even the places where we were happiest, but had been instead that house in East Liberty, where we never really lived in any permanent sense but only visited. Will our children remember the house in Vermont as their true home? Or are the words *true home* perhaps too much to apply to even the happiest home that lies within our power to create? Are they words that always point to a reality beyond themselves?

In a novel called *Treasure Hunt*, which I wrote some years ago, there is a scene of homecoming. The narrator, a young man named Antonio Parr, has been away for some weeks and on his return finds that his small son and some other children have made a sign for him that reads WELCOME HONE with the last little leg of the *m* in *home* missing so that it turns it into an n. "It seemed oddly fitting," Antonio Parr says when he first sees it. "It was good to get home, but it was home with something missing or out of whack about it. It wasn't much, to be sure, just some minor stroke or serif, but even a minor stroke can make a major difference." And then a little while later he remembers it a second time and goes on to add, "WELCOME HONE, the sign said, and I can't help thinking again of Gideon and Barak, of Samson and David and all the rest of the crowd ... who, because some small but crucial thing was missing, kept looking for it come hell or high water wherever they went till their eyes were dim and their arches fallen.... In the long run I suppose it would be to think of everybody, if you knew enough about them to think straight."* The reference, of course, is to the

---

Treasure Hunt, in The Book of Bebb (San Francisco: HarperSanFrancisco, 1990), p. 529.

eleventh chapter of the Letter to the Hebrews, where, after listing some of the great heroes and heroines of biblical faith, the author writes, "These all died in faith, not having received what was promised, but having seen it and greeted it from afar, and having acknowledged that they were strangers and exiles on the earth. For people who speak thus make it clear that they are seeking a homeland" (vv. 13–14).

If we are lucky, we are born into a home, or like me find a home somewhere else along the way during childhood, or, failing that, at least, one hopes, find some good dream of a home. And, if our luck holds, when we grow up, we make another home for ourselves and for our family if we get married and acquire one. It is the place of all places that we feel most at home in, most at peace and most at one in, and as I sketched out in my mind that scene in my novel, I thought of it primarily as a scene that would show Antonio Parr's great joy at returning to his home after such a long absence. But then out of nowhere, and entirely unforeseen by me, there came into my mind that sign with the missing leg of the *m*. I hadn't planned to have it read *hone* instead of *home*. It was in no sense a novelistic device I'd contrived. It's simply the way I saw it. From as deep a place within me as my books and my dreams come from, there came along with the misspelled sign this revelation that, although Antonio Parr was enormously glad to be at home at last, he recognized that there was something small but crucial missing which if only for a moment made him feel, like Gideon and Barak before him, that he was in some sense a stranger and an exile there. It is when he comes home that he recognizes most poignantly that he is, at a deep level of his being, homeless, and that whatever it is that is missing, he will spend the rest of his days longing for it and seeking to find it.

The word *longing* comes from the same root as the word *long* in the sense of length in either time or space and also the word *belong*, so that in its full richness *to long* suggests to yearn for a long time for something that is a long way off and something that we feel we belong to and that belongs to us. The longing for home is so universal a form of longing that there is even a special word for it, which is of course homesickness, and what I have been dealing with so far is that form of homesickness known as nostalgia, or longing for the past as home. Almost all of the photographs I have managed to find of my grandparents' house in Pittsburgh show simply the house itself. There is a view from the front with the long brick terrace and the French windows, and another from the rear with the sleeping porch over the kitchen porch beneath it and the bay window of my grandparents' bedroom and the tall, arched window on the first landing of the central staircase. There is an interior shot of the living room with Lavinia Holt gazing out over the grand piano, which has a fringed shawl draped over it and which, as far as I can remember, Naya was the only one of us ever to use, picking out tunes with one finger every once and so often because that was as near as she ever came to knowing how to play it, and another shot shows the library with the wicker peacock chair at one side of the fireplace and the white sofa at the far end where Naya used to let me help her do the Sunday crossword puzzle. But there is one photograph that has a person in it, and the person is Naya herself.

It is winter and there has been a thaw. Wet snow clings to the bare branches of the trees, and the air is full of mist. Naya is standing on the front terrace in profile. She is looking pensively out toward the lawn. She is wearing a short fur jacket and a fur hat with her hands in the jacket pockets. She has on galoshes, or arctics, as they were called in those days. The terrace is covered with snow except in the foreground where it has melted away in patches, and you can see her reflection in the wet brick. When I look at that photograph I can almost literally feel the chill air of Pittsburgh on that winter day in 1934 or whenever it was and smell wet fur and wet wool mittens and hear the chink of arctics when you walk in them without doing the metal fasteners all the way up. I can almost literally feel in my stomach my eight-year-old excitement at having the ground deep in snow and at being in that marvelous house and at Naya's being there. If it's true that you can't go home again, it is especially true when the home in question has long since gone and been replaced by another and when virtually all the people who used to live there have long since gone too and are totally beyond replacing. But sometimes I can almost believe that if I only knew the trick of it, I could actually go back anyway, that just some one small further movement of memory or will would be enough to transport me to that snowy terrace again where Naya would turn to me in her fur jacket and would open the front door with her gloved hand and we would enter the cinnamon, lamp-lit dusk of the house together. But it is a trick that I have never quite mastered, and for that reason I have to accept my homesickness as chronic and incurable.

The house in Vermont, on the other hand, is still very much there, but about seven years ago we moved out of it into what used to be my wife's parents' house down the hill a few hundred yards, so that now it has returned to being the guest house that it originally was before we became the permanent guests. Our children still use it from time to time, but I don't go back to it very often myself. Not long after we moved out, I remember apologizing to it for that. The house was empty except for me, and I stood in the living room and told it out loud not to be upset that we don't live there anymore and rarely return to visit. I said it must never think that it failed us in any way. I told it what wonderful years we had had there and how happy we'd been and tried to explain that we would always remember it with great gratitude and affection, all of which is true. But what keeps me from going back except on rare occasions is that it is so full of emptiness now—the children's rooms still littered with their stuffed animals and crayons and books and pictures, but the children themselves the mothers of their own children now, so that it is as if the children they themselves used to be simply ceased to exist along with the young man I once was. There is no telling the sweet sadness of all that—of the Woodland Road house gone as completely as a dream when you wake up and as haunting as a dream, and the Vermont house still there but home no longer.

Where do you look for the home you long for if not to the irrecoverable past? How do you deal with that homesickness of the spirit Antonio Parr speaks of, that longing for whatever the missing thing is that keeps even the home of the present from being true home? I only wish I knew. All I know is that, like Antonio, I also sense that something of great importance is missing, which I cannot easily name and which perhaps can never be named by any of us until we find it, if indeed it is ever to be found. In the meanwhile, like Gideon and Barak and the others, I also know the sense of sadness and lostness that comes with feeling that you are a stranger and exile on the earth and that you would travel to the ends of that earth and beyond if you thought you could ever find the homeland that up till now you have only glimpsed from afar. Where do you go to search for it? Where have I myself searched?

I have come to believe that for me the writing of books may have been such a search, although it is only recently that I have thought of it that way. For forty years and more I have been at it, sitting alone in a room with a felt-tip pen in my hand and a notebook of unlined white paper on my lap for anywhere from three to five hours a day on the days when I work. Whether it is a novel I'm writing or a work of nonfiction, at the start of each day I usually have some rough idea of where I plan to go next, but at least as often as not that is not where I end up going, or at least not in the way I foresee or at the pace I intend. Time slows down to the point where whole hours can go by almost without my noticing their passage and often without writing anything at all. Sounds tend to fade away—somebody running a power mower, a dog barking in the driveway, voices speaking in another part of the house. Things that have been bothering me disappear entirely—the television set that needs to be repaired, the daughter we haven't heard from for over a week so that I am certain some terrible disaster has befallen her, my wretched defeat in a political argument at a dinner party the evening before.

In between periods of actually writing down words on the white page before me, my eyes almost always glance off to the left toward the floor, but it is not the floor that I am seeing. I am not really seeing anything or doing anything in the usual sense of the term. I am simply *being*, but being in what is for me an unusually intense and unfocused manner. I am not searching for the right way to phrase something, or for the next words to have a character speak, or for how to make a graceful transition from one paragraph to another. As nearly as I understand the process, I am simply letting an empty place open up inside myself and waiting for something to fill it. And every once and so often, praise God, something does. The sign that reads WELCOME HONE. The character who speaks something closer to the truth than I can imagine having ever come to on my own. A sentence or two in a sermon, perhaps, that touch me as usually only something I haven't seen coming can touch me or that feed me as if from another's hand with something that I hadn't realized I was half starving for. I think it is not fanciful to say that among the places I have searched for home without realizing what I was doing is that empty and fathomless place within myself and that sometimes, from afar, I may even have caught a glimpse of it in the shadows there.

Sometimes, I suspect, the search for home is related also to the longing of the flesh, to the way in which, both when you are young and for long afterward, the sight of beauty can set you longing with a keenness and poignance and passion, with a kind of breathless awe even, that suggest that beneath the longing to possess and be possessed by the beauty of another sexually—to *know* in the biblical idiom—there lies the longing to know and be known by another fully and humanly, and that beneath that there lies a longing, closer to the heart of the matter still, which is the longing to be at long last where you fully belong. "If ever any beauty I did see, / Which I desir'd, and got, 'twas but a dream of thee," John Donne wrote to his mistress ("The Good Morrow"), and when I think of all the beautiful ones whom I have seen for maybe no more than a passing moment and have helplessly, overwhelmingly desired, I wonder if at the innermost heart of my desiring there wasn't, of all things, homesickness.

Finally, as I ask myself where I have searched, I think of another winter—not the winter of 1934 in East Liberty, but the winter of 1953 in New York City, when I was a twenty-seven-year-old bachelor trying to write a novel, which for one reason or another refused to come to life for me, partly, I suspect, because I was trying too hard and hadn't learned yet the importance of letting the empty place inside me open up. Next door to where I lived there happened to be a church whose senior minister was a man named George Buttrick, and depressed as I was about the novel and with time heavy on my hands, I started going to hear him preach on Sunday mornings because, although I was by no means a regular churchgoer, somebody told me he was well worth hearing, as indeed he proved to be. What I discovered first was that he was a true believer, which in my experience a great many preachers are not. Maybe in some intellectual, theological way they believe everything I do, but there is no passion in their belief that either comes through to me or seems to animate them. Buttrick couldn't have been less of a pulpit-pounder, but his passion was in his oddly ragged eloquence and in the way he could take words you had heard all your life and make you hear them and the holiness in them as though for the first time. These were also the days before ministers were supposed to be everybody's great pal and to be called by their first names from the word go, the trouble with which, at least for me, is that it's not another great pal that I go to church looking for, but a prophet and priest and pastor. Buttrick for me became, wonderfully, all three, and although I have never met a warmer, kinder man, we never became pals, for which I am grateful, and if there was anybody in his congregation who called him George, I never happened to hear it.

It was toward the middle of December, I think, that he said something in a sermon that has always stayed with me. He said that on the previous Sunday, as he was leaving the church to go back to the apartment where he lived, he happened to overhear somebody out on the steps asking somebody else, "Are you going home for Christmas?" and I can almost see Buttrick with his glasses glittering in the lectern light as he peered out at all those people listening to him in that large, dim sanctuary and asked it again— "Are you going home for Christmas?"—and asked it in some sort of way that brought tears to my eyes and made it almost unnecessary for him to move on to his answer to the question, which was that home, finally, is the manger in Bethlehem, the place where at midnight even the oxen kneel.

Home is where Christ is was what Buttrick said that winter morning, and when the next autumn I found myself to my great surprise putting aside whatever career I thought I might have as a writer and going to Union Seminary instead at least partly because of the tears that kept coming to my eyes, I don't believe that I consciously thought that home was what I was going there in search of, but I believe that was the truth of it.

Where did my homeward search take me? It took me to the Union Seminary classrooms of four or five remarkable teachers as different from each other as James Muilenburg of the Old Testament department, who was so aflame with his subject that you couldn't listen to him without catching fire yourself, and John Knox of the New Testament department, who led us through the Gospels and Paul with the thoroughness and delicacy of a great surgeon, yet who were alike in having a faith that continues to this day to nourish mine although it has been almost forty years since the last time I heard their voices. When I was ordained in Dr. Buttrick's church in 1958, the search set me on a path that has taken me to places both in the world and in myself that I can't imagine having discovered any other way.

It took me to Phillips Exeter Academy in the 1960s, where I tried to teach and preach the Christian faith to teenage boys, a great many of whom were so hostile to the idea of religion in general and at the same time so bright and articulate and quick on their feet that for nine galvanizing, unnerving years I usually felt slow-witted and tongue-tied and hopelessly square by comparison. It took me and continues to take me every now and then to people in the thick of one kind of trouble or another who, because they know of my ordination, seek me out for whatever they think I may have in the way of comfort or healing, and I, who in the old days would have shrunk with fear from any such charged encounter, try to find something wise and hopeful to say to them, only little by little coming to understand that the most precious thing I have to give them is not whatever words I find to say, but simply whatever, spoken or unspoken, I have in me of Christ, which is also the most precious thing they have to give me. All too rarely, I regret to say, my search has taken me also to a sacred and profoundly silent place inside myself, where it is less that I pray than that, to paraphrase Saint Paul, the Holy Spirit itself, I believe, prays within me and for me "with sighs too deep for words" (Rom. 8:26).

In recent years the homeward search has taken me as a writer to distant worlds I never before would have guessed were within the range of my imagination. In eleventh-century England I have heard an old hermit named Godric, aghast at how he has come to be venerated, say, "To touch me and to feel my touch they come. To take at my hands whatever of Christ or comfort such hands have. Of their own, my hands have nothing more than any man's and less now at this tottering, lame-wit age of mine when most of what I ever had is more than mostly spent. But it's as if my hands are gloves, and in them other hands than mine, and those the ones that folk appear with roods of straw to seek. It's holiness they hunger for, and if by some mad chance it's mine to give, if I've a holy hand inside my hand to touch them with, I'll touch them day and night. Sweet Christ, what other use are idle hermits for?"*

I have stood by the fifth-century Irish saint Brendan the Navigator as he preached to some ragged bog people he had just converted and have heard him "tell them news of Christ like it was no older than a day.... He'd make them laugh at how Christ gulled the elders out of stoning to death a woman caught in the act of darkness. He'd drop their jaws telling them

---

Godric (San Francisco: Harper & Row, 1983), p. 43.

how he hailed Lazarus out of his green grave and walked on water without making holes. He'd bring a mist to their eyes spinning out the holy words Christ said on the hill … and how the Holy Ghost was a gold-eyed milk-white dove would help them stay sweet as milk and true as gold."*

And I have traveled back to that day, somewhere in the second millennium B.C. perhaps, when Jacob stole Esau's blessing from their blind old father, Isaac, and heard him say, "It was not I who ran off with my father's blessing. It was my father's blessing that [like a runaway camel] ran off with me. Often since then I have cried mercy with the sand in my teeth. I have cried ikh-kh-kh to make it fall to its knees to let me dismount at last. Its hind parts are crusted with urine as it races forward. Its long-legged, hump-swaying gait is clumsy and scattered like rags in the wind. I bury my face in its musky pelt. The blessing will take me where it will take me. It is beautiful and it is appalling. It races through the barren hills to an end of its own."†

Those are some of the places the search has taken me, and what can I honestly say I have found along the way? I think the most I can claim is something like this. I receive maybe three or four hundred letters a year from strangers who tell me that the books I have spent the better part of my life writing have one way or another saved their lives, in some cases literally. I am deeply embarrassed by such letters. I think, if they only knew that I am a person more often than not just as lost in the woods as they are, just as full of darkness, in just as desperate need. I think, if I only knew how to save my own life. They write to me as if I am a saint, and I wonder how I can make clear to them how wrong they are.

But what I am beginning to discover is that, in spite of all that, there is a sense in which they are also right. In my books, and sometimes even in real life, I have it in me at my best to be a saint to other people, and by saint I mean life-giver, someone who is able to bear to others something of the Holy Spirit, whom the creeds describe as the Lord and Giver of Life. Sometimes, by the grace of God, I have it in me to be Christ to other people. And so, of course, have we all—the life-giving, life-saving, and healing power to be saints, to be Christs, maybe at rare moments even to ourselves.

---

*Brendan (San Francisco: Harper & Row, 1988), pp. 49, 48.
†The Son of Laughter (San Francisco: HarperSanFrancisco, 1993), pp. 85–86.

I believe that it is when that power is alive in me and through me that I come closest to being truly home, come closest to finding or being found by that holiness that I may have glimpsed in the charity and justice and order and peace of other homes I have known, but that in its fullness was always missing. I cannot claim that I have found the home I long for every day of my life, not by a long shot, but I believe that in my heart I have found, and have maybe always known, the way that leads to it. I believe that Buttrick was right and that the home we long for and belong to is finally where Christ is. I believe that home is Christ's kingdom, which exists both within us and among us as we wend our prodigal ways through the world in search of it.

28.
The Great Dance

After this Jesus revealed himself again to the disciples by the Sea of Tiberias; and he revealed himself in this way. Simon Peter, Thomas called the Twin, Nathanael of Cana in Galilee, the sons of Zebedee, and two others of his disciples were together. Simon Peter said to them, "I am going fishing." They said to him, "We will go with you." They went out and got into the boat; but that night they caught nothing.

Just as day was breaking, Jesus stood on the beach; yet the disciples did not know that it was Jesus. Jesus said to them, "Children, have you any fish?" They answered him, "No." He said to them, "Cast the net on the right side of the boat, and you will find some." So they cast it, and now they were not able to haul it in, for the quantity of fish. That disciple whom Jesus loved said to Peter, "It is the Lord!" When Simon Peter heard that it was the Lord, he put on his clothes, for he was stripped for work, and sprang into the sea. But the other disciples came in the boat, dragging the net full of fish, for they were not far from the land, but about a hundred yards off.

When they got out on land, they saw a charcoal fire there, with fish lying on it, and bread. Jesus said to them, "Bring some of the fish that you have just caught." So Simon Peter went aboard and hauled the net ashore, full of large fish, a hundred and fifty-three of them; and although there were so many, the net was not torn. Jesus said to

them, "Come and have breakfast." Now none of the disciples dared
ask him, "Who are you?" They knew it was the Lord. Jesus came and
took the bread and gave it to them and so with the fish.

—JOHN 21:1–13

Several winters ago my wife and I and our then twenty-year-old daughter, Sharmy, went to that great tourist extravaganza near Orlando, Florida,
called Sea World. There is a lot of hoopla to it—crowds of people, loud
music, Mickey Mouse T-shirts, and so on, but the main attraction makes it
all worthwhile. It takes place in a huge tank of crystal clear, turquoise water
with a platform projecting out into it from the far side and on the platform
several pretty young women and handsome young men in bathing suits
who run things. It was a gorgeous day when we were there, with bright
Florida sunlight reflected in the shimmering water and a cloudless blue sky
over our heads. The bleachers where we sat were packed.

The way the show began was that at a given signal they released into
the tank five or six killer whales, as we call them (it would be interesting to
know what they call us), and no creatures under heaven could have looked
less killerlike as they went racing around and around in circles. What with
the dazzle of sky and sun, the beautiful young people on the platform, the
soft Southern air, and the crowds all around us watching the performance
with a delight matched only by what seemed the delight of the performing
whales, it was as if the whole creation—men and women and beasts and
sun and water and earth and sky and, for all I know, God himself—was
caught up in one great, jubilant dance of unimaginable beauty. And then,
right in the midst of it, I was astonished to find that my eyes were filled
with tears.

When the show was over and I turned to my wife and daughter beside
me to tell them what had happened, their answer was to say that there had
been tears also in their eyes. It wasn't until several years later that I happened to describe the incident at a seminar at the College of Preachers in
Washington, and afterwards a man came up to me who turned out to be the
dean of Salisbury Cathedral in England and who asked me if I would take a
look at part of a sermon he had preached a few weeks earlier. The passage he

showed me was one that described how he had recently gone to a place near Orlando, Florida, called Sea World, and how he had seen an extraordinary spectacle there, in the midst of which he had suddenly discovered that his eyes were filled with tears.

My wife and I and our daughter Sharmy and Hugh Dickinson—I believe there is no mystery about why we shed tears. We shed tears because we had caught a glimpse of the Peaceable Kingdom, and it had almost broken our hearts. For a few moments we had seen Eden and been part of the great dance that goes on at the heart of creation. We shed tears because we were given a glimpse of the way life was created to be and is not. We had seen why it was that "the morning stars sang together, and all the sons of God shouted for joy" when the world was first made, as the book of Job describes it (38:7), and of what it was that made St. Paul write, even when he was in prison and on his way to execution, "Rejoice in the Lord always; again I will say, Rejoice" (Phil. 4:4). We had had a glimpse of part at least of what Jesus meant when he said, "Blessed are you that weep now, for you shall laugh" (Luke 6:21).

The world is full of darkness, but what I think we caught sight of in that tourist trap in Orlando, Florida, of all places, was that at the heart of darkness—whoever would have believed it?—there is joy unimaginable. The world does bad things to us all, and we do bad things to the world and to each other and maybe most of all to ourselves, but in that dazzle of bright water as the glittering whales hurled themselves into the sun, I believe what we saw was that joy is what we belong to. Joy is home, and I believe the tears that came to our eyes were more than anything else homesick tears. God created us in joy and created us for joy, and in the long run not all the darkness there is in the world and in ourselves can separate us finally from that joy, because whatever else it means to say that God created us in his image, I think it means that even when we cannot believe in him, even when we feel most spiritually bankrupt and deserted by him, his mark is deep within us. We have God's joy in our blood.

I believe that joy is what our tears were all about and what our faith is all about too. Not happiness. Happiness comes when things are going our way, which makes it only a forerunner to the unhappiness that inevitably follows when things stop going our way, as in the end they will stop for all of us. Joy, on the other hand, does not come because something is happening or not happening, but every once in a while rises up out of simply being alive, of being part of the terror as well as the fathomless richness of the world that God has made. When Jesus was eating his last meal with his friends, knowing that his death was only a few hours away, he was in no sense happy, nor did he offer his friends happiness any more than he offers happiness to you and me. What he offers is more precious than happiness because it is beyond the world's power either to give or take away. "These things have I spoken to you," he said, "that my joy may be in you" (John 15:11)—joy, as poignant as grief, that brings tears to the eyes as it did to mine that afternoon in the crowded bleachers.

Could anyone guess by looking at us that joy is at the heart of what goes on in church Sunday after Sunday? Are we given any glimpses there of what it was that blazed forth with such power in Orlando? I hope so. I pray so. Maybe in the freshness and fragrance of the flowers on the altar we catch some flicker of it, and in the candles' burning. Maybe we can feel some reverberation of it in just all of us being together as human beings longing for and reaching out for we are not quite sure what. Maybe every once in a great while something joyful stirs in us as the taste of wine touches our tongues or some phrase of a hymn or prayer or sermon comes alive for a second and touches our hearts. The crimson and peacock blue of a stained-glass window with the sun shining through it can sometimes speak of it the way jewels do. But in all honesty I have to confess that I for one have found little joy like that in the churches we go to year after year, very little of what made the great whales leap into the sky.

We are above all things loved—that is the good news of the gospel—and loved not just the way we turn up on Sundays in our best clothes and on our best behavior and with our best feet forward, but loved as we alone know ourselves to be, the weakest and shabbiest of what we are along with the strongest and gladdest. To come together as people who believe that just maybe this gospel is actually true should be to come together like people who have just won the Irish Sweepstakes. It should have us throwing our arms around each other like people who have just discovered that every single man and woman in those pews is not just another familiar or unfamiliar face but is our long-lost brother and our long-lost sister because despite the fact that we have all walked in different gardens and knelt at different graves, we have all, humanly speaking, come from the same place and are heading out into the same blessed mystery that awaits us all. This is the joy that is so apt to be missing, and missing not just from church but from our own lives—the joy of not just managing to believe at least part of the time that it is true that life is holy, but of actually running into that holiness head-on the way my wife and my daughter and the English dean and I each ran into it in the splendor of that moment we shared. I think maybe it is holiness that we long for more than we long for anything else.

In the last chapter of John's Gospel there is another moment that has certain features in common with the moment at Sea World. It, also, has water in it and fish in it, and the sun, and the sky, and, unless I miss my guess, tears in the eyes of at least some of the ones who were there when it happened. The water was the Sea of Tiberias, where the fishermen disciples carried on their trade. The crucifixion had taken place over a week earlier. Jesus had appeared to some of them since then and had said things and promised things—Thomas had even touched his hand—but then again he was gone.

One night Peter rounded up six of his friends, and together they went out fishing. They failed to catch anything, but maybe it was less fish they were after than just a way of getting through another night without the one they had lost. Then "just as day was breaking," John says, about a hundred yards away on the beach, they saw the glow of a charcoal fire and a man standing by it whom at first they didn't recognize. The man asked them if they had had any luck, and when they said they had not, he told them to try throwing their nets off the starboard side, and this time they were lucky to the tune of what John says were a hundred and fifty-three fish, as if he had actually counted them at the time and never forgotten the number. Then one of the disciples saw that the man on the beach was Jesus, and when he told Peter, Peter hurled himself into the water like a whale and somehow swam and scrambled his way to shore ahead of everybody else.

The brief conversation he had with Jesus is a haunting one, because what Peter says is so close to what I suspect you and I would have said if we had been there ourselves, and because what Jesus says to Peter is so close to what he says to all of us. Jesus asks Peter if he loves him, and Peter says yes, he does. He says he loves him. Even when you have never seen Jesus, as you and I have never seen him, it is hard not to love him, at least a little. Even when you are not sure who Jesus is or what you are supposed to believe about him—even when you have never been very good, God knows, at following him, whatever that means—even then, I think, you can't help loving him in at least some half-embarrassed, half-hidden way. Three times Jesus makes Peter say he loves him, and each time Jesus answers him virtually the same way. "Feed my lambs," he says. "Tend my sheep," he says. "Feed my sheep" (John 21:15–17).

I think the kind of joy that brings tears to our eyes has much to do with what Jesus means by feeding each other. There are people who are literally starving for want of food, and there are other people, closer to home, who may be starving for want of nothing so much as whatever we ourselves can give them in the way of God only knows what small but life-restoring act of kindness and understanding. Literally or figuratively, for you and me to feed each other, to tend to each other's needs, one way or another to take care of each other, is more and more to become part of that dance of earth and sky and men and women and water and beasts that according to the psalmist makes the floods clap their hands and the hills sing together for joy.

"Feed my sheep," Jesus said to Peter as the first rays of the sun went fanning out across the sky, but, before that, he said something else. The six other men had beached the boat by then and had come up to the charcoal fire knowing that it was Jesus who was standing there and yet not quite knowing, not quite brave enough to ask him if he was the one they were all but certain he was. He told them to bring him some of the fish they had just hauled in, and then he said something that, if I had to guess, was what brought tears to their eyes if anything did. The Lamb of God. The Prince of Peace. The Dayspring from on High. Instead of all the extraordinary words we might imagine on his lips, what he said was, "Come and have breakfast."

I believe he says it to all of us: to feed his sheep, his lambs, to be sure, but first to let him feed us—to let him feed us with something of himself. In the sip of wine and crumb of bread. In the dance of sun and water and sky. In the faces of the people who need us most and of the people we most need. In the smell of breakfast cooking on a charcoal fire. Who knows where we will find him or whether we will recognize him if we do? Who knows anything even approaching the truth of who he really was? But my prayer is that we will all of us find him somewhere, somehow, and that he will give us something of his life to fill our emptiness, something of his light to drive back our dark.

29.

The News of the Day

Woe to you that are rich, for you have received your consolation.

Woe to you that are full now, for you shall hunger.

Woe to you that laugh now, for you shall mourn and weep.

—LUKE 6:24-25

It gets to be six-thirty or seven in the evening, say, and we switch the TV on to CBS or NBC or ABC or PBS if we are really serious about it, and then settle back and listen to the news of the day. It is a way of keeping in touch with reality, of maintaining perspective, of taking stock. It is a way of reminding ourselves that beyond the little world we live in, there is another, wider world that we are all part of, although we get so caught up in the business of our own worlds that we tend to forget about it.

Every evening the news is different, of course, and yet there seem to be certain major themes that keep on recurring day after day and year after year. There are always wars going on somewhere. In the Middle East, in Africa, in our own streets, there are always people fighting other people for control, for power, for revenge, for freedom, for a bigger slice of the pie.

On the other side of the coin, the news of the day always involves also the search for peace. Heads of state get together to air old grievances and consider new possibilities of accommodation and compromise. The Arab sits down with the Jew. Labor sits down with management. Just as much as the world is always fighting, the world is also always searching for a way to bring the fighting to an end and to have peace.

And the world is always hungry. Hunger is another of the great recurring themes. The statistics are so appalling that we cannot keep them in our heads or choose not to. Not just in the Third World, but all over the world people are starving to death, hundreds of thousands of them, and thousands of them children. In Manchester, Vermont, near where I live, a crowd of people line up at the senior center on School Street every week to pick up enough of the food collected by the local churches to keep the wolf from their doors because even in this country, surrounded by affluence, there are countless families that can afford either a home to live in or food to eat but not both.

And that leads to the last of the recurring themes, which is homelessness. When I was a child in New York, if you wanted to see people sleeping on the streets, you had to go down to places like the Bowery to see them. Nowadays there are people sleeping in all the streets—not just the slum streets but the fancy streets too, and not just in New York, God knows, but in cities all over this country. They lie on the sidewalks, on hot-air gratings, in station waiting rooms till somebody kicks them out, in doorways, and on the steps of churches. Even on the coldest winter nights you see them there in their cardboard boxes and filthy clothes padded out with old newspaper for extra warmth. They are the dispossessed and forgotten ones. They are the ones without shelter, without any place that belongs to them or where they belong. As someone once put it, home is the place where, if you have to go there, they have to take you in, and these people have no such place anywhere in the world.

The fighting. The search for peace. Hunger. Homelessness. Every evening we sit in our living rooms and watch on the flickering screen what has gone on in the world that day. What we choose to do about it, you and I—what worthy causes, if any, get our time and energy, what political candidates get our votes, how much money we give away or could afford to give away if our hearts were really in it—those are all issues of the greatest and most far-reaching importance not just for the saving of the world but for the saving of our own souls. But without leaving those issues behind, we would do well to focus also on another kind of news of the day—another kind of taking stock, another kind of reality to keep in touch with.

Beyond what goes on in the world that makes the headlines, there is also what goes on in the small, private worlds that you and I move around in and the news of our own individual days in those worlds. Some of the things that happen in them are so small that we hardly notice them, and some of them shake the very ground beneath our feet, but, whether they are great or small, they make up the day-by-day story of who we are and of what we are doing with our lives and what our lives are doing to us. Their news is the news of what we are becoming or failing to become.

Maybe the best time to look at that news is at night when we first turn out the light and are lying in the dark waiting for sleep to come. It is a time to look back at the wars that you and I have been engaged in for the last twenty-four hours, or twenty-four years for that matter, because there are none of us who do not one way or another wage war every day, if only with ourselves. It is a time to look back at our own searches for peace because deep beneath the level of all the other things we spend our time searching for, peace, real peace, is the treasure for which maybe we would all of us be willing to trade every other treasure we have. As we lie there in the dark, we might ask ourselves, what battles, if any, are we winning? What battles are we losing? Which battles might we do better not to be fighting at all, and which, in place of surrender, should we be fighting more effectively and bravely? We are churchgoers. We are nice people. We fight well camouflaged. We are snipers rather than bombardiers. Our weapons are more apt to be chilly silences than hot words. But our wars are no less real for all of that, and the stakes are no less high.

Perhaps the stakes are nowhere higher than in the war we all wage within ourselves—the battles we fight against loneliness, boredom, despair, self-doubt, the battles against fear, against the great dark. In the whole Bible there are perhaps no words that everybody, everywhere, can identify with more fully than the ones St. Paul wrote to the Roman church: "I do not do the good I want, but the evil I do not want is what I do" (7:19). That is as rich a summation as any I know of the inner battle that we are all involved in, which is the battle to break free from all the camouflaged and not so camouflaged hostilities that we half deplore even as we engage in them, the battle to become what we have it in us at our best to be, which is wise and loving friends both to our own selves and to each other as we reach out not only for what we need to have but also for what we need to give.

These are the wars that go on within families, within marriages, the wars we wage with each other sometimes openly but more often so hiddenly that even in the thick of them we are hardly aware of what we are doing. These are the wars that go on between parents and children, between people who at one level are friends but at another level are adversaries, competitors, strangers even, with a terrible capacity for wounding each other and being wounded by each other no less deeply and painfully because the wounds are invisible and the bleeding mostly internal. Sometimes we fight to survive, sometimes just to be noticed, let alone to be loved. Sniping and skirmishing, defensive maneuvers, naked aggressions, and guerrilla subversions are part of the lives of all of us.

In Ken Burns's television series on the Civil War, the narrator describes a remarkable scene that took place on the fiftieth anniversary of the Battle of Gettysburg in 1913, when what was left of the two armies decided to stage a reenactment of Pickett's charge. All the old Union veterans up on the ridge took their places among the rocks, and all the old Confederate veterans started marching toward them across the field below, and then the extraordinary thing happened. As the old men among the rocks began to rush down at the old men coming across the field, a great cry went up, only instead of doing battle as they had half a century earlier, this time they threw their arms around each other. They embraced each other and openly wept.

As we lie in the dark looking back over the news of one more day of our lives coming to an end, we might ask ourselves which of the obscure little wars we all engage in could end that same way if only we had eyes to see what those old men saw as they fell into each other's arms on the field of Gettysburg. If only we could see that the people we are one way or another at war with are, more often than not, less to blame for the bad blood between us than we are, because, again more often than not, the very faults we find so unbearable in them are apt to be versions of the same faults that we are more or less blind to in ourselves.

One evening at dinner not long ago I found myself sitting next to a woman I have known for years. She is someone I have valued and admired in all sorts of ways, but for one reason or another, as much because of me as because of her, the air between us was often shadowed and bent. I found myself telling her a dream I had had about her a few nights before. I told her I had dreamed that I was sitting beside her, much as I was sitting beside her there at the dinner table telling her about it, and that suddenly I had turned to her and said, "I love you." I then told her something else I don't think I fully realized until that moment. I told her that what I had said to her in the dream was true. I saw immediately that she was as moved as I was, and all at once the air between us was no longer bent but was full of healing and kindness. It was only a very small moment, but in terms of the news of that day of my life, it marked the end of a war and gave me at least a glimpse of the peace that she and I and all of us hunger above all else to find.

Hunger in the literal sense is unknown to you and me. In a world where thousands starve to death every day, we live surrounded by plenty. With full bellies we watch the TV footage of Third World children with their bellies swollen, their legs and arms like sticks, eyes vacant in their ancient faces, and may God have mercy on us as a nation, as a civilization, as whatever it means to call us Christendom, if we do not find some way to wipe their hunger from the face of the earth. And may God have mercy upon us too if we fail to recognize that even in the midst of plenty, we have our own terrible hungers.

We hunger to be known and understood. We hunger to be loved. We hunger to be at peace inside our own skins. We hunger not just to be fed these things but, often without realizing it, we hunger to feed others these things because they too are starving for them. We hunger not just to be loved but to love, not just to be forgiven but to forgive, not just to be known and understood for all the good times and bad times that for better or worse have made us who we are, but to know and understand each other to the point of seeing that, in the last analysis, we all have the same good times, the same bad times, and that for that very reason there is no such thing in all the world as anyone who is really a stranger.

When Jesus commanded us to love our neighbors as ourselves, it was not just for our neighbors' sakes that he commanded it, but for our own sakes as well. Not to help find some way to feed the children who are starving to death is to have some precious part of who we are starve to death with them. Not to give of ourselves to the human beings we know who may be starving not for food but for what we have in our hearts to nourish them with is to be, ourselves, diminished and crippled as human beings.

We lie in our beds in the dark. There is a picture of the children on the bureau. Our clothes hang in the closet. There is a patch of moonlight on the carpeted floor. We live surrounded by the comfort of familiar things, sights, sounds. When the weather is bad, we have shelter. When things are bad in our lives, we have a place where we can retreat to lick our wounds and pull ourselves back together again, while tens of thousands of people, thousands of them children, wander the streets looking for some doorway to lie down in out of the wind. "Woe to you that are rich," Jesus said, "for you have received your consolation. Woe to you that are full now, for you shall hunger. Woe to you that laugh now, for you shall mourn and weep." It is a text that is not often preached on to people like us because it cuts too close to the bone, but woe to us indeed if we forget the homeless ones who have no vote, no power, nobody to lobby for them, and who might as well have no faces even, the way we try to avoid the troubling sight of them in the streets of the cities where they roam like stray cats. And as we listen each night to the news of what happened in our lives that day, woe to us too if we forget our own homelessness.

To be homeless the way people like you and me are apt to be homeless is to have homes all over the place but not to be really at home in any of them. To be really at home is to be really at peace, and our lives are so intricately interwoven that there can be no real peace for any of us until there is real peace for all of us. That is the truth that underlies not just the news of the world, but the news of every one of our own days.

30.

The Secret in the Dark

That very day two of them were going to a village named Emmaus, about seven miles from Jerusalem, and talking with each other about all these things that had happened. While they were talking and discussing together, Jesus himself drew near and went with them. But their eyes were kept from recognizing him. And he said to them, "What is this conversation which you are holding with each other as you walk?" And they stood still, looking sad. Then one of them, named Cleopas, answered him, "Are you the only visitor to Jerusalem who does not know the things that have happened there in these days?" And he said to them, "What things?" And they said to him, "Concerning Jesus of Nazareth, who was a prophet mighty in deed and word before God and all the people, and how our chief priests and rulers delivered him up to be condemned to death, and crucified him. But we had hoped that he was the one to redeem Israel. Yes, and besides all this, it is now the third day since this happened. Moreover, some women of our company amazed us. They were at the tomb early in the morning and did not find his body; and they came back saying that they had even seen a vision of angels, who said that he was alive. Some of those who were with us went to the tomb, and found it just as the woman had said; but him they did not see." And he said to them, "O foolish men, and slow of heart to believe all that the prophets have spoken! Was it not necessary that the Christ should suffer these things and enter into his glory?" And beginning with Moses and all the prophets, he interpreted to them in all the scriptures the things concerning himself.

So they drew near to the village to which they were going. He appeared to be going further, but they constrained him, saying, "Stay with us, for it is toward evening and the day is now far spent." So he went in to stay with them. When he was at table with them, he took the bread and blessed, and broke it, and gave it to them. And their eyes were opened and they recognized him; and he vanished out of their sight.

—LUKE 24:13–31

It has always struck me as remarkable that when the writers of the four Gospels come to the most important part of the story they have to tell, they tell it in whispers. The part I mean, of course, is the part about the resurrection. The Jesus who was dead is not dead anymore. He has risen. He is here. According to the Gospels there was no choir of angels to proclaim it. There was no sudden explosion of light in the sky. Not a single soul was around to see it happen. When Mary Magdalene arrived at the tomb afterward, she thought at first that it must be a gardener standing there in the shadows, and when she saw who it really was and tried to embrace him, he told her not to, as if for fear that once she had him in her arms she would never let him go, the way I suspect that if you and I were ever to have him in our arms, we would never let him go either. When the disciples heard he was alive again, they tended to dismiss it as too good to be true, and even when they finally saw him for themselves, Thomas still wasn't convinced until Jesus let him touch his wounds with his own hands. Later on, when they were out fishing at daybreak, they saw him standing on the beach, and there again they failed to recognize him until he asked them to come join him at the charcoal fire he had started on the sand and cooked them breakfast.

The way the Gospel writers tell it, in other words, Jesus came back from death not in a blaze of glory, but more like a candle flame in the dark, flickering first in this place, then in that place, then in no place at all. If they had been making the whole thing up for the purpose of converting the world, presumably they would have described it more the way the book of Revelation describes how he will come back again at the end of time with "the armies of heaven arrayed in fine linen, white and pure" and his eyes "like a flame of fire, and on his head many diadems" (19:14, 12). But that is not the way the Gospels tell it. They are not trying to describe it as convincingly as they can. They are trying to describe it as truthfully as they can. It was the most extraordinary thing they believed had ever happened, and yet they tell it so quietly that you have to lean close to be sure what they are telling. They tell it as softly as a secret, as something so precious, and holy, and fragile, and unbelievable, and true, that to tell it any other way would be somehow to dishonor it. To proclaim the resurrection the way they do, you would have to say it in whispers: "Christ has risen." Like that.

Down through the centuries the Christian church, needless to say, has not whispered it but shouted it, and who can blame it? It was St. Paul who was blunt enough to come straight out and write to the Corinthians: "If Christ has not been raised [from the dead], then our preaching is in vain and your faith is in vain" (1 Cor. 15:14). So when churches all over the world proclaim that he has been raised indeed and our faith gloriously vindicated, they naturally do so at the top of their lungs and with all flags flying. Banks of lilies on the altar. A full choir singing Bach or Handel. A resounding sermon. Fancy clothes. Packed pews. It can be a very powerful and beautiful occasion proclaiming that even in a mad and murderous world like ours, which no longer believes in much of anything, there are still people who believe that this miracle of all miracles actually took place, or who at least long to believe it, at least believe that it is of all miracles the one that would be most wonderful to be able to believe if only they could. But the shadow side of the great Easter celebration is that sometimes the very fanfare and fortissimo of it are apt to leave us feeling like the only guests at a great New Year's Eve party who are not having the time of our lives. All the wonderful things that are going on around us on Easter Sunday can sometimes make us more conscious than usual that nothing even close to all that wonderful is going on inside ourselves.

That is why the Sundays after Easter are so precious, and precious because, in their comparatively subdued, low-key way, they seem not only closer to how the resurrection actually took place as the Gospels describe it but, more important still, closer to the reality of the resurrection as you and I are apt to experience it. These everyday Sundays without all the flowers and music and exaltation are like the kind of day that Luke describes in his account of the two disciples on their walk from Jerusalem to Emmaus some seven miles away.

They had heard the women's report about finding the tomb of Jesus empty that morning, but as Luke writes, it "seemed to them an idle tale, and they did not believe them." They did not believe the women because they found what the women said unbelievable, and then as they trudged along with the evening approaching and the sun starting to set, Jesus himself—risen from the dead and alive again—joined them on their way, only they did not know it was Jesus because, again as Luke puts it, "their eyes were kept from recognizing him," and I think those eyes are almost the most haunting part of the whole haunting story because they remind me so much of my own eyes and because I suspect they may remind you also of yours. How extraordinary to have eyes like that—eyes that look out at this world we live in but, more often than not, see everything except what matters most.

In Florida, in the winter, there is a walk that I take early in the morning before breakfast most days. It doesn't go to Emmaus exactly, unless maybe that's exactly where it does go, but in the literal sense it takes me some three miles or so along a completely uninhabited stretch of the inland waterway that separates the barrier island where we live from the mainland. I do not know any place lovelier on the face of this planet, especially at that early hour when there is nobody else around and everything is so fresh and still. The waterway drifts by like a broad river. The ponds reflect the sky. There are wonderful birds—snow-white egrets and ibis, boat-tail grackles black as soot—and long, unbroken vistas of green grass and trees. It is a sight worth traveling a thousand miles to see, and yet there is no telling how hard I have to struggle, right there in the midst of it, actually to see it.

What I do instead is think about things I have been doing and things I have to do. I think about people I love and people I do not know how to love. I think about letters to write and things around the house to get fixed and old grievances and longings and regrets. I worry and dream about the future. That is to say, I get so lost in my own thoughts—and *lost* is just the word for it, as lost as you can get in a strange town where you don't know the way—that I have to struggle to see where I am, almost to be where I am. Much of the time I might as well be walking in the dark or sitting at home with my eyes closed, those eyes that keep me from recognizing what is happening around me.

But then every once in a while, by grace, I recognize at least some part of it. Every once in a while I recognize that I am walking in green pastures that call out to me to lie down in them, and beside still waters where my feet lead me. Sometimes in the way the breeze stirs the palms or the way a bird circles over my head, I recognize that even in the valley of the shadow of my own tangled thoughts there is something holy and unutterable seeking to restore my soul. I see a young man in a checked shirt riding a power mower, and when I wave my hand at him, he waves his hand at me and I am hallowed by his greeting. I see a flock of white birds rising, and my heart rises with them.

And then there is one particular tree, a tree that I always see because it is the northernmost one I come to and marks the spot where I turn around and start for home. The label on it says that it is a Cuban laurel, but its true and secret name has nothing to do with labels. It has multiple trunks all braided and buttressed, and roots that snake out over the ground as widely as its branches snake out into the air. Here and there from one of the larger branches it has sent down a slender air-root, which in time turns into another trunk that supports its weight like a sinewy old arm. There are one or two places where the leaves have gone brown and brittle, but the tree holds them high into the sky as proudly and gallantly as it holds the green ones. At the risk of being spotted as a hopeless eccentric, I always stop for a moment and touch the coarse-grained, gray bark of it with my hand, or sometimes with my cheek, which I suppose is a way of blessing it for being so strong and so beautiful. Who knows how many years it has been standing there in fair weather and foul, sending down all those extra trunks to keep itself from breaking apart and wearing its foliage like a royal crown even though part of it is dying? And I think it is because of that quality of sheer endurance that on one particular morning I found myself touching it not to bless it for once, but to ask its blessing, so that I myself might move toward old age and death with something like its stunning grace and courage.

"When I was hungry, you gave me food, when I was naked you clothed me," Jesus said. "When I was a stranger, you welcomed me" (Matt. 25:35–36). And "When I was a tree," he might have said, "you blessed me and asked my blessing." To believe that Christ is risen and alive in the world is to believe that there is no place or person or thing in the world through which we ourselves may not be made more alive by his life, and whenever we *are* made more alive, whenever we are made more brave and strong and beautiful, we may be sure that Christ is present with us even though more often than not our eyes, like the two disciples' eyes, are kept from recognizing him.

What kept them from recognizing him, of course, was that they thought he was dead and gone, and when he asked them what they had been talking about, that is what they told him in words as full of pathos as any in the New Testament. "We had hoped that he was the one to redeem Israel," they said, but by then their hope was as dead as they believed he was himself. They had gone to the tomb to see if he was alive as some believed but had found no trace of him. Like me on my walk, they were so lost in their sad and tangled thoughts that they did not recognize him any more than you and I would probably recognize him as we walk through the world because, like theirs, our eyes are too accustomed to darkness and our faith not strong enough to believe in the reality of light even if it were to blaze up before us.

Schindler's List is a movie about the Holocaust. It is a movie about Oskar Schindler, who was a wartime profiteer, a womanizer, a boozer, a good friend of the Nazis, yet who for reasons even he apparently didn't understand became obsessed with the idea of saving as many Jews as he could from the gas ovens of Auschwitz by commandeering them to work in one of his factories and ended up saving some eleven hundred of them. It is about Oskar Schindler, the Nazi saint. It is about a dark and anguished world where again and again in the faces of the persecuted Jews as they appear on the screen you see the face of Christ while their persecutors saw only a people to be wiped from the face of the earth. It is about an inhuman, ex-human young commandant of a Nazi death camp who has the face of a fallen angel, the face of someone in whom the Christ who dwells in all of us is as dead as the Christ who dwells in all of us can ever be. And it is also about a little girl in a red dress.

The movie is filmed almost entirely in black and white like a documentary or an old newsreel, but every once in a while, usually in some crowd scene of children playing or people running or being herded into freight cars, you see, flickering like a candle flame in the seething grayness, one single touch of color in the form of a little girl dressed in red. You see her in her red dress hiding herself under a bed while the Nazis set about systematically shooting all the Jews they can lay their hands on in the Krakow ghetto, and then again here, then there, until finally for the last time you see a patch of the same red dress buried almost out of sight in a mountain of the dead left when the massacre has been completed.

I believe that although the two disciples did not recognize Jesus on the road to Emmaus, Jesus recognized them, that he saw them as if they were the only two people in the world. And I believe that the reason why the resurrection is more than just an extraordinary event that took place some two thousand years ago and then was over and done with is that, even as I speak these words and you listen to them, he also sees each of us like that. In this dark world where you and I see so little because of our unrecognizing eyes, he, whose eye is on the sparrow, sees each one of us as the child in red. And I believe that because he sees us, not even in the darkness of death are we lost to him or lost to each other. I believe that whether we recognize him or not, or believe in him or not, or even know his name, again and again he comes and walks a little way with us along whatever road we're following. And I believe that through something that happens to us, or something we see, or somebody we know—who can ever guess how or when or where?—he offers us, the way he did at Emmaus, the bread of life, offers us a new hope, a new vision of light that not even the dark world can overcome.

That is the word that on Easter Sunday is sounded forth on silver trumpets. And when Easter is past and the silver trumpets have faded away to hardly more than a distant echo, that is the word that is whispered to us like a secret in the dark, the saving and holy word that flickers among us like a red dress in a gray world.

31.
The Seeing Heart

On the evening of that day, the first day of the week, the doors being shut where the disciples were, for fear of the Jews, Jesus came and stood among them and said to them, "Peace be with you." When he had said this, he showed them his hands and his side. Then the disciples were glad when they saw the Lord. Jesus said to them again, "Peace be with you. As the Father has sent me, even so I send you." And when he had said this, be breathed on them, and said to them, "Receive the Holy Spirit. If you forgive the sins of any, they are forgiven; if you retain the sins of any, they are retained."

Now Thomas, one of the twelve, called the Twin, was not with them when Jesus came. So the other disciples told him, "We have seen the Lord." But he said to them, "Unless I see in his hands the print of the nails, and place my finger in the mark of the nails, and place my hand in his side, I will not believe."

Eight days later, his disciples were again in the house, and Thomas was with them. The doors were shut, but Jesus came and stood among them, and said, "Peace be with you." Then he said to Thomas, "Put your finger here, and see my hands; and put out your hand, and place it in my side; do not be faithless, but believing." Thomas answered him, "My Lord and my God!" Jesus said to him, "Have you believed

because you have seen me? Blessed are those who have not seen and
yet believe."

—JOHN 20:19–29

There was a great teacher of the Old Testament at the seminary where I
studied for the ministry years ago, and one thing he told us that I have
always remembered is that we really can't hear what the stories of the
Bible are saying until we hear them as stories about ourselves. We have
to imagine our way into them, he said. We have to imagine ourselves the
prodigal son coming home terrified that the door will be slammed in his
face when he gets there, only to have the breath all but knocked out of
him by the great bear hug his father greets him with before he can choke
out so much as the first word of the speech he has prepared about how
sorry he is and how he will never do it again, not unlike the way Sunday
after Sunday you and I say in our prayers how sorry we are and how we
will never do it again. We have to put ourselves in the place of the good
thief spread-eagled in the merciless sun saying to the one who is dying
beside him, "Jesus, remember me when you come in your kingly power,"
the way at the heart of every prayer we have ever prayed or will ever pray,
you and I are also saying it in one form or another: *Remember* me. *Remember* me. Jesus, *remember*.

I don't know of any story in the Bible that is easier to imagine ourselves
into than this one from John's Gospel because it is a story about trying to
believe in Jesus in a world that is as full of shadows and ambiguities and
longings and doubts and glimmers of holiness as the room where the story
takes place is and as you and I are inside ourselves.

It is the evening after the resurrection, and all but one of the disciples are
gathered together in this shadowy room. The door is bolted tight because
they are scared stiff that the ones who seized Jesus in the night will come
and seize them next, and every sound they hear—the creaking of the house,
the stirring of air through the trees, a dog barking—becomes for them the
dreaded sound of footsteps on the stair. If they speak at all, you can imagine
them speaking almost too quietly to hear. The room is small and crowded

and the air acrid with the smell of their fear. That morning just after dawn, Mary Magdalene told them that she had seen Jesus alive again, but even the ones who believed her were not much comforted because he was not alive again with them there where they needed him. Then suddenly he *was* there. "He came and stood among them," John says, and he spoke to them.

"Shalom," was what he said, "Peace be with you," which was of all words the one that in their un-peace they needed most to hear, but the way John tells it, it is as if they were too stunned to understand what they had heard, even to know who had spoken. So Jesus had to show them what had been done to his hands and to his side, and it was only then that they recognized him. "As the Father has sent me, even so I send you," he said, and then he breathed on them.

Can we imagine ourselves into that part of the story, I wonder? Can we put ourselves into their place as they breathed his breath into themselves, his life into their lives? I think we are often closer to their experience than we believe we are. I think that Christ dwells deep down in all of us, believers and unbelievers both, and that again and again, whether we realize it or not, he brings us healing and hope. I think there have been moments for all of us when the hand we reached out to another's need was not our hand but Christ's hand, and moments when the tears that have come to our eyes at another's sadness or joy, or even at our own sadness, our own joy, were Christ's tears. "Receive the Holy Spirit," he said to them there in the shadows, and I think we have all of us received more of that spirit into our own shadows than we dream.

The one disciple who wasn't in the room when Jesus appeared was Thomas, of course, although he was as much a friend and follower of Jesus as any of them. As far as Thomas knew, Jesus was dead and that was the end of it. He was aware of what Mary Magdalene claimed she had seen, and now, that evening, his friends were claiming the same thing, but Thomas himself had not seen him, and the words he spoke when they told him about it have the ring of unvarnished truth. "Unless I see in his hands the print of the nails, and place my finger in the mark of the nails, and place my hand in his side," he said, "I will not believe." Thomas is called the Twin in the New Testament, and if you want to know who the other twin is, I can tell you. I am the other twin, and unless I miss my guess, so are you.

How can we believe that Christ is alive when we haven't seen him? I believe the sun rose this morning because there it is in the sky above us. I believe you and I are alive because here we are looking at each other. But when it comes to this central proclamation and holiest mystery of Christian faith that after his death Jesus returned to life and is alive to this day, how can we believe that?

There are lots of other things we *can* believe about him. We can believe that of all good people, he was the goodest. We can believe that no one else in history embodied the love of God so movingly and unforgettably. We can believe that although down through the centuries endless follies and barbarities have been committed in his name, the beauty and holiness of his life remain somehow untouched, and that of all the great saints the world has produced, he remains the loveliest and the one most worth following. But when Thomas says that unless he sees him with his own eyes, he will not believe that he is actually alive the way you and I are actually alive, I think we all know in our hearts what he is talking about.

What we have to remember is that our eyes are not all we have for seeing with, maybe not even the best we have. Our eyes tell us that the mountains are green in summer and in autumn the colors of flame. They tell us that the nose of the little girl is freckled, that her hair usually needs combing, that when she is asleep, her cheek is flushed and moist. They tell us that the photographs of Abraham Lincoln taken a few days before his death show a man who at the age of fifty-six looked as old as time. Our eyes tell us that the small country church down the road needs a new coat of paint and that the stout lady who plays the pump organ looks a little like W. C. Fields and that the pews are rarely more than about a quarter filled on any given Sunday.

But all these things are only facts because facts are all the eye can see. Eyes cannot see truth. The truth about the mountains is their great beauty. The truth about the child is that she is so precious that without a moment's hesitation we would give our lives to save her life if that should somehow ever become necessary. The truth about Abraham Lincoln is a humanness so rich and deep that it's hard to stand in his memorial in Washington without tears coming to our eyes, and the truth about the shabby little church is that for reasons known only to God it is full of holiness. It is not with the eyes of the head that we see truths like that, but with the eyes of the heart.

Eight days after Jesus's first appearance to the disciples, John says, Jesus came back to them again in the same room, and this time Thomas was with them. Again Jesus said "Peace" to them. Then he turned to Thomas and spoke only to him as if there was no one else in the world just then who mattered, and you can imagine the two of them standing there looking at each other with maybe no more than an oil lamp to see by and their shadows flickering on the wall. Less as a reproach the way I hear it than as an enormous kindness, Jesus said, "Put your finger here, and see my hands; and put out your hand, and place it in my side. Do not be faithless, but believing." It was an extraordinary thing for him to offer, but it is as though Thomas didn't even hear him. It's as though maybe for the first time in his life it wasn't just the fact of Jesus that he saw but the truth of Jesus and the truth of who Jesus was for him. In light of that truth everything else became suddenly unimportant, and there was no need to touch him with his hands to make sure he was real because suddenly Thomas was so moved by the reality he was experiencing within himself that all he could do was to say something that I suspect he said in a whisper—"My Lord and my God!" He had seen him with the eyes of his heart, and there was nothing more he could say, nothing more he needed to say. Can we imagine ourselves into that part of the story? Have we ever even come close to seeing the truth of Jesus the way Thomas did just then?

I believe we have, more than we know, and I believe that, in the last analysis, those glimpses more than anything else are what bring us to church Sunday after Sunday. I believe we have glimpsed the truth of Jesus in the faces and lives of people we know who have loved him and served him, and let each of us name their names silently to ourselves. I believe we have glimpsed him in the pages of the Gospels when by some miracle of grace those pages come alive for us and it is as if we ourselves are the ones he is speaking to when he says, "Come to me, all who labor and are heavy laden, and I will give you rest" (Matt. 11:28). I believe we have caught sight of him in works of art that have been created to honor him, like the St. Matthew

Passion of Bach, or the flaking, faded frescoes of old European churches where he moves like a dream across the walls.

I believe we have seen him once in a while even in our own churches, especially when there is a pause in our endless babbling about him and for a moment or two he is present in the silence of waiting and listening. I remember how once when the minister was administering the chalice to me he made my heart skip a beat by calling me by name and saying "The blood of Christ, Freddy, the cup of salvation," and I saw suddenly that Christ not only remembers us but remembers each one of us by name as surely as he remembered the good thief, and that he welcomes us to his table not in some sort of impersonal, churchly sense but as if the party wouldn't be complete without every last one of us the way the father in his story threw his arms around the prodigal and welcomed him home.

I believe we have seen him in those rare moments when, moved by his spirit alive within us, we have been able to be Christs to one another and also at those moments when we have resisted his spirit within us and turned away from each other full of a kind of dimness and sadness. Most of all, I believe, we have seen him in our endless longing for him even when we don't know who it is we are longing for.

"Have you believed because you have seen me?" Jesus asked Thomas, our twin, and my guess is that Thomas believed not because of what his eyes had seen but because of what his heart had seen. With his eyes he had seen only Jesus the son of Joseph and Mary, a man much like any other man—so many inches tall, so many pounds heavy, hair this color, eyes that color—but with his heart he saw, maybe for the first time in his life, the one he was destined to love and search for and try to follow as best he could for the rest of his days when Jesus was no longer around for him to see with his eyes any more than he is around for us to see with ours.

The last thing of all that Jesus said to his disciples that day was, "Blessed are those who have *not* seen and yet believe," and I think that among others he meant you and me. We have not seen him with our eyes the way Thomas did, but precious as that sight would have been, I wonder in the long run what difference it would have made. What makes all the difference in the world is the one whom from time to time, by grace,

I believe we have seen with our hearts or who is there to see always if we will only keep our hearts peeled for him.

To see him with the heart is to know that in the long run his kind of life is the only life worth living. To see him with the heart is not only to believe in him but little by little to become bearers to each other of his healing life until we become finally healed and whole and alive within ourselves. To see him with the heart is to take heart, to grow true hearts, brave hearts, at last. That is my dearest hope and prayer for all of you and also for me.

32.

Let Jesus Show

"Little children, yet a little while I am with you. You will seek me; and as I said to the Jews so now I say to you, 'Where I am going you cannot come.'"... Simon Peter said to him, "Lord, where are you going?" Jesus answered, "Where I am going, you cannot follow me now; but you shall follow afterward.... Let not your hearts be troubled; believe in God, believe also in me. In my Father's house are many rooms; if it were not so, would I have told you that I go to prepare a place for you? And when I go and prepare a place for you, I will come again and will take you to myself, that where I am you may be also. And you know the way where I am going." Thomas said to him, "Lord, we do not know where you are going; how can we know the way?" Jesus said to him, "I am the way, and the truth, and the life; no one comes to the Father, but by me"

—John 13:33, 36; 14:1–6

When Jesus sat down to eat for the last time with a handful of his closest friends, he knew it was the last time, and he didn't have to be the Messiah to know it—they all did. The Romans were out to get him. The Jews were out to get him. For reasons that can only be guessed at, one of his own friends was out to get him, and Jesus seems to have known that too. He knew, in other words, that his time had all but run out and that they would never all of them be together again.

It is an unforgettable scene there in that upper room—the shadows, the stillness, the hushed voices of people speaking very carefully, very intently, because they wanted to get it all said while there was still time and to get it said right. You can only imagine the way it must have haunted them for the rest of their lives as they looked back on how they had actually sat there with him, eating and drinking and talking; and through their various accounts of it, including this morning's passage from John, and through all the paintings of it, like the great, half ruined da Vinci fresco in Milan, and through two thousand years of the church's reenactment of it in the Eucharist, it has come to haunt us too. But I think of the Last Supper as haunting in another way as well—not just as a kind of shadowy dream of an event long past but also as a kind of foreshadowing of an event not all that far in the future, by which I mean our own last suppers, the last time you and I will sit down with a handful of our own closest friends.

It's hard not to believe that somehow or other there's always going to be another time with them, another day, so the chances are we won't know it's the last time, and therefore it won't have the terrible sadness about it that the Last Supper of Jesus must have had. But not knowing is sad in another way because it means that we also won't know how precious this supper is, how precious these friends are whom we will be sitting down with for the last time whether we know it or not.

Who are these friends for you, who are they for me? We have to picture them for ourselves, of course—to see their faces, hear their voices, feel what it's like to be with them. They are our nearest and dearest—our husband or wife, our children, a few people we can't imagine living without or their living without us—and the sadness is that we have known them so long and so well that we don't really see them anymore for who they truly are let alone who they truly are to us, who we truly are to them. The sadness is that we don't see that every supper with them—even just a bowl of cornflakes in the kitchen some night after the movies—is precious beyond all telling because the day will come beyond which there will be no other supper with them ever again. The time will come when time will run out for us too, and once we see that, we see also that for the eighteen-year-old at McDonald's as well as for the old crock in the retirement-home cafeteria, every one of our suppers points to the preciousness of life and also to the certainty of death, which makes life even more precious still and is precious in itself because under its shadow we tend to search harder and harder for light.

There in that shadowy room the disciples turned to Jesus, who was their light, with greater urgency and passion than maybe ever before because, with all hell about to break loose, they had no other place to turn. They had drunk the wine he told them was his blood and put into their mouths the bread he told them was his body, and thus with something of his courage in them they asked him a question they had never risked asking so helplessly and directly before. It was Simon Peter who asked it, and what he said was, "Lord, where are you going?"

As if they didn't know. As if they didn't know. As if you and I don't know—both where he was going and where all of us are going too. He was going down the stairs and out the door. He was going into the night. He was going to pray in a garden to the God he called Father not to let the awful thing happen to him that he knew was already happening, and the Gospels do not record that he got so much as a whisper in reply. He was going alone, and he was going against his will, and he was going scared half out of his wits. He sweated blood is the way the Gospels put it.

The Last Supper not only prefigures our own last suppers wherever and whenever they are to be. It also is our last supper. You cannot read the account of it without in some measure being there, and the table where he sits with his friends is our table, and as they drew close to the light of him, we too try to draw close as if maybe in the last analysis he is the one who is our nearest and dearest—or our farthest and dearest because he is always just too far away to see very well, to take hold of, too far away to be sure he sees us. If we have any hope at all, he is our hope, and when Peter asks him, "Lord, where are you going?" the question within his question is "Are you going anywhere at all or just going out, like a light," and that is also our question both about him and about ourselves. When time runs out, does life run out? Did Jesus's life run out? Do you and I run out?

"You will seek me," Jesus says, and no word he ever spoke hits closer to home. We seek for answers to our questions—questions about life and about death, questions about what is right and what is wrong, questions about the unspeakable things that go on in the world. We seek for strength, for peace, for a path through the forest. But Christians are people who maybe more than for anything else seek for Christ, and from the shabbiest little jerry-built meeting house in the middle of nowhere to the greatest cathedrals, all churches everywhere were erected by people like us in the wild hope that in them, if nowhere else, the one we seek might finally somehow be found.

A friend of mine told me about a Christmas pageant he took part in once as the rector of an Episcopal church somewhere. The manger was down in front at the chancel steps where it always is. Mary was there in a blue mantle and Joseph in a cotton beard. The wise men were there with a handful of shepherds, and of course in the midst of them all the Christ child was there, lying in the straw. The nativity story was read aloud by my friend with carols sung at the appropriate places, and all went like clockwork until it came time for the arrival of the angels of the heavenly host as represented by the children of the congregation, who were robed in white and scattered throughout the pews with their parents.

At the right moment they were supposed to come forward and gather around the manger saying, "Glory to God in the highest, and on earth peace, good will among men," and that is just what they did except there were so many of them that there was a fair amount of crowding and jockeying for position, with the result that one particular angel, a girl about nine years old who was smaller than most of them, ended up so far out on the fringes of things that not even by craning her neck and standing on tiptoe could she see what was going on. "Glory to God in the highest and on earth peace, good will among men," they all sang on cue, and then in the momentary pause that followed, the small girl electrified the entire church by crying out in a voice shrill with irritation and frustration and enormous sadness at having her view blocked, "Let Jesus show!"

There was a lot of the service still to go, but my friend the rector said that one of the best things he ever did in his life was to end everything precisely there. "Let Jesus show!" the child cried out, and while the congregation was still sitting in stunned silence, he pronounced the benediction, and everybody filed out of the church with those unforgettable words ringing in their ears.

There is so much for all of us that hides Jesus from us—the church itself hides him, all the hoopla of church with ministers as lost in the thick of it as everybody else so that the holiness of it somehow vanishes away to the point where services of worship run the risk of becoming only a kind of performance—on some Sundays better, on some Sunday worse—and only on the rarest occasions does anything strike to the quick the way that little girl's cry did with every last person who heard her realizing that Jesus didn't show for any of them—the mystery and miracle of Jesus with all his extraordinary demands upon us, all his extraordinary promises.

Let Jesus show in these churches we have built for him then—not just Jesus as we cut him down to size in our sermons and hymns and stained-glass windows, but Jesus as he sat there among his friends with wine on his breath and crumbs in his beard and his heart in his mouth as he spoke about his death and ours in words that even the nine-year-old angel would have understood. "Let not your hearts be troubled," he said in the midst of his own terrible troubles. Take it easy. Take it easy. Take heart. "Believe in God," he said. "Believe also in me."

Well, we are believers, you and I, that's why we're here—at least would-be believers, part-time believers, believers with our fingers crossed. Believing in him is not the same as believing things about him such as that he was born of a virgin and raised Lazarus from the dead. Instead, it is a matter of giving our hearts to him, of come hell or high water putting our money on him, the way a child believes in a mother or a father, the way a mother or a father believes in a child.

"Lord, where are you going?" Peter asked from where he was sitting, and Jesus answered, "I go to prepare a place for you ... that where I am you may be also." Can we put our money on that? Are we children enough to hear with the ears of a child? Are we believers enough to believe what only a child can believe?

Three years ago, not long after my only brother, Jamie, died, I found myself one summer afternoon missing him so much, needing him so much, that I decided to call up his empty New York apartment. I knew perfectly well there wasn't anybody there to answer and yet of course I couldn't know it for sure because nothing, nothing, is for sure in this world, and who could say that at least some echo of him mightn't be there, and I would hear him again, hear the sound of his voice again, the sound of his marvelous laugh. So I sat there in the Vermont sunshine—this skeptical old believer, this believing old skeptic, who you would have thought had better sense—and let the phone ring, let it ring, let it ring.

Did Jamie answer it? How wonderful to be able to say that by some miracle he did and that I heard his voice again, but of course he didn't, he didn't, he didn't, and all I heard was the silence of his absence. Yet who knows? Who can ever know anything for sure about the mystery of things? "In my Father's house are many rooms," Jesus said, and I would bet my bottom dollar that in one of those many rooms that phone rang and rang true and was heard. I believe that in some sense my brother's voice was in the ringing itself, and that Jesus's voice was in it too.

Jesus said, "I go to prepare a place for you ... that where I am you may be also," speaking about death because that is what was uppermost in his mind as it was uppermost in the minds of all of them that last time they had supper together and as I suspect it is uppermost in our minds too more often than we let on. He says he is not just going out like a light. He says he is going on. He says he is going ahead. He says we will go there too when our time comes. And who can resist giving our hearts to him as he says it?

"You know the way where I am going," he says, and then Thomas speaks out for every one of us in a voice that my guess is had all the irritation and frustration and sadness of the little girl's. "Lord, we do not know where you are going; how can we know the way?"

If I were as brave as the rector at that Christmas pageant, I would stop talking precisely here with those starkly honest words. When it comes to the mystery of death, like the mystery of life, how can any of us know anything? If there is a realm of being beyond where we now are that has to do somehow with who Jesus is, and is for us, and is for all the world, then how can we know the way that will take us there?

"I am the way, and the truth, and the life," is how he answers. He does not say the church is the way. He does not say his teachings are the way, or what people for centuries have taught about him. He does not say religion is the way, not even the religion that bears his name. He says he himself is the way. And he says that the truth is not words, neither his words nor anyone else's words. It is the truth of being truly human as he was truly human and thus at the same time truly God's. And the life we are dazzled by in him, haunted by in him, nourished by in him is a life so full of aliveness and light that not even the darkness of death could prevail against it.

How do we go where he is? How do we who have a hard enough time just finding our way home in the night find the way that is his way, the way that is he? Who of us can say, and yet who of us doesn't search for the answer in our deepest places?

As for me, I think what we are to do is to keep on ringing and ringing and ringing, because that ringing—and the longing, the faith, the intuition that keeps us at it—is the music of the truth trying to come true even in us. I think that what we are to do is to try to draw near to him and to each other any way we can because that is the last thing he asked of us. "Love one another as I have loved you" (John 15:12) is the way he said it, and that is exactly what the little girl asked too on that Christmas Day. By believing against all odds and loving against all odds, that is how we are to let Jesus show in the world and to transform the world.

33.
Jairus's Daughter

Then one of the leaders of the synagogue named Jairus came and, when he saw Jesus, fell at his feet and begged him repeatedly, "My little daughter is at the point of death. Come and lay your hands on her, so that she may be made well, and live." So he went with him. And a large crowd followed him and pressed in on him. Some people came from the leader's house to say, "Your daughter is dead. Why trouble the teacher any further?" But overhearing what they said, Jesus said to the leader of the synagogue, "Do not fear, only believe." He allowed no one to follow him except Peter, James, and John, the brother of James. When they came to the house of the leader of the synagogue, he saw a commotion, people weeping and wailing loudly. When he had entered, he said to them, "Why do you make a commotion and weep? The child is not dead but sleeping." And they laughed at him. Then he put them all outside, and took the child's father and mother and those who were with him, and went in where the child was. He took her by the hand and said to her, "Talitha cum," which means, "Little girl, get up!" And immediately the girl got up and began to walk about (she was twelve years of age). At this they were overcome with amazement. He strictly ordered them that no one should know this, and told them to give her something to eat.

—MARK 5:22–24, 35B–43, NRSV

The story Mark tells takes place on the western shores of the Sea of Galilee, which isn't a sea at all, of course, but a large freshwater lake some thirteen miles long and eight miles across surrounded by high mountains and apparently roughly in the shape of a heart, which is rather wonderful if you stop to think about it—a heart-shaped lake at the heart of where it all happened. After leaving Nazareth Jesus seems to have spent most of what was left of his short life in the city of Capernaum, which was on the northern shore of the lake and the center of its fishing industry. A number of his best friends lived there including Zebedee's two sons, James and John, together with Peter and his brother Andrew, who were all of them partners in some sort of fishing enterprise that employed other people whose names we don't know and that seems to have owned at least two boats.

When Mark gives his account of what happened by the lake on this particular day, he puts in so many details that Matthew's parallel account leaves out that it seems possible he was actually there at the time or at least had talked to somebody who was. It has the ring of an eyewitness account, in other words, and that makes it a little easier for us all these centuries later to see it with our eyes too, which is what I think we should always try to do with all these stories about Jesus. Hearing them preached on in church year after year and reading them in the dreary double columns of some Bible, we tend to think of them as dreary themselves—as little stained-glass stories suitable for theologizing about and moralizing about but without much life in them or much relevance to the reality of our own lives and to us.

But that is not at all the kind of story that Mark is telling us here if you think about it, or maybe if you don't so much think about it as just listen to it, let it take you wherever it is going. It is a quiet, low-key little story and in some ways so unclear and ambiguous that it's hard to know just why Mark is telling it or just what he expects us to make out of it or made out of it himself. It's a story not about stained-glass people at all but about people who lived and breathed and sweated and made love and used bad language when they tripped over furniture in the dark and sometimes had more troubles than they knew what to do with and sometimes laughed themselves silly over nothing in particular and were thus in many ways very much like the rest of us.

Jesus had just crossed over in a boat from the other side of the lake, Mark writes, when he found himself surrounded by some of them right there at the water's edge where there were nets hanging up to dry and fish being gutted and scaled and stray cats looking around for anything they could get their paws on. He doesn't say there was any particular reason for the crowd, so it's probably just that they had heard about Jesus—probably even knew him, some of them—and were there to gawk at him because there were a lot of wild stories about who some people said he was and what he was going around the countryside doing and saying, and they were there to see what wild things he might take it into his head to say or do next.

There are so many people around him it's hard to pick out which one Jesus is, but it's worth giving it a try. Is he the one with his hand in the air signaling to somebody he can't get to on the far edge of the crowd? Is he the thin, sad-eyed one who looks a little like Osama bin Laden, of all people? Is he the one leaning down and reaching out to take something a child is trying to hand him? What did it feel like to be near enough to touch him if you dared? If his eyes happened to meet yours for a moment, what would you say if you could find the right words for saying it, and how would he answer you if he could so much as hear you in the midst of all the babbling and jostling? What if just for a moment as he tried to shoulder his way out of the crowd he brushed against you so that for a second or two you actually felt the solid flesh and bone of him, smelled the smell of him?

I think that is part of what all these stories about Jesus in the Gospels are trying to tell us if we keep our ears open. They're trying to tell us who he was and what it was it like to be with him. They're trying to tell us what there was about him that made at least some of the people there by the lake that day decide to give up everything they had or ever hoped to have, in some cases even their own lives, maybe just for the sake of being near him.

Matthew's account doesn't give us the name *Jairus*, but Mark's does. There was a man named Jairus there, he says, who somehow made his way to Jesus and threw himself at his feet, as Mark describes it, fell to his knees perhaps, or touched his forehead to the ground in front of him. He was a synagogue official of some kind, Mark says, whatever exactly that means, but an important man anyway, which is possibly why the crowd gave way enough to let him through. But he doesn't behave like an important man, though. He behaves like a desperate man, a man close to hysteria with fear, grief, horror, God knows what.

The reason is that his daughter is on the point of death, Jairus says, only he doesn't say "my daughter," he says "my little daughter." She is twelve years old, going on thirteen, we're told, so she wasn't all that little really, but to Jairus she would presumably always be his little daughter the way even when they've grown up and moved away long since, we keep on speaking of our sons and daughters as children because that is what they were when we knew them first and loved them first.

His child is dying is what Jairus is there to get through somehow to this man some say is like no other man. She is *dying*—he says it repeatedly, Mark tells us, dying, dying—and then he says, "Come and lay your hands on her," because he's seen it done that way before and has possibly even tried doing it that way himself, except that it did absolutely no good at all when he tried it, as for all he knows it will do absolutely no good now either. But this is the only card he has left to play, and he plays it. "Lay your hands on her, so she may be made well, and live," he says—live, he says, live, not die, before she's hardly had more than a glimpse of what living is. It's a wonder Jesus even hears him what with all the other things people are clamoring to him for, but somehow he does, and so does a lot of the crowd that follows along as Jairus leads the way to where his house stands.

They follow presumably because for the moment Jesus is the hottest ticket in town and because they don't have anything better to do and because they're eager to see if the man is all he's been cracked up to be. But before they get very far, they run into some people coming the other way who with the devastating tactlessness of the simple souls they are come right out and say it. "*Your* daughter *is dead,*" they tell Jairus. They have just come from his house, where she died. They saw it with their own eyes. There is nothing anybody can do about it now. They have come too late. "Why trouble the teacher any further?" they ask her father, and it is Jesus who finally breaks the silence by speaking, only it's just Jairus he speaks to.

"*Do not fear,*" he says. Don't be afraid. Don't be afraid. And then, "*Only believe.*"

The question is what is a man to believe when his whole life has blown up in his face? Believe that somehow life makes sense even in the face of a twelve-year-old's death? Believe that in some unimaginable way all will be well no matter what? Believe in God? Believe in Jesus? Jairus doesn't ask what he is to believe or how he is to believe and Jesus doesn't tell him as they stand there in the road. "*Only believe*" is all he says, meaning maybe only "Believe there's nothing you have to be afraid of," and then he tells everybody to go home except for his three particular friends, who Mark tells us were Peter and James and John. And everybody goes home.

When the five of them finally get to Jairus's house, they find it full of people "weeping and wailing loudly," as Mark describes it because this is not the twenty-first century but the first century and people apparently hadn't started yet saying things like "It's really a blessing" or "She is in a better world now" because for the most part they didn't believe in any better world but just some sort of limbo world under the earth where the ghosts of the dead drift like dead leaves. Instead, they wept and wailed because they didn't have it in them to pretend that the death of a child is anything but the tragic and unspeakable thing that it is, and Jesus didn't say anything to make them change their minds, didn't tell them that it was God's will or anything like that. What he did instead was to say something that it's hard to know how to understand.

"The child is not dead," he said, "but sleeping."

Was he speaking literally? Did he mean she had lapsed into some kind of coma? Or was he only trying to comfort her father with the thought that death is only a kind of eternal sleep? Who knows what he meant, but the people in the house seemed to think he was either a fool or a madman. They had been there when it happened. They knew death when they saw it, and because the line between weeping and laughing is sometimes a very tenuous one, they stopped their weeping and wailing and of all things *laughed* at him, Mark said, laughed because they didn't know what else to do, until Jesus finally "put them all outside," the way Mark tells it, so that only the three fisherman friends along with Jairus and the child's mother were left there with him, and together they went on to the room where the child lay.

It is the deafening stillness of it, I think, that you can imagine best—the mother with her face in her hands, Jairus on his knees at the bedside, the child like the waxwork of a child, hair brushed, face washed, hands folded one on top of the other on her chest.

Then the moment of magic, if magic is what it was. It's the child herself that Jesus speaks to. He reaches down and picks up one of her hands in his hand, and Mark reports the words he used not in Greek, which is what the rest of his Gospel is written in, but in Aramaic, which was the language Jesus actually spoke, so somebody who was there at the time must have heard them and remembered them—the actual words he used as he reached out and lifted up the child's hand in his.

"*Talitha cum,*" Jesus says. "*Talitha cum,*" and you hardly need the translation to understand him. "Little girl"—*Talitha*—"get up," is what he said, and then according to Mark "immediately the girl got up and started to walk about.... At this they were overcome with amazement."

It was not just the *child's* life that had been given back, of course, but the lives of the mother and father, who stood there with no words they knew how to say. The worst thing that had ever happened to them had suddenly become the best thing that had ever happened to them, and you can imagine their hardly daring so much as to breathe for fear of breaking the spell. You can imagine her walking around the room touching familiar things—a chair, a comb, a flower somebody had left, a chipped plate—trying to get the world back, trying to get her self back.

For whatever the reason, Jesus asked them never to tell a soul what had happened—maybe because he wasn't ready for the secret of who he was to be known yet, maybe because he wasn't sure he knew the secret of who he was yet himself. Who can say? Then he told them to go get the child something to eat, something for the child to eat, and that is where Mark's story ends.

The question is what kind of a story is it? If the little girl had actually died the way the people who were there in the house believed she had, then it is the story of a miracle as dazzling as the raising of Lazarus and bears witness to the power Jesus had over even the last and darkest power of all. If she was only sleeping as Jesus said—in a coma or whatever he may have meant—then it is a story about a healing, about the power of Jesus's touch to make the blind see and the deaf hear and the lame walk. Either way it is a story about a miracle, but about a miracle that doesn't end with an exclamation point the way you would expect, but with a question mark or at most with the little row of dots that means unresolved, to be continued, to figure out somehow for ourselves.

Who can say for sure exactly what it is that Jesus did in that house where Jairus lived or how far down into the darkness he had to reach to do it, but in a way who cares any more than her mother and father can have cared. They had their child back. She was alive again. She was well again. That was all that mattered. I picture her looking something like the photographs we have of Anne Frank—a wry, narrow little Jewish face full of irony and wit and a kind of bright-eyed exhilaration; I picture how it would be to have the child that was Anne Frank back again somehow, the way she was before the gates of the concentration camp closed behind her. I picture how one way or another, if such a thing were to happen, we would all of us fall to our knees. The whole world would fall to its knees.

Who knows what kind of story Mark is telling here, but the enormously moving part of it, I think, is the part where Jesus takes the little girl's hand and says, *"Talitha cum"*—"Little girl, get up"—and suddenly we ourselves are the little girl.

Little girl. Old girl. Old boy. Old boys and girls with high blood pressure and arthritis, and young boys and girls with tattoos and body piercing. You who believe, and you who sometimes believe and sometimes don't believe much of anything, and you who would give almost anything to believe if only you could. You happy ones and you who can hardly remember what it was like once to be happy. You who know where you're going and how to get there and you who much of the time aren't sure you're getting anywhere. "Get up," he says, all of you—all of you!—and the power that is in him is the power to give life not just to the dead like the child, but to those who are only partly alive, which is to say to people like you and me who much of the time live with our lives closed to the wild beauty and miracle of things, including the wild beauty and miracle of every day we live and even of ourselves.

It is that life-giving power that is at the heart of this shadowy story about Jairus and the daughter he loved, and that I believe is at the heart of all our stories—the power of new life, new hope, new being, that whether we know it or not, I think, keeps us coming to places like this year after year in search of it. It is the power to get up even when getting up isn't all that easy for us anymore and to keep getting up and going on and on toward whatever it is, whoever he is, that all our lives long reaches out to take us by the hand.

34.

Waiting

Jesus said, "There will be signs in the sun, the moon, and the stars, and on the earth distress among nations confused by the roaring of the sea and the waves. People will faint from fear and foreboding of what is coming upon the world, for the powers of the heavens will be shaken. Then they will see 'the Son of Man coming in a cloud' with power and great glory. Now when these things begin to take place, stand up and raise your heads, because your redemption is drawing near."

Then he told them a parable: "Look at the fig tree and all the trees; as soon as they sprout leaves you can see for yourselves and know that summer is already near. So also, when you see these things taking place, you know that the kingdom of God is near."

—LUKE 21:25–31, NRSV

I don't know any other passage in the Gospels that is harder to understand, to feel our way into, to know how to respond to, than these words of Jesus about the Second Coming. He is speaking about the end of the world and about the coming of the Kingdom of God as the climactic last act of history, and he is speaking in words and images as foreign to our whole way of thinking as his subject itself. As the day approaches, there will be a great cosmic upheaval, he says, with signs in the sun and moon and stars, and the powers of the heavens themselves shaken. Is he speaking literally or simply in poetic hyperbole? Does he mean there will be real eclipses and strange comets that have never been seen before, maybe a reordering of the constellations themselves to scrawl some fateful starlit message across the night sky? Or is he speaking symbolically of some upheaval not of the world without but of the world within—an upheaval of the hearts and minds and spirits of the human race? The seas will go wild, he says, and at their roaring the nations will be terrified by whatever it is that is happening or about to happen, and then, most extraordinary of all—as the cause and climax of everything that has preceded it—the Son of Man will appear, he says, in a cloud, "with power and great glory."

What does he mean by the Son of Man? Whom does he mean? It is an ambiguous term as it is used in the Bible and can mean various things at various times. Does he use it here to mean the Messiah, and if so, is he using it to refer to himself? Does he mean that he himself will appear in glory at the end of time? And if that is the case, what is his reason for using this enigmatic phrase instead of declaring it directly? Who does Jesus believe that he is, and who is he asking us to believe that he is?

His words leave us confused and uncertain, and the confusion is only compounded by the apparently contradictory ways he describes the effect that these cataclysmic events are to have. On the one hand, he says, people will "faint from fear and foreboding" at the sight of them, and on the other hand, he says, "stand up and raise your heads, because your redemption is drawing near," and likens them to the way in springtime a fig tree puts out leaves as a sign that summer is near, a time of fruition and fulfillment. Does he mean that the Second Coming will be terrifying to some and redeeming to others, that when the Kingdom finally comes, some will be in it and some will not? Or does he mean that redemption itself has an element of terror in it maybe: after years of being sick—soul-sick, heartsick, sick of ourselves—the terror of becoming suddenly well and not knowing what to do with our wellness, the terror of becoming truly human at last, which means being purged of everything that all our lives long has made us less than human—our half-heartedness, our hopeless self-centeredness? Who knows what he means in this troubling passage? Who can fathom what he is saying about what it is that the future holds for us?

Whenever we are tempted to think that we understand Jesus and have him in our pocket, that after all these years of being haunted by him and calling out to him in our need and at least *trying* to believe in him, to follow him, words like these remind us that he remains always a mystery beyond our comprehension. And yet at the heart of this apocalyptic passage, I think, there is something that we can comprehend because it is close to the heart also of our own experience as Christians, and because it is something that churches like this one bear witness to.

Look at the windows that burn like fire when the sun shines through them, and at the images of Christ and his saints, at the flowers and candles on the altar. Consider the silent space that these walls enclose and also the sounds that break the silence like the choir, the organ, the sounds of our own voices singing or praying, the voices of the men and women who stand up in this pulpit doing their best to proclaim the gospel. What does it all add up to? What is it that we are essentially doing here in this building? The immediate answer is that we are worshiping God here. We are trying to speak to God here and to speak about God. We are trying to listen for God. We are searching for something of God's peace, trying somehow to take God into our lives the way we take the wine and the bread into our mouths. But deep beneath all of this, in our innermost hearts, I think we are doing something else.

I think we are waiting. That is what is at the heart of it. Even when we don't know that we are waiting, I think we are waiting. Even when we can't find words for what we are waiting for, I think we are waiting. An ancient Advent prayer supplies us with the words. "Give us grace," it says, "that we may cast off the works of darkness and put upon us the armor of light." We who live much of the time in the darkness are waiting not just at Advent, but at all times for the advent of light, of that ultimate light that is redemptive and terrifying at the same time. It is redemptive because it puts an end to the darkness, and that is also why it is terrifying, because for so long, for all our lives, the darkness has been home, and because to leave home is always cause for terror.

A church like this one is full of darkness and light both. The light of it is the beauty of it. The light of it is the windows, the music, the candles, the silence, and the way in which they can all point beyond themselves to unimaginable beauty itself. Preachers like me are just as much in the dark as everybody else and more often than not know less about the mystery they are proclaiming than their congregations do because they have come to believe that through their endless attempts to make the mystery understandable, they have somehow managed to understand it; but even so, every once in a while some word that preachers speak here for a moment stirs to life the holiness we long for and wait for and stuns us with its truth; and that too is part of the light of this place. Every once in a while there are moments when we feel that the God we are speaking to here has heard us, that the God we are listening for has spoken to us, that the God we hunger for has fed us with more than just the sip of wine, the bit of bread.

The darkness of a church, on the other hand, is that very often there are no such moments, so that all the beauty seems artificial and theatrical and, instead of testifying to the presence of God among us, testifies to nothing so much as God's absence, not only in this place but also in ourselves. Darker still is the sense a church can give us that a church is somehow an end in itself, that all the hymns and prayers and preaching, all the ways we have of being religious here, are the only light there is and that instead of merely foreshadowing God's Kingdom, realistically speaking they may well be all the kingdom that God has. Let us never forget how the book of Revelation tells us that when the Kingdom of Heaven finally comes like a bride adorned for her husband, there will be no church in it at all because in the Kingdom of Heaven it is God's presence itself that is the church, and all our ways of worshiping God, all our attempts to body forth the glory of God in song and stained glass and sermon are at best only fingers pointing to a glory we know best by how we miss it and in our hearts long for it even when we don't know we are longing.

"There *will be* signs in the sun, the moon, and the stars," Jesus says. You "*will see* the Son of Man coming in a cloud with power and great glory." When the fig tree starts to put out leaves, you know that summer *will come.* Will be, will see, will come—if we take the words of Jesus as seriously as he asks us to take them, then the realest, truest, most authentic thing we can do as Christians is to wait—to wait with passion, to wait with hope against hope for these mysterious words of Jesus to be fulfilled. If we forget that we are waiting, if we come to believe that the best we have found of God here in these shadows is the best there is, if we come to believe that the most God wants of us is to be religious the way we are religious in a church, then we have lost touch with the living depths of our faith.

When Jesus said that we must become like children, I wonder if part of what he meant was that we must learn to wait like children. I think of the way my younger brother and I waited for the coming of Christmas when we were children. I remember the Advent cards our grandparents used to send us every year—with a sprinkling of tinsel dust on the roofs of the little village for snow, and windows that you opened, one each day, to show a candy cane or a teddy bear or a rocking horse. I remember how we hung it on a lampshade so the light shone through, and I can still feel the excitement in the pit of my stomach as it got closer and closer to the twenty-fourth day when you opened not just another window, but the doors of a stable, and inside the stable there was a baby asleep in the straw. Then on Christmas morning we would drive from wherever we were living at the time into New York City, where our grandparents lived, and along with my father's two brothers and their families we would start waiting all over again in the dim hallway of our grandparents' apartment with a Tiffany lamp on a round table and the curtained glass doors to the living room closed until finally our grandfather appeared ringing a handbell like a Salvation Army Santa Claus and opened them onto unutterable magic—a whole Arabian Nights' worth of treasure with the lights of the tree glimmering and cider and German Christmas cookies and so many presents that they had to be set out all around the walls of the room with a pile for each of us marked with our names. It was worth vastly more than all the weeks we had spent waiting for it, and though I've long since forgotten almost every present I ever got, I remember still the dazzling light of it and the presence of all those people I one way or another loved and who one way or another loved me, and the feeling that life simply could never get any better than this, and the almost unbearable excitement of it.

That was the light of it, but tucked away in certain corners and out beyond the curtained doors there was also of course darkness, because that is the way life is. A month before my tenth Christmas, my father committed suicide, and only a few days later my grandfather, the one who rang the bell and opened the doors, died as much of a broken heart as anything else.

And only a few years after that, my father's youngest brother committed suicide too.

What I think about now is how even before those dark things happened, they had all been somehow there in that magical room—along with the tree and the presents and the uncles and aunts and cousins—waiting to happen. I think of how not all the love there was in that room was enough to keep them from happening. There was not Christmas enough to save the day. There was not Christ enough. There never has been Christ enough—not just for my family way back then, but for all of us right now and always. And yet at some unknowable point in the future, there will be Christ enough. That is what Jesus is saying in this apocalyptic passage that is our text. That is our wild and beautiful hope.

In the meantime, if there is not Christ enough to save the day, there is Christ enough at least to make it bearable. Much of what goes on in churches, I'm afraid, is as shallow and lifeless as much of its preaching, and as irrelevant to the deep needs of the people who come to church hungering for a sense of God's presence that they more often than not never find. The church is not just in the hands of the charlatans and clowns who are apt to be the ones who represent it to millions on television, but in the hands also of good and faithful people who nonetheless often seem to be going about the business of church, the busyness of church, with so little real conviction or passion or joy that it is no wonder pews tend to be emptier every year. And yet, in spite of all this, the church is also, in St. Paul's unforgettable metaphor, the Body of Christ. On this planet at least, church is the only body that for the time being Christ has, which is to say that you and I are the only bodies Christ has. He has no hands to reach out to people with except our hands, no feet to go to them with except our feet, no other eyes to see them with, no other faces to show them his love.

So to wait for Christ to come in his fullness is not just a passive thing, a pious, prayerful, churchly thing. On the contrary, to wait for Christ to come in his fullness is above all else to act in Christ's stead as fully as we know how. To wait for Christ is as best we can to be Christ to those who need us to be Christ to them most and to bring them the most we have of Christ's healing and hope because unless we bring it, it may never be brought at all, as it was never brought to those two young men and that one old man whom I shared Christmas with all those Christmases ago.

God grant that we may each of us cast off our own works of darkness, whatever they are, however we can, and put upon ourselves the armor of something at least a little like light as we wait for the truth of Christ to come finally and fully true at last.

35.

The Word of Life

We declare to you what was from the beginning, what we have heard, what we have seen with our eyes, what we have looked at and touched with our hands, concerning the word of life—this life was revealed, and we have seen it and testify to it, and declare to you the eternal life that was with the Father and was revealed to us—we declare to you what we have seen and heard so that you also may have fellowship with us; and truly our fellowship is with the Father and with his Son Jesus Christ. We are writing these things so that our joy may be complete.

—1 JOHN 1:1–4, NRSV

The author of First John starts out by proclaiming the most precious thing he has to proclaim—the most precious reality he knows, the most precious part of his own life, the most precious part of himself as a human being. It is not something fuzzy and elusive. It is not something you have to believe in to be saved. On the contrary, he says. It is something that has happened and keeps on happening. It is real enough to hear, real enough to see, real enough to touch with our own hands the way we touch each other with our own hands. He is so caught up in telling us about it that he keeps repeating himself. He gets his syntax so confused that nobody knows quite how to translate him right.

It is "the word of life" that he is talking about, he says—in Greek the *logos* of life, which is the truth of life, the meaning of life, the innermost source and purpose of life. It is the way life was created to be lived. It is the life he has heard, seen, touched in Jesus Christ, he says. And the reason that he is proclaiming it, he says, is so that we may all of us live it. Live it! he says. And live it *how?* Live it by falling in love with it. Live it not so much by worrying about it and talking about it, but by letting it fill our sails like the wind.

And live it *why?* Live it so that we may have *koinonia* with each other, a word that has been translated *fellowship,* but that is a word that has become so stale and overused by churches that it summons up little more than drinking coffee in paper cups with each other after the eleven o'clock service. So let's say *friendship* instead. He is urging us to live this Christ-life that he has seen and heard and touched so that at long last we may be not just coffee-hour friends, social friends, but true friends. And not just true friends of each other but *true* friends of God, true friends of Christ, who are also our Friends as they are Friends too of people we wouldn't touch with a ten-foot pole.

He is writing about all this, John says, "so that our joy may be complete." Of all the things he might say, the thing he says is *joy.* This life he has seen and touched and heard is not another religious obligation. It is not a matter of believing certain things and doing certain things in order to be saved. *Joy* is his word. To be called to this life is not like being called to order or called to account or called to church. It is like being called to a great jamboree where everybody including the host is our oldest and dearest friend. "Beloved, let us love one another," he says later (4:7), and that is saying the same thing. Let us rejoice in our variety as well as in our sameness and have a wonderful time together, he says, because God himself made time wonderful and God is our friend, for God's sake. "He who does not love abides in death," he says somewhere else (3:14), and you can't put it any more strongly, any more clearly, than that. That is what the word of life is.

He wrote his Letter to a divided church, a torn-apart church, and thus to a church very much like our own, very much like ourselves with all our disagreements about issues such as abortion, and about how to read the Bible, and about who should be ordained, and heaven only knows what all else. "Be friends" is what he tells us, by which I take him not to mean that we are somehow to sweep our disagreements under the rug—they are too serious and too important for that and have to be worked out and somehow resolved. He means we are to be friends at a deeper level than we are adversaries. "Beloved, let us love one another," he says. That is the kind of friends he urges us to be—friends like the people we know whom we love even though there are times when we don't seem to see eye to eye with them about much of anything.

Sometimes by the grace of God we even manage to have friendships like that, or maybe it is more accurate to say that sometimes by the grace of God friendships like that manage to happen among us despite everything we do or fail to do. Let me tell you about one of those times when I saw it happen with my own eyes and heard it and touched it and was deeply touched by it.

Last spring my wife and I went to what amounted to a wedding although the word used in the invitation was not wedding but celebration— "a celebration of love and commitment," the invitation said. The reason the word wedding was not used was that the couple in question were not a man and a woman but two women. One of them was a childhood friend of our youngest daughter, whom we had known since she was five years old or so, a pigtailed, freckled-faced, plump little thing who grew up to become in her thirties a warm-hearted, spontaneous, outgoing woman who has had great success as a teacher and coach at a secondary school near where we live. The other, her friend, was a year or two older, an intelligent, well-educated woman who tends to be more reserved at first but is full of the same kind of wit and strength and human warmth when you get to know her.

It is hard to convey the mixed feelings I had when the invitation arrived. With part of myself, I could only rejoice not only that two people I liked and admired had each found in the other a companion she wanted to spend the rest of her life with, but that instead of keeping it as a guilty secret between them, they were prepared to stand up and declare it in the midst of a small town that they surely knew could no more be depended upon to view it with tolerance and understanding than any small town anywhere in this country or anywhere else.

With part of myself, I found it hard to believe that Jesus himself would do anything but bless a commitment as honest and brave as the one they were making to each other. The Bible has hard things to say about homosexuality in the sense of prostitution and lust and exploitation—just as it has equally hard things to say about heterosexuality in the sense of prostitution and lust and exploitation—but about homosexuality in the sense of the kind of loving, faithful, monogamous relationship that these two women were entering upon, it seems to leave it to us to search our own hearts, and with part of my own heart I was nothing but happy for them and wished them nothing but well.

But that was with only part of my heart. With the other part I was afraid for these two people and ambivalent in all sorts of ways about what they were doing and confused by my own ambivalence. I am as much the product of my own generation with all its prejudices and preconceptions and hang-ups as anybody else, and I couldn't help wishing that things had turned out differently for them. I wished my daughter's childhood friend had found a man to fall in love with and to have babies with the way my daughter did. I wished that in a world that God knows is dangerous and complicated enough as it is she and her friend had chosen a safer, simpler, more well-marked path, and as I thought ahead to the celebration we were bidden to, I couldn't help believing that a great many others—the parents, the friends, everybody who loved them—probably wished the same thing. So with all this going on inside me, I went to the ceremony full of misgivings. I felt awkward and divided inside myself. I felt awkward about what to say when I got there, about what to think, about what to be.

Some of the people I would have expected to find there were not there. Did they stay away because they felt awkward too? Did they stay away because they were scandalized? Did they stay away because of what other people would think if they went? Maybe they just hadn't been invited. Who knows? But a lot of people did go, well over a hundred anyway. The ceremony took place outside on the lawn in front of the house of the parents of my daughter's friend. There was the usual milling around and chatting while we waited for the musicians to arrive. There was a tent set up for the reception. It had been threatening rain, but the sun came out at the last minute. The service was conducted by a minister and his wife whom most of us knew. There was a homily based on the words of Ruth to Naomi— "Whither thou goest, I will go; and where thou lodgest, I will lodge; thy people shall be my people, and thy God my God. Where thou diest, will I die, and there will I be buried" (Ruth 1:16–17, KJV). Vows were exchanged, the couple embraced, and the minister blessed them.

How to describe such an occasion in Vermont of all places and in the presence of some people who looked right out of Norman Rockwell and others who looked as if they'd never heard of Norman Rockwell and would have looked down their noses at him if they had? How to guess what they felt about what they were there to witness except that probably no two of them felt quite the same way? But there was one feeling that I am as certain as you can be about such things that we all shared, and that was the feeling that something honest and loving and brave was happening before our eyes, and that something kind and affirming and hopeful was happening inside ourselves, and that grace, never more amazingly, was somehow in the very air we breathed. In other words, for a few moments that summer afternoon, it seemed to me that we were what I believe the church was created to be.

We all of us hunger for church to be like that always. We hunger for a sense of the presence of God. We hunger for God's grace to be as palpable as it seemed to be at that offbeat little celebration in Vermont where, no matter what our misgivings were about what it was that was being celebrated, we were all of us truly friends in Christ there, and Christ was truly our friend there and the friend as well of the two young women who were being blessed in his name. It is St. John's "word of life" that we hunger for and St. John's joy. But too often the churches we know seem lifeless and joyless. Too often the preachers we hear seem to know *about* the holy truth they proclaim, but not to be hearing and seeing and touching it in their own lives, not to be in touch with the living heart of that truth, which is that we were created to love one another despite all the differences between us the way God loves us despite all the differences between us.

I wish the church could be as open-hearted and open-minded and free as it was on that little patch of front lawn as the sun came out from behind the clouds. I wish that we could affirm as truly as we did there that wherever people love each other and are true to each other and take risks for each other, God is with them and for them and they are doing God's will.

36.
A 250th Birthday Prayer

On that day, when evening had come, he said to them, "Let us go across to the other side." And leaving the crowd, they took him with them, just as he was, in the boat. And other boats were with him. And a great storm of wind arose, and the waves beat into the boat, so that the boat was already filling. But he was in the stern, asleep on the cushion; and they woke him and said to him, "Teacher, do you not care if we perish?" And he awoke and rebuked the wind, and said to the sea, "Peace! Be still!" And the wind ceased, and there was a great calm. He said to them, "Why are you afraid? Have you no faith?" And they were filled with awe, and said to one another, "Who then is this, that even wind and sea obey him?"

—MARK 4:35–41

The year 1997 marks not only the 250th anniversary of Princeton's founding but also the 50th reunion of my class, and I come back to this loveliest of all chapels, which like most of my friends I avoided like the plague during my undergraduate days, with a strong sense of history—of Princeton's history, my class's history, and the histories of all of us who have gathered here this morning. I don't remember much about our commencement all those years ago, but I remember a few things, or think I do. Unless I'm mistaken, General Omar Bradley received an honorary degree and so did Catherine Cornell. I remember my surprise at reading in the program that I had been given an obscure award for writing called the Manners Prize, which everybody assumed was because I always took my hat off in the elevator when there were ladies present and kept my mouth closed when I chewed. I remember it was a beautiful June day.

But what I remember best was something that happened when we were all lined up behind Nassau Hall in our caps and gowns trying to keep the tassels out of our eyes as we waited for the signal to start marching to our seats out front to the music of Purcell or whatever they played that day. Some member of the class—I wish I could remember who—decided to walk the whole length of the long line asking everybody the same question, and the question was "What are you going to do now?"

It was an unsettling thing to be asked. What I took him to mean was what job did we have lined up for ourselves, or what graduate school, or what travel plans, something relatively simple like that, and I for one had a ready answer. I said what I was going to do was start teaching English at Lawrenceville in the fall, which indeed I did, but unless I have it wrong, a lot of people in my part of the line anyway didn't seem to be sure, which may have meant either that they didn't have anything at all lined up for the moment or that they understood the question as something much more fateful than I had.

Maybe they thought that what they had been asked wasn't just what were they going to do in the immediate future but what were they going to do with the rest of their lives, and if that was indeed what the young man meant, no wonder everybody clammed up. God knows I would have clammed up too. I don't think I had the faintest idea what I was going to do with the rest of my life if I had ever even considered the matter, and I wonder if any of us did as we stood there feeling a little unreal in our mortar boards with the hot New Jersey sun shining down on us and all those parents and friends and assorted well-wishers fanning themselves with their programs as they waited out front in their folding chairs for the show to begin. The question now, of course, is what *did* we do with the rest of our lives, and that is more unsettling still.

Well, one thing we did was to survive, some of us for longer than others, and that in itself is nothing to sneeze at. We survived physically, and maybe we even survived humanly, which is no mean feat in a world that is forever either tempting us to be less than human or looking to us to be more than human in ways that are beyond our reach—to be heroes, to be saints, to be big-time winners, to be perpetually wise and loving and brave, when the best we can possibly do is every once and a while to be things like that and the rest of the time to settle for being no better and no worse than what we hopelessly, helplessly are.

We also got married, some of us. We found another human being to ride out the storm with, and maybe it worked and maybe it didn't work, and many a marriage either ended so sadly or dragged on so sadly that those of us who chose to ride out the storm all by themselves found reason to believe that maybe they were the smart ones after all, as maybe indeed we were. Who knows? It is one of life's greatest mercies that it is not given us to know the might-have-been of things.

And what else did we do, those young men who graduated all those years ago? Well, some of us had children, and those of us who did discovered, as the chances are we wouldn't have discovered any other way, what it is to hold another life so dear that without a moment's hesitation we would lay down our own lives to save that life if ever things should come to such a pass. And if those of us who did not have children never discovered that farthest reach of love, the love that I suspect comes closest to God's love for the world, we were at least spared the discovery that what you suffer when a child you love suffers is incomparably worse than anything you can suffer on your own. So I suppose childlessness too has its compensations.

One way or another we all of us found work to do, including presumably the unknown classmate himself who was probably feeling a little shaken and hungover still from the festivities of the night before as he made his way from one of us to the next. The question is, Was the work we found for our own good only, or was it at least a little for the world's good too? Were our hearts in our work, or did we do it only to make money enough to be able to enjoy ourselves when we weren't working?

Did we ever learn to speak in our own true voices rather than in the voices that we thought would be most impressive, most persuasive, that would best keep hidden from the world the secret of who we really were inside ourselves?

Those of us who were as timid and uneasy about our sexuality as later generations seem open and natural and glad about it, did we gain more than we lost by to one extent or another repressing so rich a part of what it is to be human?

If we were religious, did we move beyond churchgoing into some sense of the mystery and holiness of life, including the individual lives of all of us?

If we wrote off religion as superstitious and irrelevant, was it because we had the wit to see that that is often exactly what religion is, or was it because for one reason or another we were reluctant to look where religion points us, which is beneath the surface of ourselves into the deep places where angels do battle with demons and souls are saved and lost?

All of this is something to think about anyway, and it is something for Princeton to think about too. I think of this venerable old campus as Jonathan Edwards knew it and James Madison and Woodrow Wilson, not to mention F. Scott Fitzgerald and Jimmy Stewart. I think of Chancellor Green while it was still full of books and so quiet you could hear a page turn, and McCosh 50, where I once sat directly behind Albert Einstein listening to Bertrand Russell give a lecture on the laws of chance, of which I understood not so much as a single word. I think of Alexander Hall with the snow falling and of the magnolias blossoming on University Place and of squirrels chasing each other up and down the tall elms. But, more than anything, I think of the generations of teachers—some of them mad as hatters, some of them dry as dust, some of them unforgettably patient and eloquent and learned—and how some of them labored so hard through the decades, and some of them labored not nearly hard enough, to pass on to generations of students the accumulated wisdom of the human race.

So what have they added up to, these two hundred and fifty years? Did the young who studied here leave not only smarter than they were before they came but maybe even wiser and with something more of honor, of courage, of the resolve, however dimly recognized, to do something with the rest of their lives that might ease the world's pain a little, might add something to the never quite extinguished capacity of the world to be just, to be beautiful, to be worth having lived in and died in as all of us have lived in it and all of us will someday die in it? Has this chapel and the chapels that preceded it been just window dressing, just the relic of a faith that to many seems as remote and implausible as it did to me fifty years ago, or has it for some of us come to point beyond itself to that innermost reality, east of the sun and west of the moon, where the morning stars sing together and all the sons and daughters of God shout for joy? All we can do I suppose is answer, each one, for our single selves.

But all of this has to do with the past, and it wasn't the past that was on the mind of the beery boy in his mortar board. "What are you going to do *now?*" was his question, and it is the question still, and it is also the question implicit in the Gospel reading for this first Sunday in June. Jesus has apparently spent the day teaching by the Sea of Galilee with the usual crowd gathered to hear him, but then evening comes and a kind of lull descends and with it the question of what were they going to do next.

Start for home maybe? Find a place to lie down and get some rest, sign off for the day, because God knows the day has been long and hard and nobody can keep going forever? But that is not what Jesus says though there can't have been any of them readier to call it a day than he was, the star of the show. He is standing at the water's edge with his tired fishermen friends, and what he says to them is "Let us go across to the other side." His answer to the question of what to do next, what to do with the rest of their lives, is simply stated. What he says to them is *Go.*

Go when you're in your seventies at your fiftieth reunion? Go when for better or worse your work is mostly done and your life is mostly behind you? Go when you're young with your life mostly ahead of you and you haven't decided yet what your life's work will be? Go when you're not sure where to go or how or why? Go when you're a great university that surely after two hundred and fifty years no longer has to prove itself but can rest on its laurels at last? Yes, precisely that, Jesus says. Go for God's sake, and for your own sake too, and for the world's sake. Climb into your little tub of a boat and keep going. And to us too he says it, because these Gospel stories are like dreams, and like dreams they are about ourselves, and everything in them tells us about who we are the way everything in our dreams does.

You can preach your own sermons to yourselves from here on out. You don't need a preacher. Remember your own going over the years. Remember the crazy winds that have blown you off course as again and again they have blown me off mine. Remember the scudding clouds that have blotted out the moon and the cruel white lip of the wave curling over the gunnels. Remember the fear at your own helplessness, at being lost in a storm very often of your own making. Remember what it's like to be old with death ahead of you and what it's like to be young with life ahead of you. These are among the storms for each of us to preach about to ourselves, remembering always too that somehow we have survived the storm and that even at the worst of it there was something in us that clung on for dear life because even at its worst life is dear.

Keep going, Jesus says, because to keep going is to keep living and to stop going is to stop living in any way that much matters. "Let us go across to the other side," he says, though who knows how far the other side is or what awaits us when we get there, if anything awaits us at all. And go bravely because if we are the boat and the storm and the fishermen in their helplessness, we are also, we have in us also, the holy one asleep in the stern with a pillow under his head whose presence gives us hope and courage.

There are Christians among us and Jews among us, and some of us believe in God under one name or another and some of us have never found it in our hearts to believe in much of anything, but no matter. I think there is a holiness that sleeps in the heart of all of us even when we do not know its name or seek to know it. I think that, however dimly, we have all of us glimpsed that holiness especially at those moments when we were wiser or braver or more loving than left to ourselves we know how to be, at those moments when we are overwhelmed by the joy of life and the tragedy of life and the indestructible beauty and holiness of life that lie deeper than either. I think that just our longing for it, our listening for it, can stir that holiness to life within us. So let us long for it. Let us listen for it. Let us shelter it with our hands like a flame in the wind, because it is the innermost mystery of who we are as human beings and what makes us human. It is the power within us to live with charity, honor, grace, the power to keep going even when we are tempted to go no place that matters, to go no farther.

"What are you going to do with the rest of your life?" the boy asked half a century ago, if that's what he meant with his terrible question. Which of us knew how to answer him? Which of us knows how to answer him now, whether the rest of our lives is to be only a few more years or many a long year to come? I don't know what any of us is going to do let alone what I'm going to do myself. But I think I know this.

I think I know that, recognized or unrecognized, Christ sleeps in the deepest selves of all of us, and whatever we do in whatever time we have left, wherever we go, may we in whatever way we can call on him as the fishermen did in their boat to come awake within us and to give us courage, to give us hope, to show us, each one, our way. May he be with us especially when the winds go mad and the waves run wild, as they will for all of us before we're done, so that even in their midst we may find peace, find him.

And I wish the same for Princeton, two hundred and fifty years old this year. May Christ be present here among these tall trees and these spring days that all but break the heart with their beauty. May he be present in these old buildings and musty classrooms and green playing fields.

Whether or not they call upon his name or even honor it, may he be present especially in the hearts of all who teach here and all who learn here because without him everything that goes on here is in the long run only vanity. May he be alive in this place so that something like truth may be spoken and heard and carried out into the world. So that something like love may be done.

37

The Newness of Things

When I was a preppy like you during the second administration of Ulysses S. Grant, it was fashionable to greet the reopening of school in September with a series of terrible groans. The same old grind was beginning all over again. The same inept, malevolent teachers would be back teaching the same infinitely boring courses and handing out the same grotesquely unfair grades. The same inedible food would be served up to us laced heavily with saltpeter to subdue our adolescent libidos. It would all come flooding back over us again—the nit-picking rules and regulations, the irritating talk about school spirit, the mangy campus and the dumb little town it was located in and the unspeakable weather. Not wanting to seem any more of an oddball than I feared I was, I'm sure I groaned right along with the rest of them, but it was just camouflage. The truth of it was that I loved getting back to school in September.

First of all, the fall always seemed to me to be not just the beginning again of school, but the beginning again of life itself. Spring is traditionally when that's supposed to happen with the crocuses and the first robin and all that, but spring always seemed to me more a sort of lovely, vague in-between time. Then summer came like a long, hazy dream with days floating endlessly by and intermingling the way clouds do, and everything sleepy and green and buzzing like bees in honeysuckle and nobody getting much of anything done, least of all myself. When fall came, on the other hand, everything started rolling again, including me. The crisp fall air felt full of excitement and promise, and for me the most exciting part of it all was getting back to school again, though I wouldn't have admitted it for the world. In some ways it was the same old grind all over again as the groaners complained, but in other ways it always seemed wonderfully new to me, and it's that newness I want to draw your attention to this morning.

I draw your attention to new pencils, for instance—I assume they're still making them the way I remember—long, yellow pencils with pink erasers that haven't been chewed or worn down yet and soft lead that makes everything you write look like the Declaration of Independence. Or if you are pen people instead of pencil people, I urge you not to stick to just the old blue ones or black ones, which will mark you as hopeless squares, but, especially if you go in for felt-tips as I do, to cut loose with new green ones or purple ones or even pink ones, which will turn even your least inspired offerings into the *Rubaiyat of Omar Khayyam*. When my brother and I were small boys, we started something called the Be Kind to Animals Club with a couple of friends, and although as far as I can remember we never got around to locating so much as a single animal to be kind to, we loved accumulating the sort of office supplies that we considered essential to our humanitarian purposes—things like brand-new pads of snowy white paper and loose-leaf notebooks and file cards and paper clips and rubber bands, and I have rejoiced in such things ever since and encourage you to see them as part of the magical newness of these opening days of classes.

I commend to you also the newness of the books you will be reading. Open them up and savor the enchanted smell of the paper they're printed on and the glossy photographic plates, if they happen to have any, and the rich, dark ink, and the stiff, uncracked binding. Riffle through the pages that possibly not another human being in the entire world has ever riffled through before and marvel at whatever you may find there in the way of new ideas, or new facts, or new ways of looking at old facts that you thought you knew inside and out until you discovered otherwise—like the nature of matter, including our own material bodies, which I for one always thought were as solid and uncomplicated as eggplants or manhole covers until I found out that, like everything else, you and I ourselves are composed of a whirl of subatomic particles, which relative to their size are as far apart as the planets in the solar system, so that to see us as we really are would be to see not a collection of individual bodies of varied size and shape, but a whole interdependent universe as vast and mysterious as the one we live in. Some of your new books may strike you as about as exciting as binomial equations or grammar—Mark Twain once said he would rather decline three free drinks in a saloon than a single German noun—but you never know when you may find in them a new line of poetry that can give you goose bumps, such as Emily Dickinson's writing that a snake is like "a whiplash unbraiding in the sun," or some new word from the ancient past that for all you know may change the whole course of your life like the apostle John writing, "He who does not love remains in death" (1 John 3:14).

And then of course there are also your new teachers. Teachers are an exotic species, as I know not only from having observed a good many of them over the years but also from having from time to time been one myself. They're apt to talk too much and listen too little. They are also apt to think they know a great deal more than they do and their students a great deal less, and to tell corny jokes, and to give brutal, unannounced tests, and, in my day anyway, to do antisocial things like throwing chalk at you or crawling under the table and crowing like a rooster if you gave a wrong answer. But most of them anyway are in the business of teaching because they're fascinated by their subjects, and every once in a while if you're not careful (or maybe if you are) you may catch something of their fascination from them, and then there's no way of telling where it may take you. Every once in a while too something quite extraordinary happens in a classroom when the yawning chasm that exists between teachers and students closes over for some mysterious reason and suddenly you and they both are all caught up together in talking to each other with a degree of openness and intensity and unself-consciousness and mutual respect that is almost unparalleled anywhere else and that gives you as valuable a glimpse of what being human is all about as anything you're apt to find anywhere.

You can't be really human all by yourself, of course. You need other people to talk to and listen to and share your secrets with and laugh yourself silly with and, when you really get to know each other well, even to be able to be silent together with without embarrassment. That is what friends are all about, needless to say, and along with new stationery and new books and new teachers this new year, you may find a few new ones of them too if you're lucky. Sometimes you can spot right from the start who your new friends are going to be, but sometimes it doesn't work out that way at all. Every once in a while people turn up in school, or anywhere else for that matter, who have nothing about them to make you take a second look. They come from different worlds from yours and have different interests and different views on almost everything and might as well speak a different language. But you never know when one of them may turn out to be somebody you'll hang on to for the rest of your life. Think about Laurel and Hardy in their derby hats, for instance—Laurel, the skinny one who gets everything wrong and has a way of bursting into falsetto tears at moments of adversity, and Hardy, the fat one who thinks he's got everything right and keeps on twiddling his necktie at the ladies. They are direct opposites in almost every way, and that is of course what makes them such a great comic team as they squabble and bungle their way through the world creating mayhem wherever they go. But what makes them so much more than just funny, I think, and what has kept their movies alive all these years is the sense they somehow manage to convey that underneath all the differences between them they love each other. So keep your eyes peeled as this new year begins, because you never know what unlikely new candidate for friendship may turn out to be the Hardy to your Laurel, or the other way around.

This year, 1997–1998, is the newest year there is, but it won't be new always, and that's worth thinking about. In a few hundred years from now historians and archaeologists will look back at our 1997 world with as much fascination as we look back on the world of Julius Caesar or Billy the Kid. They would give their eyeteeth for just one glimpse of the way things were in the United States on the eve of the twenty-first century when William Clinton was president and outer space hadn't been colonized yet and there were people still around who remembered the assassination of Martin Luther King and had heard Caruso sing and watched Joe DiMaggio play for the New York Yankees. What wouldn't they do, those men and women of centuries yet to come, to be able to witness at first hand not just the great public events and superstars of our time, but simply what it was like be alive in Mercersburg, Pennsylvania, for instance, all those years ago. What did 1997 look like and sound like and taste like? What did it feel like to ride around in a twentieth-century automobile of all things and to look up at the moon before McDonald's had a franchise there. Future generations would give their eyeteeth to know such things whereas to you it is given to know them like the back of your hand. So pay attention to what's going on this newest year no matter how humdrum and unimportant it may seem. Keep your eyes and ears open, because new as today always seems while you're living it, in a few years from now it will exist only in your memories of it, and in a few centuries it will have vanished like a dream.

In fifteen years from now you'll be in your unimaginable thirties somewhere, and that's worth thinking about too. What will you remember about this year, I wonder? Will you remember important things or, like me, only disconnected bits and pieces of things like part of a movie you saw, maybe, or getting caught in a thunderstorm on your way back from gym. Try writing a letter to the person you will have turned into in fifteen years from now, and in that letter jog your memory about at least a few of the important things. Write to yourself who the person is right now that you would rather spend a day with than anybody else in the world. Write to yourself what you hope you'll be doing with your life fifteen years from now and also the kind of thing you hope you won't be doing. Some people say there is a God and some people say there isn't; set down in your letter which side you would put your money on today and why. Set down the last thing that made you cry, and the most beautiful place you've ever seen up to now, and the nicest thing anybody has ever done for you and the nicest thing you have ever done for somebody else. The letter should have things like that in it so that you won't lose track of them, and then give it to somebody to mail to you somewhere in 2012, and my bet is that it will turn out to be one of the most interesting and useful letters you'll ever receive.

Finally, at the end of the letter, you might add a P.S. saying that 1997 was the year the school got a new headmaster, and let me end with him.

First of all, he's as good a listener as he is a talker, and good listeners don't grow on trees. As far as I can tell, most people I know hardly listen at all when I try to tell them something, but seem instead just to be waiting till it's time for them to start talking again, and that always makes me feel terribly lonely, as if the only one of us who gives a hoot about who I am and what I think is me. But if you try to tell Mr. Hale something—something about yourself maybe, about what's on your mind, or how you're feeling about something—he listens, I think, not just because he's a Southern gentleman and very polite, but because he's really interested and takes in what you say and remembers it, so that the next time you meet, you don't have to start at square one again, but can go on from where you left off the last time, which is a lot of what friends are all about.

The second reason why I value him as a friend is that when he talks to you, you get the feeling that he's not putting on an act the way some people do. He's not talking to impress you, or to sound like the kind of person he thinks you want him to be, or to tell you the kind of thing he thinks you want him to say. On the contrary, as much as just about anybody I know, he seems to me to be talking out of the truth of who he is and to be telling you what he truly thinks and feels because that's the way he's made.

The third reason is that he's kind. I don't mean kind just on the surface with a lot of less than kind things going on behind the scenes, or kind for the sake of being popular and getting your vote, or kind because that's what's expected of him. I mean that as I've observed him, he's kind in the sense of genuinely wishing people well and of being willing to do what he can for their welfare, even if sometimes it may not be what they themselves might choose for him to do. I'm sure he has his bad moments like the rest of us, but my guess is that they don't come easy for him and that he has to work at it to bring them off successfully.

There are a lot of other things I could say about him, but I'll limit myself to just one more, which is that his wife is a winner in exactly these same ways and a good deal better looking, so what you're really getting is two new friends for the price of one. Be good to them as they start out this new year with you, this new chapter in the school's history and your own individual histories, and I think I can promise that they will be good to you because that is their nature. Finally, may God bless them and you and everyone who teaches here and learns here, so that you may all grow in grace and truth together.